Restoring America's Future

by
Gene Gordon

Islewest Publishing
Dubuque, Ia.

I want to thank all the writers, economists, and authors who investigated, reported, and wrote about the many incidents, details, and facts cited in this book. Years of research and many hours of creative thinking brought this book to life. The solutions to America's economic, social, and government problems will come from creative concepts which can easily do what many years of taxing and tinkering will never achieve.

This book is written for my children and grandchildren with the hope that it can make a difference in their future. I deeply appreciate my wife Virginia's assistance and patience while this project took shape. Many thanks also to Project Manager Mary Jo Graham, Editor Joan Lyon, and the efforts of many friends who are helping deliver the book into the hands and minds of people who can make a change in our country's future.

Credits:

Illustrations
Dick Locher and Jeff MacNelly, reprinted
with permission of Tribune Media Services

Rob Rogers reprinted by permission of
United Feature Syndicate Inc.

Jerry Holbert reprinted by permission of
Newspaper Enterprises Association Inc.

Project management Islewest Publishing
4242 Chavenelle Dr. Dubuque, Ia. 52002.

96-094282

ISBN 1-88461-00-4

Table of Contents

finding it necessary to have large layoffs or go out of business entirely? Why are so few jobs available for 21-to 35-year-old college graduates? Why do criminals seem to have more rights than society? Why can't we create more productive jobs? Why should campaign contributions, by special interests, to politicians—who make laws—be legal, when bribery of judges is illegal? Why does our civil tort law system cost four to ten times more than legal systems in other major countries? Why did our dollar devaluate over 400% against the Japanese yen? Why will children born after 1990 be required to pay 82%[1] of their lifetime earnings in net taxes? Why do we believe they can pay that much? Why did federal government costs and regulations raise our cost of living so much? What does COLA (cost of living adjustment set yearly by the consumer price index) do to the economy? Why is the rate of inflation or COLA now over 260%[3] higher than the worker productivity rate? Why hasn't the government lived within its income? Why are government agencies so inefficient? Why is the Japanese labor management system more productive and efficient than ours? When and why did it become so much higher? Why is the Federal Reserve Board so concerned about inflation?

There are easily understood answers to all of these questions. The research and data regarding them generated many possible, innovative opportunities to improve our society, economy, and government. When the questions were answered, it became apparent why the old Congress acted as it did:

•Foremost, the old Congress wanted to remain in power.

•Congress voted money it did not have for government largess in their respective districts and substantially increased the debt.

•It blatantly traded special interest favors for campaign contributions and voting blocks. Some voting blocks and interests wanted business and industry to become subject to the federal government by means of laws, regulations, consumer protection, and litigation.

Congress then passed unprecedented legislation and our economy subsequently lost profit, jobs, growth, and personal savings. We then developed an immense debt and a cost of living that has made all our goods and services cost 263%[3] more than our country's productivity. In 30 years, violent crime increased 450%.[4] Welfare costs grew 37 times higher,[5] and our education system is not among the top 12 nations in the world in math and science.[6] The old Congress created a monster that is very much out of control.

A new Congress has taken over, promising by contract to make government smaller and less intrusive. The "1994 Contract With America" is shown in Appendix D. It has also promised to balance the budget in seven years. Is this promise too much and too quick, or too little and too late? If the new Congress uses innovative and creative approaches that use incentives and objectives instead of laws and regulations, it can make government and the economy much more efficient and effective. Congress must focus on rescinding the acts, laws, regulations, and practices passed in the last 30 years that have severely damaged our international competitiveness, destroyed jobs, and greatly increased our cost of living and the national debt. Chapter 1 is an overall perspective of the reasons our democracy failed economically and why we must adopt changes. *Restoring America's Future* is about these necessary changes. The last chapter compares our country's future as directed under the policies of the old Congress, and the recommendations outlined in each chapter of this book.

I want to express my appreciation to all the writers, economists, and authors who investigated, reported, and wrote about the many incidents, details, and facts cited in this book. The information fit together like pieces in a puzzle and made a whole picture understandable.

Knowledge is power. Imagination and unconventional thinking based on knowledge are the means of restoring America's future. Congress is much too comfortable with the status quo. All who read this book can make a difference in changing our country's future.

Democracy is not a form of government to survive. It will only succeed until its citizens discover they can vote themselves money from the treasury. Then they will bankrupt it. —Karl Marx

Chapter 1. Congress and the National Debt

ECONOMIC BACKGROUND

There is a growing belief that the old Congress, over 30 years, has not acted in our national interest. In 1995, two items, federal waste (as identified by the bipartisan Citizens Against Government Waste) and interest on the national debt exceeded all personal federal income tax revenues. I am deeply concerned that my children will be devastated by the consequences of past congressional actions which produced a 1995 debt of $4.962 (five) trillion[1] including borrowing ($1.4 trillion)[2] surplus Social Security trust funds which will soon be needed for baby boom retirees. According to the 1994 report of the Bipartisan Commission on Entitlements and Tax Reform, Congress allowed unfunded obligations for Medicare, Social Security, civil service employees, and military retirement to reach $14.4 trillion[3] by 1991. An audit by Arthur Andersen & Co. indicates these obligations were $17.2 trillion in 1993. Each Social Security retiree was supported by 42 workers in 1945,[4] is supported by 3.3 workers now, and will be supported by two workers by my grandchildren.[5] How can my grandchildren's generation, with a ratio of two workers for every Social Security retiree, possibly support this generational debt transfer?

The power to make laws, control spending, and control the bureaucracy is given only to Congress. Our economy and currency are nearing economic free fall. The old Congress passed the Employment Retirement Income Security Act (ERISA), requiring all U.S. pension funds be fully funded. If they are not, the corporation must amortize the unfunded portion over 30 years.

The old Congress has in the last 25 years spent all surplus ($1.4 trillion) Social Security trust funds actuarially required for the retirement of the baby boom generation. It promised benefits our children and grandchildren can't possibly fund. The new Congress just passed legislation that all laws applying to the rest of the country apply equally to Congress. This should mean, at current interest rates of about 6%, the new Congress must start reducing federal expenses at least $500 billion a year and increase retirement age, or contribute an additional $1 trillion a year to federal retirement funds. Failure to change will quickly drive our economy over a cliff.

Foreign countries held over $555 billion of federal securities in July 1994.[6] Foreign investors may require us to replace matured funds should the dollar drop. That will make interest rates rise and take needed money out of circulation.

Francis Bacon said, "Religion, justice, council, and treasure are the four pillars of government." If there is a serious debt problem, we must carefully analyze the root causes of this threat and keep our minds open for new means of bringing the debt down without a crash. We, like flies on a window, need to focus not on one single means of escape which will leave us dead on the windowsill, but on a wide variety of options and questions. How did we get in this situation? What caused it? Who caused it? What needs to be changed to correct it? How can changes be made to improve the economy without damaging it? How can we prevent it from happening again? Failure to recognize and correct the problems causing the debt will ensure a crash.

The national debt, like gravity, is the manifestation of absolute economic forces which cannot be ignored. Debt, like lung cancer, is the result of abuse. We have been abused by the most privileged and powerful people in our country. They are the old Congress, who traded legislative favors and unnecessary projects for campaign money and votes.

Saving a debt-burdened economy centers around designing a soft drop for our national debt, while stimulating the economy and reducing the bureaucracy, confrontation, regulation, litigation, and lobby money that hold it back. A great deal of focus must be on the legal profession, which produces nothing but creates mammoth and unseen economic waste. Lawyer lobbies have been the major force behind the immense growth of laws and regulations, and the major beneficiary of them. We can create jobs or we can retain regulations, but we can't, over time, have both.

COST PER SUPPORT HOUSEHOLD

All statistics demonstrate Congress has been spending our country into bankruptcy. Millions, billions, and trillions of dollars, received and spent by the federal government, are difficult for the public to comprehend and relate to. For this reason, the book will reference national incomes, expenditures, and potential savings, as costs or savings per **support household**. There are 264 million people in the United States,[7] with 98.5 million households[8] averaging 2.7 persons per household.[8] Just **50 million (about half) of these support households** earn over $22,000 and **pay 95% of all federal income tax.**[8] **A billion dollars in federal savings will save each of these households $20.**[9] Welfare begins at $15,000 for a mother and two children. Households with incomes less than $22,000 consume federal spending and are powerless to solve the federal government's financial problems. A household of four, earning under $19,703, has access to food stamps and other welfare programs. Welfare now costs $375 billion ($7,500 per year per support household).[10] All households earning less than $22,000 contribute $32 billion in income taxes and receive 12 times more from the government.[9] The average taxable income of "support households" is $60,000.[9] They pay $3,700 FICA tax, $11,120 federal income tax, and $3,000 state and local taxes.[9] This leaves a $42,180 balance of spendable income. The employers of these support households pay $3,700 FICA, plus state and federal taxes,[9] and $3,000 (est) health care costs. Our support household presently saves $3,000 per year. In order to balance the budget and pay back half of the deficit in 10 years, the federal government will be short revenues of $10,000 per support household annually.[12] This is over three times their normal savings and would reduce their spendable income from $42,180 to $32,180. Even if we could tax ourselves this much, it would require our children and grandchildren to pay substantially higher lifetime taxes than we paid.

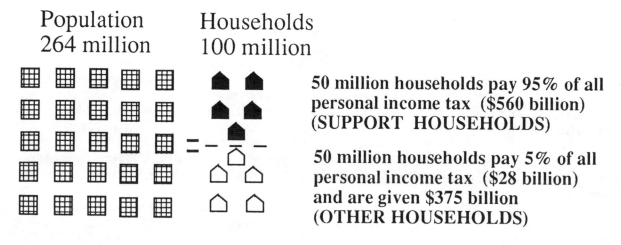

Population
264 million

Households
100 million

50 million households pay 95% of all personal income tax ($560 billion) (SUPPORT HOUSEHOLDS)

50 million households pay 5% of all personal income tax ($28 billion) and are given $375 billion (OTHER HOUSEHOLDS)

FROM RICHES TO RAGS

In 1900 the debt was $14 per person.[13] We were the wealthiest country in the world,[14] had the strongest economy, and paid the highest wages.[13] Only 7% of the births were to unwed mothers,[15] about the same as Europe. Minor taxes accounted for all government funds. The first permanent income tax began February 25, 1913, as a "temporary" tax. A senator, speaking against the "temporary tax" said, "If we allow this one percent, foot-in-the-door tax, it might rise to five percent." The federal debt remained "minimal" until the Depression of 1929. From then until now, the federal revenue has exceeded expenditures only seven times, by minimal amounts. The $5 trillion national debt has risen exponentially since 1960 when it was $290 billion. The support household's share of this debt is $99,231,[16] and it grows over $6,660 per year ($334 billion for 1995).[18] In comparison, the average Japanese worker saves over $5,000 per year. It will simply be impossible for those born after 1992 to pay a projected 82% of their lifetime earnings in net taxes because presently 50% of our households pay 95% of all personal income tax.

Prior to 1932 the prevailing national belief was that government should stay out of everything not specifically allowed in the Constitution. As a result, our government was very frugal. Franklin Roosevelt changed that concept and from 1932 to 1944, the government policy was to provide help to those in need through work projects and regulations to make business conform to government requirements. By 1944 the debt was $260 billion or about $1,900 per person after costly World War II ended. The debt grew only $31 billion in the next 16 years.

From 1935 to 1944, politicians and the new Supreme Court accepted federal laws and regulations the courts held unconstitutional prior to 1932. This growth in government and political power reignited in the mid-1960s and has continued until November 1994. Federal efforts to control the economy with regulations have been a major cause of the decrease in manufacturing jobs (primary source of "new" money), a decrease in international competitiveness, and higher costs of American products. It is long past time to see how regulations affected the economy. Small businesses, the major creators of jobs, are stifled by regulations related to discrimination, paperwork, hiring, firing, OSHA, EEOC, and EPA to name a few. Two additional employees, a lawyer and an accountant, are necessary additions to a start-up business.

Our national debt jumped in the 1960s when the Great Society started a War on Poverty and expanded Social Security entitlements to include Medicare, Medicaid, AFDC, WIC, Head Start, rent subsidies, federal employee benefits, and many others. The interest on the $322 billion federal debt in 1965 was $9 billion, and was 18% of federal personal income tax. By 1975 interest on the debt was $33 billion, or 27% of federal personal income tax. By 1985 interest on the debt was $179 billion, or 54% of federal personal income tax. In 1995 interest on the $5 trillion debt was $334 billion, which is 57% of all federal personal income tax.[17] Interest is now larger than the 1965 debt. The old Congress then promised an additional $14.4 trillion of unfunded retirement benefits, added deficit to debt, and passed the debt to future generations for payment.

If you were born in 1930, your net taxes have been 28% of your lifetime income. If you were born in 1960, they have been 32% of your lifetime income.[19] Page 25 of the *1994 Budget of the United States Government* Analytical Perspectives projects that those born after 1992 will pay 82% of their lifetime income in net taxes. Future support household incomes of $60,000 would have only $10,800 for living expenses using these projections. In 1994, the Senate Bipartisan Committee on Entitlements and Tax Reform stated that funding for Medicare will run out in 2001 and, by 2012, entitlements and interest on the national debt will consume all federal tax revenues.

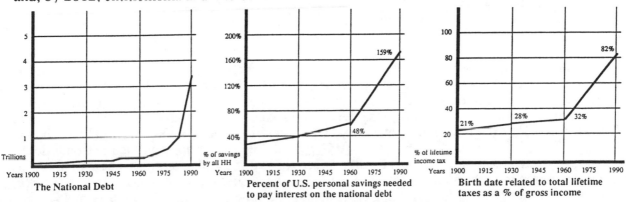

The National Debt	Percent of U.S. personal savings needed to pay interest on the national debt	Birth date related to total lifetime taxes as a % of gross income

Federal Revenue and Expense Graph 1950-1995

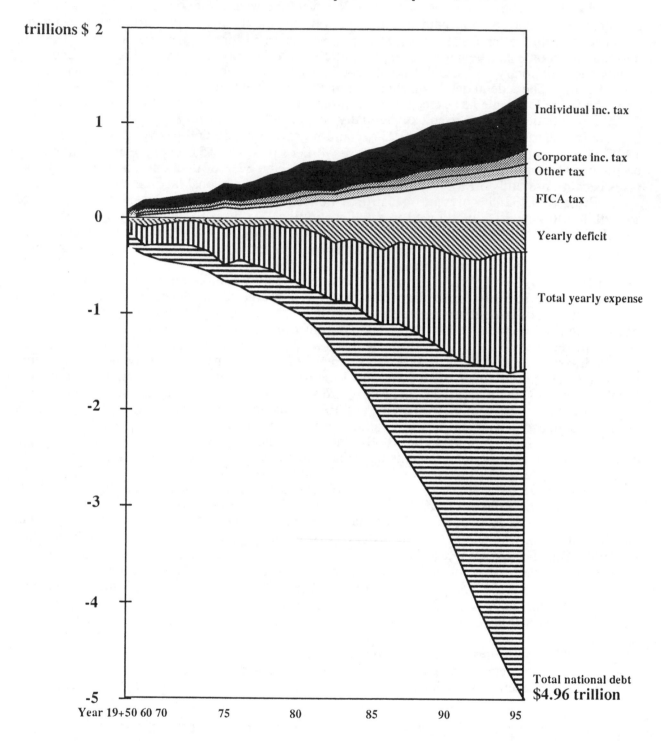

The national debt is out of control. The chart shows corporate income tax of $125 billion is a minor part of federal revenues. In reality it pays half ($246 billion) of the FICA tax. Labor has been driven 263% higher than worker productivity by laws and regulations passed since 1965. Nongovernment labor is 76% of our gross domestic product (GDP) which is $7.2 trillion. That $5.5 trillion is $3.39 trillion higher than worker productivity since 1965. The total penalty on business is $3.8 trillion a year (over half of the GDP and 75% of our accumulated national debt). The laws, regulations, and deficit spending approved by the old Congress have made U.S. corporations much less competitive internationally and have cost millions of good jobs. (Source, *Statistical Abstract of the United States,* Department of Commerce, 1993, p 319, 1994, p 451.)

The Historical Tables of the *1996 Budget of the United States* project that from 1995 to 2000, the interest rate on the national debt will increase from $334 billion to $447 billion, an increase of 34%. This is more than twice the current rate of inflation. The congressionally-imposed debt will devastate the coming generation unless major changes are made by the new Congress immediately. What caused the old Congress to be so irresponsible?

CONGRESS AND CAMPAIGN CONTRIBUTIONS

Congressional and special interests:
Tort reform, tax exemptions, unions, corporations,
balanced budget, abortion, NAFTA, GATT,
welfare, health care, education, crime, gay rights
$$

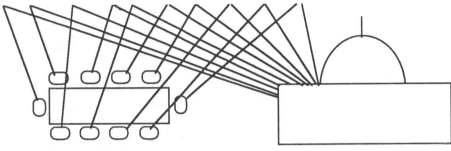

Congressional committees   **Congress**

Special interests and lobbies fund 40% of all congressional reelections. It is mother's milk for politicians. The ideal solution for Congress is to never pass any legislation and never let the issues go away. This keeps contributions flowing in from special interests on both sides of the issue, forever. Confrontation, polarization, and gridlock are the necessary basic tools of Congress, to preserve their seats in power. Obtaining local congressional pork, franking privileges, and special interest election contributions ensured 95% incumbent reelection of the old Congress until 1994.

The political system has stretched "freedom of speech" to become "freedom to bribe Congress." If you were in court in a malpractice suit against an attorney who contributed 40% of the judge's reelection funds, would you believe the judge would be impartial? It is time to ask ourselves if we believe laws and regulations that were made by a Congress that received 40% of its funds from special interests can be fair to all.

Accepting major campaign contributions from special interests has caused Congress to act as agents of special interests instead of representatives of the people. It has caused Congress to gridlock and become contentious and it has caused them to pass much too much legislation for the special interests, to the detriment and expense of the public. Campaign contributions of any kind by lobbies, PACs, or special interest groups should be abolished. This would make Congress more responsive to voters. Lobbies spend $300 billion[21] per year to influence federal, state, and local governments. Attorney lobbies benefit thousands of times more than their election contributions. Total lobby gifts raise yearly costs a minimum of $6,000 per support household. James Madison, in a letter to Thomas Jefferson, wrote, "Wherever the real power in government lies, there is danger of oppression."

THE CAUSE AND THE PRICE
Virtually all of our present unimaginable financial problems were brought on by the old Congress during the last 30 years.
1. It passed an unprecedented mountain of legislation relating to poverty, welfare, environment, worker safety, equal employment, and massive rights, discrimination, and harassment laws.
This caused the number of lawyers to grow 13 times faster than the population from 1970 to 1980.
They then consumed a large portion of our economic resources, without producing any goods.
2. Congress recklessly spent funds it didn't have and made future promises it couldn't keep.

governments, the costs to business and industry, and reduce direct costs to the taxpayer. These efforts also have the ability to not only stop the increase in the cost of living, but make it decrease.

Federal reductions of $10,000 per support household will halve the $5 trillion debt in 10 years.[12] Twice this amount may be required to provide for retirement obligations.

Table 4. Total Costs and Proposed Reductions per Support Household per Year:
Note: These reductions averaged over 10 years cannot be directly added because they overlap.

Description	Current cost/support HH	Proposed cut/support HH
1. Federal cost of regulatory agencies[23]	$ 332	$ 50
2. Citizens Against Govt Waste Report '94[24]	5,208	5,208
3. Entitlements less welfare[25]	7,700	700
4. Welfare entitlements	7,500	3,750 avg
5. Federal discretionary spending[26]	11,080	2,200
6. Federal pensions[27]	2,464	1,264
7. Interest on national debt[28]	6,670	1,740 avg
8. Decentralize federal agencies[29]	10,685	1,400
9. Change COLA to WPI[30] x $1.6 trillion	2,400	2,400 avg
10. Corporate welfare	1,640	1,640
Total	$55,679	$20,352

The following will prevent our children and grandchildren from becoming government slaves:
1. Many federal regulations are necessary and helpful, such as highway or banking. Many others are unimaginably expensive to the government and the economy, with little or no benefit to the people. All regulations that increase costs, reduce economic productivity, or reduce employment should be targeted for revision. Savings in Alternative 5 will stimulate the economy.
2. Citizens Against Government Waste (CAGW) got its impetus from the Grace Commission. Their "Prime Cuts 1994" includes 556 recommendations to reduce government costs, which combine Grace Commission recommendations, CAGW, the Congressional Budget Office, the National Performance Review, and the president's current proposals. All of these should be approved by Congress with a single up or down vote, with no amendments. More detailed information can be obtained from Citizens Against Government Waste, 1301 Connecticut Ave. NW, Suite 400, Washington, D.C., 20036. Major cuts are shown in Appendix B.
3. Life expectancy has increased five years in the last 25 years. Full retirement benefits should move to age 70, within 10 years, for all employees in and out of government, in order not to dramatically raise FICA taxes. Early retirement benefits for all should move to age 65 within 6 years.
4. Welfare must be replaced with a Full Employment program. Recipients work in order to receive payments. Day care and Medicaid services will be provided as needed. Additional education may be substituted for work with limitations. Pregnant, single mothers must verify the identity of the father in order to receive child care payments. Both parents must support their children by working or the Full Employment program until the children reach 18 years of age. Fathers must make all child support payments.
5. By reverting to constitutional limitations on Congress, only "absolutely necessary" discretionary spending could be justified. It should be possible to cut expenditures 20%.
6. Federal pensions should be identical to Social Security, with equal benefits and trust fund payments by government. Presently $1.4 trillion in federal retirements are unfunded. Staffing cuts of 10% would cover the government matching payment shortfall.
7. Reducing federal costs $10,000 per support household will reduce interest on the national debt $30 billion the first year, increasing to $144 billion in 10 years and averaging $87 billion per year.
8. Decentralize, eliminate, or change Commerce, Education, Treasury, Housing, Energy, Agriculture, Transportation, EPA, and OSHA departments, to reduce costs and improve the quality of their services. Decentralized services, assumed by states, can be funded with federal taxes.
9. The worker productivity index (WPI) has been 1.5% lower than COLA for 10 years. Our government now purchases over $1.5 trillion in goods and services, which will be 1.5% less in the first year, and 15% less in 10 years. This will average 8% savings over 10 years.

10. Cato Institute identified $82 billion in annual federal subsidies to large corporations. Substantial funds from these corporations flow to congressional campaign reelection funds. Changing election laws to prohibit any lobby gifts will prohibit these subsidies.

Alternative 5. The following reductions will lower all U.S. costs to support households. These costs were artificially generated by COLA (now 263% higher than WPI since 1965). Reducing the following costs will rid the economy of 30 years of legislated economic friction holding it back.

Table 5. Current Costs and Proposed Savings per Support Household per Year:

Note: These reductions averaged over 10 years cannot be directly added because they overlap.

	Current costs/support HH	Reduction/support HH
11. Federal regulations[31]	$13,658	$2,000
12. Foreign and national lobbies[32]	6,000	3,000
13. Financing federal elections[33]	0	(6)
14. Legal tort system[34]	13,200 to 2,400	2,000
15. Defensive medicine[39]	3,600	1,800
16. Revised criminal justice system[36]	4,877	500
17. WPI cost of living savings[37]	18,085	2,408 avg.
18. Change all income tax to pay and sales tax	1,300	1,300
	Total $49,920	$13,014

11. All households pay for the hidden costs of federal regulations in goods and services they buy, taxes they pay, and the federal interest added to the increasing national debt.

12. Lobbies trade contributions for political favors far greater than their gifts. The practice is destroying our economy, and must end so that each special interest favor can be corrected on its own merits, and relate to the cost of living and the economy.

13. Taxpayers can finance federal elections, however, senate candidates must raise $600,000 and representatives $100,000 from individuals only, in contributions not over $200 each.

14. The present tort system is outdated, is very expensive, harms the economy, clogs our court system, and primarily benefits only lawyers. The excessive tort costs may exceed $13,200 per support household. Direct mediation without lawyers should be required. Our tort costs are at least five times higher than other major industrial countries.

15. Medical costs are 20% higher because doctors must practice defensive medicine to avoid civil suits. If mediation is required and doctors are not expected to always make perfect decisions, the need for most defensive medicine costs will be greatly reduced.

16. Congress should redefine the rights of the accused and require polygraph, blood, DNA, and other testing methods when they can help to determine truth. All criminal records should be public. Restitution, work, and repentance should be required of prisoners, prior to release.

17. Lobbies, laws, and congressional excesses have driven COLA 263% higher than worker productivity since 1965. Households' living costs have more than doubled because of COLA. When 20% of the most detrimental effects of regulations passed over the last 30 years are rescinded, and when WPI replaces COLA, the cost of living will average $2,408 per year.

18. A national 10% (plus average 3% state) sales tax with a revised 7.65% FICA plus 4% corporate wage tax can end _all_ personal and corporate, federal, state, and local income taxes; gift; and estate taxes and reduce all costs to taxpayers a total of $165 billion. See Appendix A for details.

THE COST OF REGULATION, LITIGATION, AND LOBBIES

Each year, every support family, and the business it works for, pays over $10,000 more than necessary in goods and services, primarily to benefit lawyers and lobbies. This increases COLA. Special interest lobbies spend at least $300 billion ($6,000 per support household) each year to influence legislation in all government entities. You can correctly assume that the benefit to the lobby is greater than their expenditures.

The biggest lobby in all government entities is the American Trial Lawyers Association. They are behind the increasing number of laws and regulations. Regulations produce new victims. As a result, product liability insurance is dramatically higher in the United States than any other country.

Beechcraft has lost over $100 million and 18,000 jobs because of excessive litigation of quality products.[38] U.S. goods and services cost an additional $182 billion to $660 billion each year because of tort suits claiming negligence.[39] This alone costs each support household $3,600 to $13,200 per year. Unrelenting litigation has driven up health care costs, as contingency fee lawyers try to win jackpots for themselves and any clients who believe their health problems did not have the result they wished.

Remember, lawyers for both sides, plus the court system, take half of the amount of all judgments or settlements. We have 5% of the world's population and 70% of its lawyers.[40] The present, expensive tort system costs over five to 10 times[41] more than those of England or Canada who have the same tort roots we have. The trial lawyers have had their hands deep in our pockets for too long, while our criminal justice system is clogged up.

Ann Landers, a no-nonsense commentator of our times, summed it up in response to a reader's complaint about lawsuits. McDonald's lost a $2.9 million lawsuit when a woman burned herself while trying to open a coffee cup, placed between her legs, while in a moving car. The courts later reduced the settlement to $640,000. Ann said, "The once noble profession of law has indeed sunk to a new low." She closed saying, "The clogging of the courts has become a national disgrace. Is it not outrageous that the two youths who allegedly killed Michael Jordan's father in 1994 are still in a North Carolina jail waiting to be put on trial because there is such a backlog of cases?" The trial is scheduled to start over two years after the murder.

Congress should do the following:

1. Supplant the tort system with immediate mediation, and require both sides to present a final mediation proposal.

2. Make professional actions performed with reasonable care "lawsuit immune." Otherwise, why not hold Congress responsible for passing imperfect laws and regulations?

3. Replace our extremely complicated regulations and laws with not more than 12 readily understood common laws, described in Chapter 6, which every citizen over age 10 would be required to know and understand. They will be the basis of tort and criminal law.

4. Limit the contingency fee to 10%.

5. Require losers of lawsuits to pay the winner's legal costs. We cannot continue to allow the existing legal system and lobbies to waste hundreds of billions of dollars.

POWER CORRUPTS

Most politicians during the early years of our country were well thought of and worked hard for a few months of the year to make our country prosperous and free. Politicians had little or no financial gain for their efforts and, for many, it took valuable time away from their home business interests. Today, the public holds professional politicians in the same regard as auto salesmen. They spend our limited resources for their reelection needs. Many are addicted to power. Power corrupts and absolute power corrupts absolutely. Once members of Congress spread their roots, and absorb the "system" in Washington, they will do almost anything to retain power. History shows congressmen need two major things to get reelected: Pork (money for projects for their district), and more campaign money than their opponent. It precipitates trading votes for money. In the judicial system it is called bribery. This bribery is supported by foreign and home grown lobbies, PACs, special interest groups, corporations, and unions, to mention a few. They have fully supported our deficit economy. End special interest or lobby gifts of any kind to legislators and government employees, just as it is not permitted in our legal system.

It should be noted here that not all politicians have abdicated fiscal responsibility. Prior to November 1994, about 25% of the members of Congress were deficit hawks who set their perspectives on the long-term good of our country. They found, until now, that the political establishment, the lobbies, and the committee chairpersons remained opposed to the significant changes necessary, and ruled with power and money.

Our political system has developed and expanded, with fundamental flaws not perceived by our founders. One flaw causes our government to spend money we don't have, for things we don't need, to benefit lobbies and politicians. Another flaw promotes waste and inefficiency in administering the federal government. Congress spent 23% of our gross national product, but collected taxes for only 73% of its spending and charged the rest to future generations. I believe the framers of the Constitution would condemn Congress for this abuse, and us for not stopping it.

FEDERAL AGENCIES

Our government agencies are expensive, wasteful, and inefficient. They do not have to be profitable and compete. They are a monopoly. They are paid based on the Government Service Administration (GSA) rating system. In federal government service, the more employees who work under you, the more you are paid. It should be no surprise then that employees search for new work to do, generate more reports, tolerate minimal employee performance, and have benefits 250% higher than the best private industry. Unlike the private sector, the government, as an employer, contributes nothing toward retirement funds.

How many times have you heard or read, in recent years, that the Postal Service or other government agency was advertising for 50 positions and there were 2,000 applicants? If wages and benefits were in line with private enterprise, you would not have to review 40 applications to hire one person. If you work for the government, however, reviewing 40 applications increases the tasks you have to do and is to your benefit. There are presently work rules that make management impossible. Necessary federal government can be much more efficient and effective by changing the regulations, efficiency incentives, and management methods. Substantial agency work (the eighth recommended reduction) should be reduced or eliminated and sent to states with compensating grants, or be privatized. It is vital and fair that federal government employees have the same retirement and medical benefits as the general public. Taxpayers must not be second class.

Federal agencies are politically well-connected. President Carter rightly wanted "sunset laws" and "zero-based budgeting" for all government agencies. Presidents Reagan and Bush wanted smaller government. Agencies, politicians, and lobbies easily won out over all these presidents. Until 1994, government grew and politicians prospered, while waste and inefficiency continued unabated. Government must become smaller, more efficient, and more productive.

BUSINESS, REGULATIONS, AND JOBS

Our international manufacturing corporations, which bring foreign revenues to the United States, have suffered major layoffs over 30 years as productivity per dollar of labor has plummeted. Major businesses and manufacturing are surviving, but have been losing strength, market share, and employees for decades. The Fortune 500 companies have lost 4.4 million jobs since 1980. This has created higher than normal unemployment. There are many reasons for this decline. After World War II in 1945, all other major manufacturing nations, except for the United States, Sweden, and Canada, were in shambles. The United States could produce any product, even with defects, and there was demand for that product. America produced unprecedented prosperity which will never return. The existing confrontational "labor versus management" style of producing goods and services is now less efficient than the Japanese "Jobs for Life" in exchange for intense worker cooperation and contribution toward producing quality products. The U.S. cost of living has grown 263% faster than our productivity and has made us uncompetitive. Decline was also due to corporations paying too much attention to annual profit and too little to customer satisfaction, research and development (R&D), long-term market share, and expansion. Generally, business and industry are now focused on quality management and customer satisfaction. Our manufacturing productivity has increased 30% in the last 10 years (3% per year), as compared to our entire economy's productivity increase (only 0.7% per year).[42] Other major countries' entire productivity averaged over 2%.

Many countries are capable of producing quality, technical products such as autos, electronics, and computers, with wages from 50% to 10% of our wages. We will have to battle them with innovation and patents. By 1990 four Japanese companies each received more U.S. patents than any American company. Their companies invest much more in R&D than ours do. They have a better education system. We desperately need to create a favorable business climate for emerging, high-tech industries. We also need to dramatically reduce the number of lawyer-promoted, federally-mandated regulations which decimate business and industry.

A FAILED EDUCATION SYSTEM

Our education system costs more than any of the other seven leading industrial nations and our test scores in math and science are the lowest. We produce 10,000 fewer engineers than Japan annually, and we have twice their population. Our students are educationally unmotivated and their minds are preoccupied with the opposite sex, sports, music, and social life, instead of grades, learning how to learn, and responsibility for one's future. The education system furnishes an inferior product, for use by business and industry, to compete with the rest of the world. The Federal Department of Education, with a total budget of $57 billion[43] (28% of all education costs), has presided over the decline of our educational system. The number of hours our children spend in school must dramatically expand and we must make children understand that their education and attitude are the pathways to good and secure jobs in their future. This expanded education program can provide over four additional years of education for our children, while they live at home. The program will save the government $37 billion each year, and will reduce student college loans an additional $1 billion each year for 12 years.

MEDIA, MORALITY, AND CRIME

We have allowed TV and other media to profit from graphically portraying every immoral, savage, and demented act known to man. Common morality is now considered "counterculture" by the media. Is it any wonder our children are preoccupied with sex, drugs, and violence? Is it any wonder they have no confidence in the future? Our children are a product of what they see, hear, or read from a believable source. They watch TV as many hours as they are in school. We are all self-programmed computers. A recent Gallup survey found 90% of all Americans pray; 75% pray daily. As a society, we are paying a high cost for not devising a system to curb the quantity and quality of input from the media into our children's minds. Japan stresses responsibility and morality at school and their education system (1,890 hours per year) leaves no time for TV or movies.

We all pay for media excesses in many ways. Teenagers circumvent their parents' concerns regarding sex, drugs, late hours, smoking, and drinking. Too many become irresponsible, pregnant, infected, addicted, violent, or dead. The government has assured a pregnant teenager will be provided with welfare. Workfare must replace welfare. A welfare recipient must accept that "everyone works for benefits." We pay for higher costs of insurance, jails and prisons, health care, justice, and we pay with our lives for the increase in drug use and the amount of money necessary to support drug habits. Criminals' sentences should be measured by the weeks they work. We also pay for the avoidable violence, imprinted in the minds of some people who are prepared to copy actions of others who act with violence. We can move toward morality, save households thousands of dollars, and society's quality of life would be much improved. Early social, moral, and personal responsibility training, in schools with expanded hours, is obviously necessary. All media must be made to stop exploiting sex and violence, for their profit and our expense.

THE DOLLAR AND THE DEBT

The value of currency is only as good as the belief that it will retain its value. The old Congress and the president opposed a balanced budget amendment. Our national debt is extreme, and threatens our currency. The Swiss franc is strong and stable. It is 100% backed up with gold. A $20,000 purchase of Swiss francs in 1970 would be worth $67,400 today, without a cent of interest. Our dollar actually dropped 337%, and our tax brackets increased accordingly.

The U.S. personal savings rate, as a percent of our net national product, has dropped from 8% to 4% in the last 25 years.[45] At the same time, our consumption has risen from 65% to 72%[46] of income. U.S. personal savings are one-fourth to one-third the personal savings of other major countries. Japan's personal savings rate, by contrast, went up to 17% in 1994. We spend as if there is no tomorrow. If we continue, there will be none. We must develop incentives to save.

ALCOHOL AND TOBACCO COSTS

Tobacco and alcohol impose two more expenses on all of us. Over 400,000 new smokers from ages 12 to 17 start smoking each year, and an equal number of smokers die prematurely each year from lung cancer, emphysema, and heart problems, all associated with smoking. Health costs for diseases brought on by smoking were $65 billion in 1992. Tobacco taxes that year were $5.8 billion,[47] and much of that went to the bureaucracy. Tobacco taxes should rise to pay additional health costs.

Alcohol taxes were $8 billion[47] in 1992. These taxes came nowhere near the penalty each of us pays in insurance costs, health costs, and lost work due to alcoholism. Columbia University in

May 1994 reported the United States will spend $16 billion treating diseases caused by smoking. Large numbers of young people take up drinking and eventually generate unnecessary social and health problems. Intoxication is the leading cause of traffic fatalities; it is a major cause of marital problems and it reduces worker productivity. Alcohol and tobacco are not taxed enough to pay for the additional costs we all have to pay in higher auto insurance premiums, health premiums, welfare, and loss of productivity. Those who choose to smoke and drink should pay for the added economic costs, by way of taxes on the products they consume.

INDEPENDENT COMPUTERIZED ACCOUNTABILITY

An article in the Washington Times, January 22, 1996, "Truth in Spending Needed for Budget to be Balanced," by former U.S. Congressman Joseph J. DioGuardi and Michael H. Granof (University of Texas), said "some of the dollar amounts used in the current budget debate are so misleading they should be tossed out. The figures are based on accounting principles that capture only a portion of the costs of federal activities."

They observed that the federal government, using 1993 data and current principles, determined its actual operating deficit to be $225 billion. In its audited financial statement for 1993 using "generally accepted accounting principles," the U.S. government reported a deficit of $386 billion (a 51% discrepancy).

The conventional measure of the federal debt holds that it was $3.2 trillion as of year end 1993. This contrasts with $5.2 trillion as reported in the latest audited financial statements (a 63% discrepancy). The difference exists because the budget is constructed on a cash basis, whereas the financial statements are prepared on a more meaningful "generally accepted accounting principles" basis. These principles take into account presently contracted government actuarial promises.

While the higher federal debt figure incorporates accounts payable and accrued civil service and military pension obligations, it still does not include total unfunded actuarial liability for Social Security of $7.6 trillion and unrecorded Medicare obligations of $3.6 trillion. In addition, it excludes contingencies, such as loan and credit guarantees and potential obligations under insurance programs, that add up to another $5.9 trillion (a total of $17.16 trillion). In the report of the 1993 statements, Arthur Andersen & Co. concluded that deficiencies in both accounting principles and information systems "make it likely that the (consolidated financial statements are) materially misstated." Experts are demanding that the government hold itself to the same standards of accountability to which it holds officers of publicly-traded corporations and taxpayers. The above 1993 report is almost $3 trillion higher than the 1994 Bipartisan Commission on Entitlement and Tax Reform report, that used 1992 data and showed $14.4 trillion of unfunded obligations.

Congress should immediately investigate the accuracy of this information because our real unfunded liabilities may be $5 trillion plus over $17 trillion instead of an imaginary $3.5 trillion. Assuming the information is true, the new Congress must quickly and realistically correct a problem six times greater than the old Congress wanted known. The yearly increased obligations must be at least triple those acknowledged by government. It must then plan and authorize an independent professional organization to assure our country's medical, retirement, revenue, and expenses accurately reflect our obligations.

Federal accounting has been fragmented, unreliable, unresponsive, and slow. It needs to be replaced with a privately held, independent, strike-free CPA/computer hardware and software firm to independently ensure that Congress cannot circumvent a balanced budget. A team of key people from major accounting firms and major U.S. computer hardware and software companies must then develop a government-wide computer network to guarantee timely information for effective management of the federal government.

Input computers should be IBM PC compatible, for economy, and the software system should be an easily modified database. It should operate on the concept that everyone from birth will have a picture ID card with fingerprints which will be reissued every five years. The card will reference transactions with employers, Social Security, federal wage records, marriage, divorce, death, criminal records, medical records, blood type, allergies, welfare, and AFDC, all keyed in with a social security number. It is vital that no personal data in the system can be recovered by unauthorized people or departments. The firm will issue all government checks. Children will need these cards to go to school; wives can track delinquent, child support payments; all entitlements will be tracked. Illegal aliens will have no cards and collect no benefits. The firm will collect all necessary data; collect, record, and disburse all funds; forecast future needs; and financially secure all trust funds, using citizen cards as the control. Failure to make this change will further cause Congress to play games with our treasury and trust funds.

A second objective would be to develop this complete, easily modified, computerized, government system for sale to other governments. The system should be fast and flawless. Stock funding for this firm can be expedited and the major profits for the company will come from sale to other countries. The firm would charge the government for all labor, plus agreed benefits, plus a percentage. Computers and hardware would be billed at direct cost, plus a bid percentage. The system must write all checks and account for all income and expenses within two years. It should have full operational capabilities within four years.

THE POSITIVE VALUES OF CHANGE

The solution to our financial problems starts with understanding their real magnitude. It next requires an analysis of what we pay for what we want from government. Lobbies have been spending $300 billion for political favors. Regulations have added $680 billion to our cost of living, and our legal services cost us $120 billion to $660 billion more than our major economic competitors. Income taxes have added $166 billion to our economic friction. Government-imposed costs directed by lobbies, laws, and regulations must be reduced or eliminated. Government has been very redundant, and must be made more efficient. Campaign financing by lobbies must end, so that all lobby benefits can be judged on their own merits, in relation to our economy.

The changes outlined in this chapter can put our financial house in order quickly. The proposed changes will trigger other presently undiscovered efficiencies and improvements to our economy, government, and debt. Our economy can recover by supporting those politicians who would balance the budget and embrace change. With these changes, the cost of living can dramatically drop, business can be much more competitive, jobs can more easily be created, and industries once closed by excessive litigation can reopen, restoring lost jobs. The faults need to be corrected as soon as possible, and they can be. Failure to move (status quo) can easily leave us amoral, bankrupt, and living in anarchy. The needed changes will only affect substantially less than 1% of the most privileged people in America. History gives us great insight into making the decisions that have to be made.

I know no way of judging the future but by the past. —Patrick Henry

Chapter 2   History

By 1774 the 2,600,000 British colonists were chafing under the heavy hand of British Colonial rule.[1] Patrick Henry made the following speech to the Virginia Assembly: "Besides, sir, we shall not fight our battles alone. There is a just God who presides over the destinies of nations, and who will raise up friends to fight our battles for us. The battle, sir, is not to the strong alone; it is to the vigilant, the active, the brave." By 1775 Thomas Jefferson wrote, "Our cause is just. Our union is perfect. Our internal resources are great; and, if necessary, foreign assistance is undoubtedly attainable. With hearts fortified with these animating reflections, we most solemnly, before God and the world, declare that, exerting the utmost energy of those powers which our beneficent Creator has graciously bestowed upon us, the arms we have been compelled by our enemies to assume, we will, in defiance of every hazard, with unabating firmness and perseverance, employ for the preservation of our liberties; being with one mind resolved to die free men rather than live slaves." That same year George Washington agreed to lead the army without pay, other than expenses.

At a public meeting of the residents of Mecklenburg County in the state of North Carolina, held at Charlotte on May 20, 1775, "it was Resolved that whenever directly or indirectly abetted, or in any way, form, or manner countenanced, the unchartered and dangerous invasion of our rights, as claimed by Great Britain, is an enemy of our country to America and to the inherent and inalienable rights of man. Resolved, That we, the citizens of Mecklenburg County, do hereby dissolve the political bonds which have connected us to the mother-country, and hereby absolve ourselves from all allegiance to the British crown, and abjure all political connection, contract or association with that nation, which has wantonly trampled on our rights and liberties and inhumanly shed the blood of American patriots at Lexington. Resolved, that we do hereby declare ourselves a free and independent people; are and of right ought to be a sovereign and self-governing association, under the control of no power other than that of our God and the general government of the Congress. To the maintenance of which independence we solemnly pledge to each other our mutual cooperation, our lives, our fortunes, and our sacred honor." In June of 1776 Congress appointed a committee to write the Declaration of Independence. Thomas Jefferson wrote it and after making some revisions, it was unanimously approved on July 4, 1776 (the first

15

portion of which and the last paragraph is as follows with bold print of statements of this and other founding documents emphasized for focus):

DECLARATION OF INDEPENDENCE

When in the course of human events, it becomes necessary for one people to dissolve the political bands which have connected them with another, and to assume, among the powers of the earth, the separate and equal station to which the laws of nature and of nature's God entitle them, a decent respect to the opinions of mankind requires that they should declare the causes which impel them to the separation.

We hold these truths to be self-evident, that all men are created equal, that they are endowed, by their Creator, with certain unalienable rights, that among these are life, liberty, and the pursuit of happiness. That to secure these rights, governments are instituted among men, deriving their just powers from the consent of the governed, that whenever any form of government becomes destructive of these ends, it is the right of the people to alter or to abolish it, and to institute new government, laying its foundation on such principles, and organizing its powers in such form as to them shall seem most likely to effect their safety and happiness. Prudence, indeed, will dictate, that governments long established should not be changed for light and transient causes; and accordingly all experience hath shown that mankind are more disposed to suffer where evils are sufferable, than to right themselves by abolishing the forms to which they are accustomed. **But when a long train of abuses and usurpations, pursuing invariably the same object, evinces a design to reduce them under absolute despotism, it is their right, it is their duty, to throw off such government, and to provide new guards for their future security.**

And for the support of this declaration, with a firm reliance on the protection of Divine Providence, we mutually pledge to each other our lives, our fortunes, and our sacred honor.

ARTICLES OF CONFEDERATION

Approved by the Congress July 12, 1776. They stated:

ARTICLE 1. The style of this confederacy shall be "The United States of America."

ARTICLE 2. **Each state retains its sovereignty, freedom, and independence, and every power, jurisdiction, and right which is not by this confederation expressly delegated to the United States in Congress assembled.**

ARTICLE 3. The said states hereby enter into a firm league of friendship with each other, for their common defense, the security of their liberties, and their mutual general welfare, binding themselves to assist each other against all force offered to, or attacks made upon them, on account of religion, sovereignty, trade, or any other pretense whatever.[2]

On March 1, 1781, the Articles of Confederation were ratified by all 13 states.

In the winter of 1777, Washington's Colonial Army was surrounded and outnumbered by the British in Yorktown, and their escape was cut off by the Potomac River. Troop morale was very low and the weather, food, and clothing were miserable. Washington continuously rallied his troops saying, "If God be with us, who can be against us?" Then on a single foggy winter night, he managed to move all of his 8,000 troops, horses, equipment, and ammunition across the river safely without being noticed until all were safe.

By 1778 the Continental Army remained in bad shape and demoralized, however the tides gradually turned and on February 27, 1782, Cornwallis surrendered at Yorktown. The Continental Congress in 1787 completed the Constitution of the United States of America, which was ratified by March 1789, and 15 amendments were later ratified. Portions of the Constitution and amendments pertaining to this work are as follows:

CONSTITUTION OF THE UNITED STATES OF AMERICA

Preamble. **We, the people of the United States, in order to form a more perfect union, establish justice, insure domestic tranquillity, provide for the common defense, promote the general welfare, and secure the blessings of liberty to ourselves and our posterity,** do ordain and establish this Constitution for the United States of America.

Article I.

Section I. 1. **All legislative powers herein granted shall be vested in a Congress of the United States,** which shall consist of a Senate and House of Representatives.

Section IV. 1. The times, places and manner of holding elections for Senators and Representatives shall be prescribed in each State by the Legislature thereof; but the Congress may at any time by law make or alter such regulations, except as to the place of choosing Senators.

Section VI. 1. The Senators and Representatives shall receive a compensation for their services, to be ascertained by law, and paid out of the treasury of the United States. They shall, in all cases, except treason, felony, and breach of the peace, be privileged from arrest during their attendance at the sessions of their respective houses, and in going to and returning from the same; and for any speech or debate in either house, they shall not be questioned in any other place.

Section VII. 1. All bills for raising revenue shall originate in the House of Representatives, but the Senate may propose or concur with amendments, as on other bills.

2. Every bill which shall have passed the House of Representatives and the Senate shall, before it become a law, be presented to the President of the United States; if he approve, he shall sign it, but if not, he shall return it, with his objections, to that house in which it shall have originated, who shall enter the objections at large on their journal, and proceed to reconsider it. If after such reconsideration two thirds of that house shall agree to pass the bill, it shall be sent, together with the objections to the other House, by which it shall likewise be reconsidered; and if approved by two thirds of that House it shall become a law.

3. Every order, resolution, or vote to which the concurrence of the Senate and House of Representatives may be necessary (except on a question of adjournment) shall be presented to the President of the United States; and before the same shall take effect shall be approved by him, or being disapproved by him, shall be repassed by two thirds of the Senate and the House of Representatives, according to the rules and limitations prescribed in the case of a bill.

Section VIII. 1. The Congress shall have power: To lay and collect taxes, duties, imposts, and excises, to pay the debts and provide for the common defense and general welfare of the United States; but all duties, imposts, and excises shall be uniform throughout the United States.

2. To borrow money on the credit of the United States.

3. To regulate commerce with foreign nations, and among the several States, and with the Indian tribes.

4. To establish a uniform rule of naturalization and uniform laws on the subject of bankruptcies throughout the United States.

5. To coin money, regulate the value thereof, and of foreign coin, and fix the standard of weights and measures.

6. To provide for the punishment of counterfeiting the securities and current coin of the United States.

7. To establish post offices and post roads.

8. To promote the progress of science and useful arts by securing for limited times to authors and inventors the exclusive rights to their respective writings and discoveries.

9. To constitute tribunals inferior to the Supreme Court.

10. To define and punish piracies and felonies committed on the high seas, and offenses against the law of nations.

11. To declare war, grant letters of marque and reprisal, and make rules concerning captures on land and water.

12. To raise and support armies, but no appropriation of money to that use shall be for a longer term than two years.

13. To provide and maintain a navy.

14. To make rules for the government and regulation of the land and naval forces.

15. To provide for calling forth the militia to execute the laws of the Union, suppress insurrections, and repel invasions.

16. To provide for organizing, arming, and disciplining the militia, and for governing such part of them as may be employed in the services of the United States, reserving to the States respectively the appointment of the officers, and the authority of training the militia according to the discipline prescribed by Congress.

17. To exercise exclusive legislation in all cases whatsoever over such district (not exceeding ten miles square) as may, by cession of particular States and the acceptance of Congress, become the seat of Government of the United States, and to exercise like authority over all places purchased by the consent of the Legislature of the State in which the same shall be, for the erection of forts, magazines, arsenals, dry docks, and other needful buildings.

18. To make all laws which shall be necessary and proper for carrying into execution the foregoing powers, and all other powers vested by this Constitution in the Government of the United States, or in any department or officer thereof.

Section IX. 4. No Capitation or other direct tax shall be laid, unless in proportion to the census or enumeration hereinbefore directed to be taken.

ARTICLE II.

Section I. 1. The Executive power shall be vested in a President of the United States of America. He shall hold his office during the term of four years, and, together with the Vice-President, chosen for the same term, be elected as follows:

ARTICLE III.

Section I. The judicial power of the United States shall be vested in one Supreme Court, and in such inferior courts as the Congress may from time to time ordain and establish. The judges, both of the Supreme and inferior courts, shall hold their offices during good behavior, and shall at stated times receive for their services a compensation which shall not be diminished during their continuance in office.

ARTICLE V.

The Congress, whenever two thirds of both Houses shall deem it necessary, shall propose amendments to this Constitution, or, on the application of the Legislatures of two thirds of the several States, shall call a convention for proposing amendments, which, in either case, shall be valid to all intents and purposes, as part of this Constitution, when ratified by the Legislatures of three fourths of the several States, or by conventions in three fourths thereof, as the one or the other mode of ratification may be proposed by the Congress; provided that no amendment which may be made prior to the year one thousand eight hundred and eight shall in any manner affect the first and fourth clauses in the Ninth Section of the First Article; and that no State, without its consent, shall be deprived of its equal suffrage in the Senate.

ARTICLE VII.

The ratification of the Conventions of nine States shall be sufficient for the establishment of this Constitution between the States so ratifying the same.

EARLY AMENDMENTS TO THE CONSTITUTION

Article I. **Congress shall make no law respecting an establishment of religion, or prohibiting the free exercise thereof; or abridging the freedom of speech or of the press; or the right of the people peaceably to assemble, and to petition the Government for a redress of grievances.**

Article II. A well-regulated militia being necessary to the security of a free state, **The right of the people to keep and bear arms shall not be infringed.**

Article III. No soldier shall, in time of peace, be quartered in any house without the consent of the owner, nor in time of war but in a manner to be prescribed by law.

Article IV. **The right of the people to be secure in their persons, houses, papers, and effects, against unreasonable searches and seizures, shall not be violated, and no warrants shall issue but upon probable cause, supported by oath or affirmation, and particularly describing the place to be searched, and the persons or things to be seized.**

Article V. **No person shall be held to answer for a capital or other infamous crime unless on a presentment or indictment of a grand jury,** except in cases arising in the land or naval forces, or in the militia, when in actual service, in time of war or public danger; **nor shall any person be subject for the same offense to be twice put in jeopardy of life or limb; nor shall be compelled in any criminal case to be a witness against himself, nor be deprived of life, liberty, or property, without due process of law; nor shall private property be taken for public use without just compensation.**

Article VI. **In all criminal prosecutions, the accused shall enjoy the right to a speedy and public trial, by an impartial jury of the State and district wherein the crime shall have been committed, which district shall have been previously ascertained by law, and to be informed of the nature and cause of the accusation; to be confronted with the witnesses against him; to have compulsory process for obtaining witnesses in his favor, and to have the assistance of counsel for his defense.**

Article VII. **In suits at common law, where the value in controversy shall exceed twenty dollars, the right of trial by jury shall be preserved, and no fact tried by a jury shall be otherwise re-examined in any court of the United States than according to the rules of the common law.**

Article VIII. **Excessive bail shall not be required, nor excessive fines imposed, nor cruel and unusual punishments inflicted.**

Article IX. The enumeration in the Constitution of certain rights shall not be construed to deny or disparage others retained by the people.

Article X. **The powers not delegated to the United States by the Constitution, nor prohibited by it to the States, are reserved to the States respectively, or to the people.**

Article XI. **The judicial power of the United States shall not be construed to extend to any suit in law or equity, commenced or prosecuted against one of the United States, by citizens of another State, or by citizens or subjects of any foreign State.**

Article XII. The electors shall meet in their respective States, and vote by ballot for President and Vice President....

Article XIII. 1. **Neither slavery nor involuntary servitude, except as a punishment for crime whereof the party shall have been duly convicted, shall exist within the United States,** or any place subject to their jurisdiction.

Article XIV. 1. All persons born or naturalized in the United States, and subject to the jurisdiction thereof, are citizens of the United States and of the State wherein they reside. **No State shall make or enforce any law which shall abridge the privileges or immunities of citizens of the United States; nor shall any State deprive any person of life, liberty, or property** without due process of law, nor deny to any person within its jurisdiction the equal protection of the laws.

Article XV. 1. The right of the citizens of the United States to vote shall not be denied or abridged by the United States or by any State on account of race, color, or previous condition of servitude.

WRITINGS OF THE FOUNDERS

Alexander Hamilton in 1784 wrote, "Nothing is more common than for a free people, in times of heat and violence, to gratify momentary passions by letting into the government principles and precedents which afterwards prove fatal to themselves. Of this kind is the doctrine of disqualification, disfranchisement, and banishment, by acts of legislature. The dangerous consequences of this power are manifest. If the legislature can disfranchise any number of citizens at pleasure by general descriptions, it may soon confine all the votes to a small number of partisans, and establish an aristocracy or an oligarchy. If it may banish at discretion all those whom particular circumstances render obnoxious without hearing or trial, no man can be safe nor know when he may be the innocent victim of a prevailing faction. The name of liberty applied to such a government would be a mockery of common sense. "

Benjamin Franklin in a speech to the Constitutional Convention in 1787 said,"I agree to this Constitution with all its faults, if they are such; because I think a general government necessary for us, and there is no form of government but what may be a blessing to the people if well administered and believe farther that this is likely to be well administered for a course of years, and can only end in despotism, as other forms have done before it, when the people shall become so corrupted as to need despotic government, being incapable of any other. I doubt, too, whether any other convention we can obtain may be able to make a better Constitution; for when you assemble a number of men to have the advantage of their joint wisdom, you inevitably assemble with those men all their prejudices, their passions, their errors of opinion, their local interests, and their selfish views. From such an assembly can a perfect production be expected? On the whole, sir, I cannot help expressing a wish that every member of the Convention who may still have objections to it would, with me, on this occasion doubt a little of his own infallibility."

Patrick Henry in 1788 said to the Virginia Ratifying Convention, "My political curiosity, exclusive of my anxious solicitude for the public welfare, leads me to ask, Who authorized them to speak the language of 'We, the people,' instead of We, the states? States are the characteristics and the soul of a confederation. If the states be not the agents of this compact, it must be one great, consolidated, national government of the people of all the states. This government will operate like an ambuscade. It will destroy the state governments and swallow the liberties of the people, without giving previous notice. If gentlemen are willing to run the hazard, let them run it; but I shall exculpate myself by my opposition and monitory warnings within these walls." Henry was very much in favor of a union of states but believed that a strong central government would become an oppressive, cumbersome, unmanageable bureaucracy. He believed the proposed Constitution would use the ruse of general welfare to displace states rights and generate enormous debt and ruinous taxes.[3]

Thomas Jefferson stated in his first inaugural address in 1801 that our government should be "a wise and frugal government, which shall restrain men from harming one another, which shall leave them otherwise free to regulate their own pursuits of industry and improvement, and shall not take from the mouth of labor the bread it has earned." Jefferson further wrote, "Government governs best which governs least."

Excerpts show the framers' religious and constitutional beliefs, desire for a frugal government, distrust of big government, and fear of being enslaved by it. The Continental Congress was very aware of English and European history, where virtually everyone but the privileged were serfs subject to the will of the powerful. The statement that all men are created equal meant to them, equal under the law, with no privilege and no bondage due to power, religious beliefs, ancestry, or any other reason. It did not mean the government should make the dull smarter and the smart duller or the sick healthier and the healthy sicker so that all would be equal in every way. The right to bear arms came directly from their history where unarmed peasants continuously became slaves of the armed monarchies, clans, and privileged class. They also clearly show that the Congress has virtually all the power in government and that it can be changed by the people. The Congress has all the powers outlined in Article I, Section VIII, and no other power as defined in the Tenth Amendment. They show that the framers of the Constitution believed in God, but wanted no part of a required national religion. They show that freedom of speech and the press functions primarily as a watchdog to prevent government abuse of power, not dubious artistic and immoral expression. Congressional limitations were upheld by the Supreme Court until Franklin Roosevelt appointed enough replacement justices to change, until now, the power of the federal government and its economic impact on our country.

SPENDING AND INDEPENDENCE

You cannot keep out of trouble by spending more than you earn. You cannot build courage and character by taking away a man's initiative and independence. You cannot help men permanently by doing for them what they could and should do for themselves.—Abraham Lincoln

The Continental Congress seriously debated whether they should tax as much as 1% or 2% through interstate tariffs to support the federal government and decided that neither should be enacted because the federal government might tax that much, whether they need it or not. The average American today pays more in taxes than for food, clothing, and shelter combined.

The old Congress, special interests, and federal agencies have defeated every president's attempt to spend less and become more efficient. Without major changes our horrendous debt will overwhelm us without notice. Our government has over $17 trillion more debts and obligations ($340,000 per support household) than assets. Any fiscal crisis could trigger a drop in America's faith in our economy or trust in our currency that could precipitate a stock free fall and depression more severe than the Great Depression of the 1930s. Stocks dropped 22.6% over two days in October 1929 and dropped 22.7% in one day in 1987.

A depression is caused by long-term economic abuse. Prior to the last depression, many Americans prospered by speculating in the market. On October 29, 1929, the stock market dropped 10 billion (1929) dollars. By the end of the year, it lost $40 billion.[4] By 1932 stocks dropped to less than 20% of their previous value. Millions of Americans lost their homes, life savings, and insurance overnight. One of every four Americans was out of work (25% unemployment). Government income plummeted, wealthy Americans had no income to report because of stock losses, and the unemployed earned no income.

If the government takes no action, the news media will talk about people's misery and riots. We must remember that only 50% of our country's households now pay 95% of its taxes. It will be impossible for half of our households to finance expanded entitlements or treasury notes.

When the government first overspends its revenues, has a strong currency, and has few debts, as in 1929, it can borrow against the future. When Congress overspends its revenues for decades and has huge debts, it can no longer borrow more money. Our currency is no longer secured with gold. It is now secured with the trust in government and its monetary policy. A stock free fall will quickly pressure the banks and the market when laid off people sell their investments and want their savings. Should this happen in the 1990s, dramatically higher tax rates will not be high enough to cover the greatly expanded expenses of unemployment and other benefits. The FDIC and FSLIC do not have enough reserves to stop a major run and will become insolvent. As more people become concerned about their jobs, sales of automobiles, airplanes, durable goods, and construction will virtually stop, triggering more layoffs. When the government is faced with a depression and cannot sell treasury notes at any reasonable interest rate, it will be forced to default on note payments or print money. Printing money will seem much more desirable than being branded as the Congress that defaulted on payments. Printing a little money will seem to be the only practical solution. It will be called monetizing the debt and it will trigger a runaway inflation that will prove to be disastrous within six months if we believe history provides any insight.

COUNTRIES WHO FACED LARGE DEBTS

In the spring of 1922 Germany monetized its debt and the value of the mark quickly dropped to 2% of its premonetized value.[5] By October 1922 it was worth less than 1/1000 of its previous value. Retirees who had government bonds saw their value drop 2000% in one day. In January 1923 (nine months later) the value of the mark was 1/4000 of its previous value. By the end of 1923, the mark was worth one-trillionth of its former value. Before World War II

Argentina was the fifth largest export nation in the world. The government sold the people the idea that it was the great provider. By the 1980s they were in debt $44 billion ($1,333 per person). The government faced three choices: default, raise taxes, or inflate currency. They printed money and within six months inflation was 100% per month. By 1990 inflation was 5,600% per year. They and the Germans both destroyed their country's economy and their people's lifetime savings by printing money instead of solving government problems. A basic economic premise is that more money chasing fewer goods always causes inflation. Printing money initially makes house payments easier, pays for all entitlements, and creates unneeded projects in order to put people to work. Retirees' savings are soon wiped out and there will be no work because the young will have their jobs. A runaway inflation can easily produce war in the streets, gang-driven chaos, and destruction similar to the Watts and Los Angeles riots. This will especially affect the disadvantaged, elderly, handicapped, and anyone without major safe savings.

The financial and other problems we have can be cured as Great Britain cured its debt problems under Prime Minister Margaret Thatcher. In 1979 Great Britain had a debt of $18 billion which was 51% of their GDP. By 1990 the debt was 27% of GDP. By contrast in 1995 our $5 trillion debt will be 68% of GDP and will continue to rise. This debt does not include immense promised unfunded retirement entitlements which will increase the debt to more than our GDP. Great Britain's unemployment was 11% in the early 1980s and dropped to 6% by 1990. Between 1981 and 1990 Great Britain created three million jobs, the GDP rose twice as fast as the previous ten years, and the pound rose against other currencies. Great Britain, however, has not fully recovered from their debt. They continue to lag behind other European countries in growth, and may never catch up. A sour economy will drive investment money out of the country. The English are now the major foreign owners of American companies.

The old Congress has changed a free and frugal government that gave individuals and states freedom to regulate their own pursuits, to a debt-bound, bloated collective in serious danger of collapsing. Business thrived under the light hand of our founders, but is now being choked by the intrusive hand of the federal bureaucracy. A self-reliant tradition has been replaced with a welfare tradition.

The dramatic political change of November 8, 1994 toward less government was made possible, and necessary, by the Continental Congress. A government projected to require all children born after 1990 to pay 82% of their lifetime income in taxes is not of the people, by the people, and for the people. It is instead an example of the corruption of congressional power and privilege by special interests. This promise or contract will grow or die depending on how much influence special interests have on the 1996 congressional elections.

Total and yearly differences in WPI and CPI since 1965 in dollars

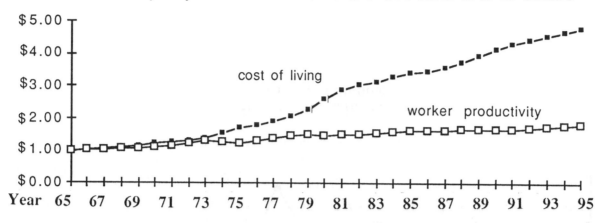

A dollar of worker productivity has increased 92 cents since 1965. The cost of living increased $3.82 in the same period. This 263% COLA increase above worker productivity severely damaged U.S. competitiveness and our economy. Source: U.S. Bureau of Labor Statistics.

Comparative Rise of Interest, Consumer Prices, and Manufacturing Productivity
Debt in billions

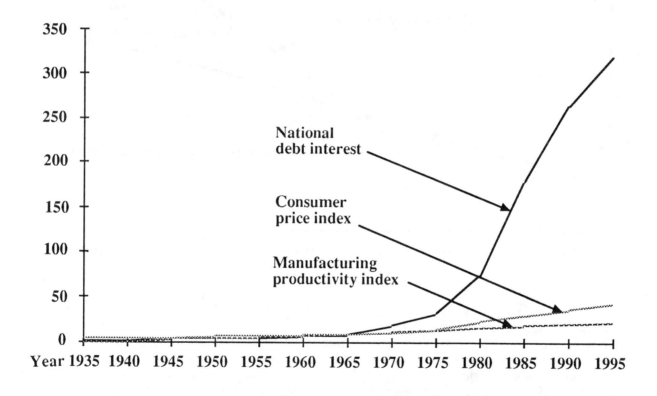

From 1945 to 1965, productivity, the consumer price index (CPI), and interest on the national debt rose together. Productivity and output per hour then continued together until 1970 when the early effects of federal economic friction set in and business started to lose productivity, a fraction of a percent each year. Accumulated CPI and COLA increases over 30 years are now 263% higher than productivity. This added a huge labor tax on business and reduced U.S. competitiveness. Source: Bureau of Labor Statistics. *Budget of the United States Government* Historical Tables 1995, p 19.

National Debt Interest Compared to All U.S. Personal Savings
in billions

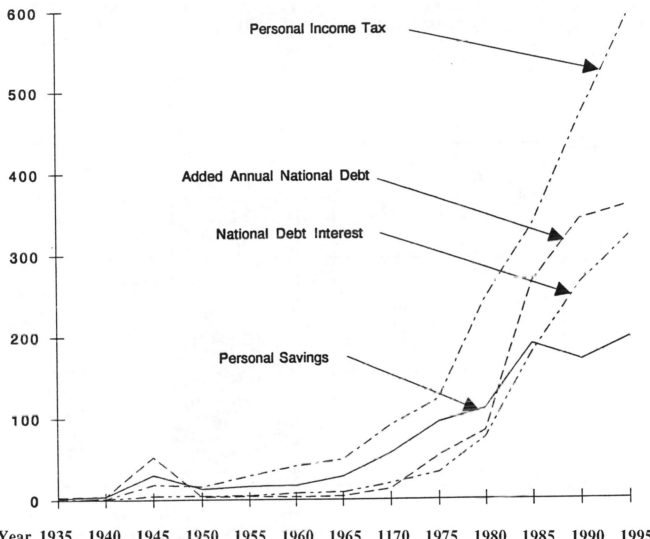

Personal Income Tax

Added Annual National Debt

National Debt Interest

Personal Savings

Year 1935 1940 1945 1950 1955 1960 1965 1170 1975 1980 1985 1990 1995

Until 1970 personal savings were about twice the size of the interest on the national debt. In 1990 they were just 64% of the interest on the debt. This year the total of all personal savings will be 60% of the yearly interest on the national debt. Future yearly federal deficits are projected to stay at $300 billion including borrowed trust funds, while annual new savings fluctuate around $200 billion. Where will the money come from for business and industry when year after year personal savings don't cover the increase on the national debt or the interest? The present administration reduced by half the amount of high-rate long-term treasury notes. This can precipitate a crisis if foreign countries do not reinvest in our short-term treasury funds because of inflation, a drop in the market, or the dollar. We now have a much higher amount of short-term treasury debt than three years ago. Isn't this why the Federal Reserve Board wants to keep inflation down at all costs? Source: *Statistical Abstract of the United States* Department of Commerce, Brief 1994, p 451; *Budget of the United States* Historical Tables, 1994, p 19, 95, 87, and Sept '95 *Survey of Current Business* p 9.

Unfunded Retirement, Medicare, and Other Liabilities

OVER $14 TRILLION IN UNFUNDED LIABILITIES: THE PROMISE OF TODAY'S ADULTS IN EXCESS OF CURRENT TRUST FUND "ASSETS" PLUS THE FUTURE TAXES TODAY'S ADULTS ARE SCHEDULED TO PAY

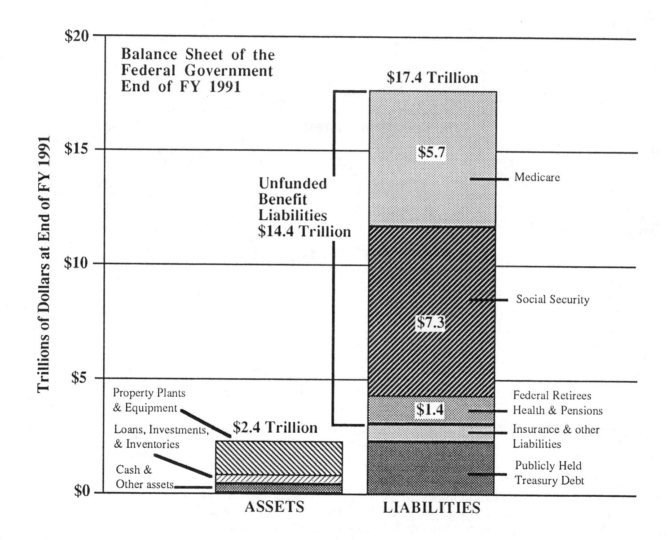

The 1994 *Bipartisan Commission on Entitlements and Tax Reform* report used this graph to illustrate how just four programs, Social Security, Medicare, Civil Service, and Military Retirement add up to $14.4 trillion in unfunded liabilities. Source: OMB 1993 data and Haeworth Robertson 1992 data. Higher unfunded liabilities and obligations of $17.2 trillion were reported by Arthur Andersen & Co, using 1993 data.

Workers Available to Support All U.S. Retirees

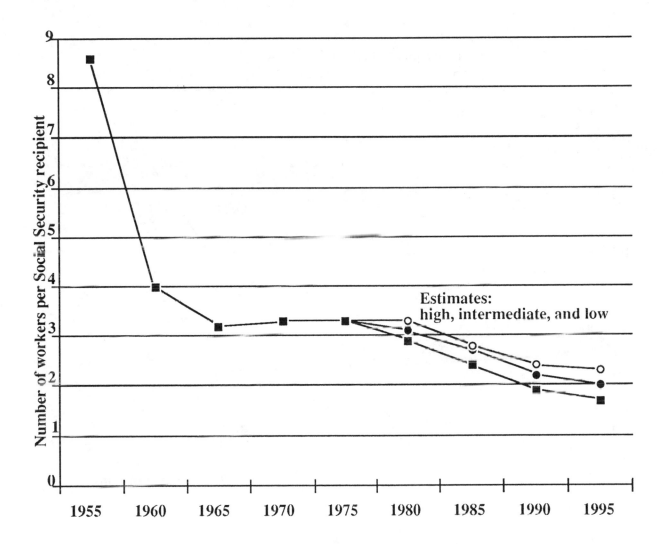

In 1935 life expectancy for men and women at birth was 60 and 64 respectively. Few lived to be 65, and many workers supported them. By 1995 life expectancy was 73 and 80, 15 years longer. In 1945 there were 42 workers supporting each retiree and almost half of the living men over 65 worked. There are now 3.3 workers per retiree, and the intermediate estimate for 2030 is 2.0 workers per retiree. The need for two incomes and smaller families reduced the number of future workers, while better health care prolonged life. The above figures do not include federal and military retirees, who taxpayers must also support. Source: *Social Security Trustees Report* 1995 p 122, 123. *Historical Statistics of the United States* from Historical Times to 1970 p 55. *1994 Statistical Abstract of the United States*, Department of Commerce, p 87.

Growth of Lawyers and Judges Compared to U.S. Population
from 1930 to 1993

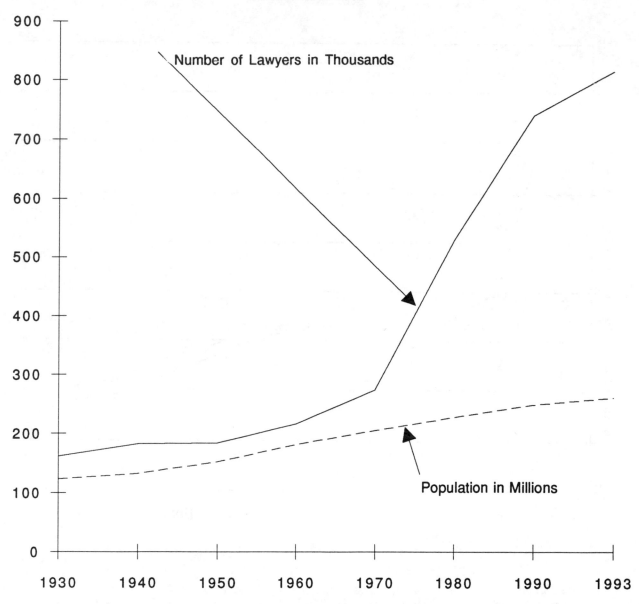

The number of lawyers has grown eight times faster than the population from 1965 to 1995, when the surge of new laws and regulations began. They are projected to be one of the fastest growing professions, and they produce nothing. The same surge of legislation caused the percent of manufacturing jobs to decline 47%, almost half. Source: Bureau of Labor Statistics; *Historical Statistics of the United States* Colonial Times to 1970. *Statistical Abstract of the United States*, Department of Commerce, 1993.

Regulations, Lawyer Growth, and Manufacturing Jobs Lost
in thousands

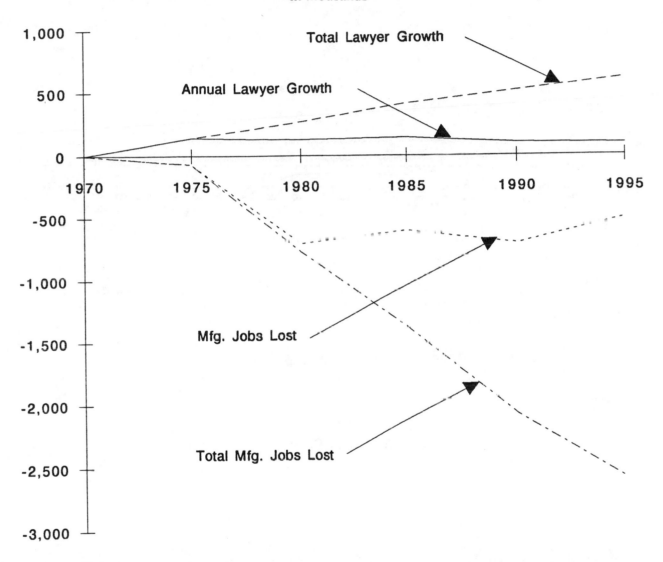

In 1970 there were 13,528,000 manufacturing workers and 260,000 lawyers in the United States. From then until now, manufacturing has lost 2,570,000 jobs and lawyers have gained 611,000 jobs. The manufacturing jobs lost add to economic friction with unemployment, welfare, and relocation costs. Unemployment puts pressure on wage increases, and it permanently reduces our GDP and savings. Stephen Magee, Professor of Finance and Economics at the University of Texas, in Austin, Texas, has studies showing that the number of lawyers above 300,000 subtract $660 billion from the economy or about 9% of our GDP. Laws and regulations enacted since 1965 must be reviewed, and some changed to reduce economic friction and cost of living. When the number of lawyers approaches 350,000, our economy will have eliminated most of the economic friction which has raised the cost of living and destroyed productive jobs. Source: Bureau of Labor Statistics.

Annual Trade Balance and Accumulated Trade Deficit
in billions

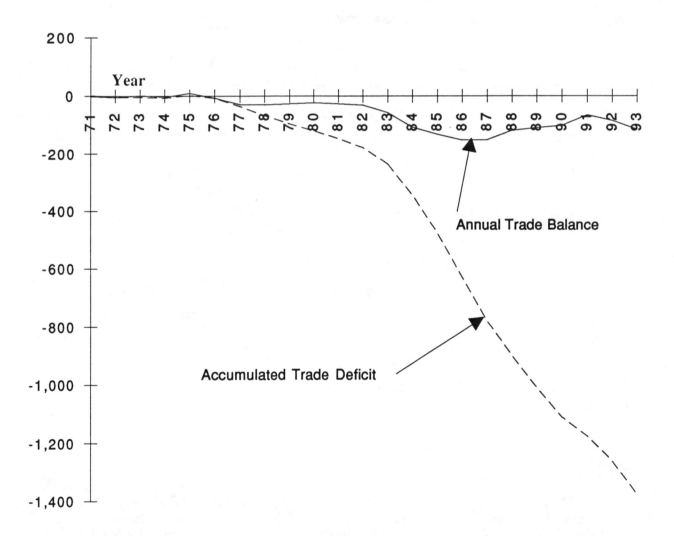

Between 1975 and 1980 we lost our positive trade balance with the rest of the world, and it coincides with our lost productivity and increased economic friction. This loss alone could repay the $1.3 trillion that the old Congress borrowed from Social Security to pay for additional federal spending programs. Source: *Historical Statistics of the United States* Colonial Times to 1970 p 895. *Statistical Abstract of the United States* Department of Commerce Brief, 1994, p 118.

Productivity of the United States

Profitability and Productivity					% change 1980-1990	% change 1989-1990
	1980	1985	1989	1990		
Intermediate input (%)	59	56	53	54	-8.5	1.9
Wages, salaries, and supplements (%)	21	21	16[e]	21	0.0	31.3
Gross operating surplus (%)	21	22	30[e]	26	23.8	-13.3
Gross output per worker ($)	96,673	130,122	161,325	163,521	69.1	1.4
Value added per worker ($)	40,078	57,191	75,527	75,555	88.5	0.0
Average wage (incl. benefits) ($)	20,044	27,955	26,356[e]	33,573	67.5	27.4

Profitability is in percent of gross output. Productivity is in U.S. $. 'e' stands for estimated value.

Profitability - 1990

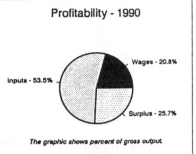

Wages - 20.8%
Inputs - 53.5%
Surplus - 25.7%

The graphic shows percent of gross output.

Productivity of Japan

Profitability and Productivity					% change 1980-1990	% change 1989-1990
	1980	1985	1989	1990		
Intermediate input (%)	65	63	60	60	-7.7	0.0
Wages, salaries, and supplements (%)	12	13	13	13	8.3	0.0
Gross operating surplus (%)	23	24	27	27	17.4	0.0
Gross output per worker ($)	88,443	102,348	202,076	200,997	127.3	-0.5
Value added per worker ($)	30,912	37,876	80,924	79,816	158.2	-1.4
Average wage (incl. benefits) ($)	11,522	13,653	26,840	26,828	132.8	0.0

Profitability is in percent of gross output. Productivity is in U.S. $. 'e' stands for estimated value.

Profitability - 1990

Inputs - 60.0%
Wages - 13.0%
Surplus - 27.0%

The graphic shows percent of gross output.

Japan had a gross manufacturing output of $971 billion in 1980. In 1990 it had $2,246 billion. The United States had $1,857 billion output in 1980 and $2,861 billion in 1990. Japan went from 52.2% of our manufacturing capacity to 78.5% in 10 years. During that time we lost 2,570,000 manufacturing jobs. At $33,573 current value each, the direct cost to our economy was $86 billion plus welfare. Their labor cost has remained at 13% while ours has been at 21% due in a large part to our cost of living index, which is substantially higher than our workers' productivity. Our value added and gross output per worker started higher than Japan's and is now lower. Japan now has more gross output and value added per worker by investing more in robots, R&D, and utilization of other costly high-tech devices. U.S. gross output per worker up 69%; Japan 127%. Japan wins!

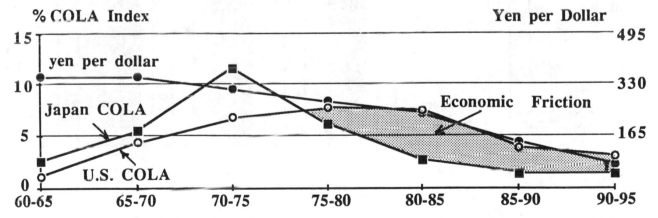

A dollar bought 360 yen in 1965 and 1970. In early 1995 it bought 83 yen. This 400% drop in value has much to do with not keeping up with Japan's productivity and efficiency. They invested early in quality technology, R&D, robots, and protection for their manufacturers. This caused their consumer price index to rise because these investments competed in the market for yen with no immediate productivity results. Our government invested in welfare, protection of citizens' rights, and regulations to control manufacturing, environment, health, and safety. Their COLA is now one-third of ours. If our economy had been as efficient as Japan's, since 1975, we would have saved over $4 trillion of economic waste. Germany's gain on the dollar is over 75% of Japan's. Source: *Statistical Abstract of the World*, 1994 p 469 & 978, *Statistical Abstract of the United States* Brief, 1994, consumer prices p 486 OECD data. *Federal Reserve Bulletin*, foreign exchange rates, p 881.

Annualized Regulatory Compliance Costs, 1977-2000 in Billions of 1995 Dollars

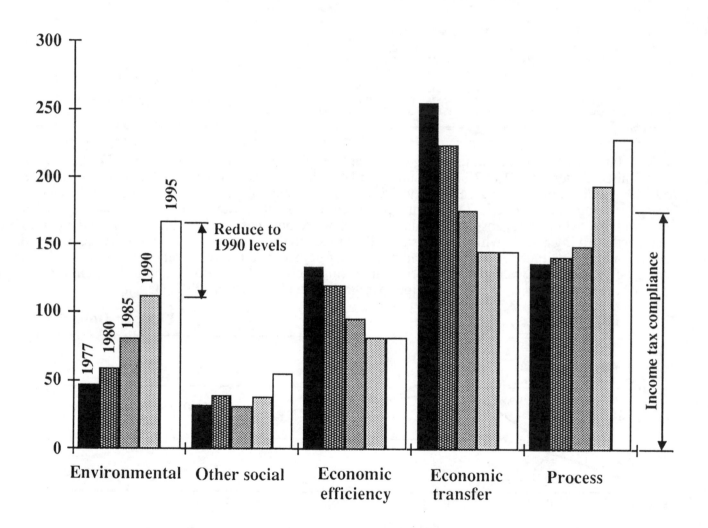

The costs we pay for federal regulations, shown in constant 1995 dollars, continue to increase as more laws are enacted than are removed. They now cost the support household over $13,000 a year. Presently, the fastest growing regulations are environmental. Process regulation (paperwork) is the other major regulatory cost. In 1992 it consumed six billion hours of private sector work and over $200 billion. Reducing the economic penalties of environmental regulations to 1990 levels, and replacing all income taxes with a 10% national sales tax, a 4% business tax on wages, and a revised 7.65% FICA tax will eliminate over $200 billion of economic friction. Source: "Profiles of Regulatory Costs" a 1995 report by Thomas D. Hopkins to the U.S. Small Business Administration.

Federal Government Costs of Regulations
in billions of 1987 dollars adjusted for inflation

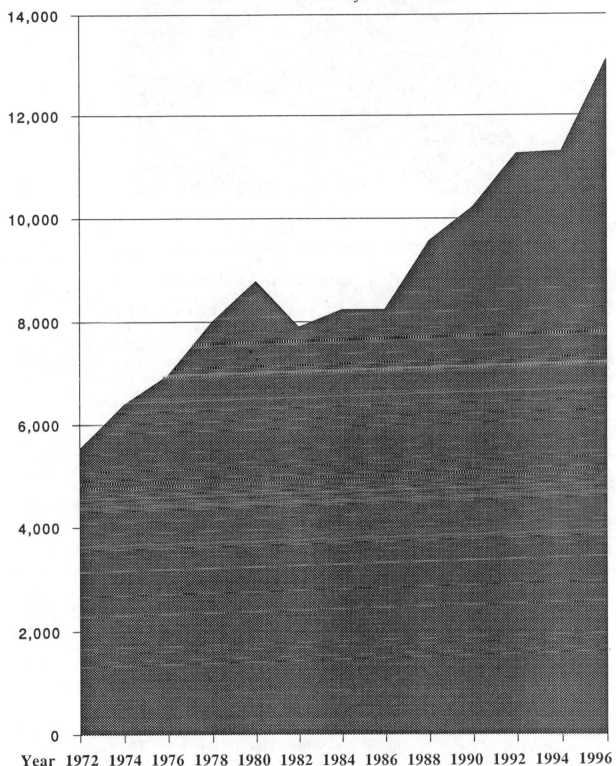

Year 1972 1974 1976 1978 1980 1982 1984 1986 1988 1990 1992 1994 1996

Federal regulatory spending is shown in constant 1987 dollars. Spending grew from $4,000 in 1970 to $11,290 in 1994. It is budgeted to jump to $16,600 in 1996. This is $14,430 in 1987 dollars and is the highest rise ever. In this 26-year period, costs have risen 350% in inflation-adjusted dollars. Source: Center for the Study of American Business, St. Louis Occasional Paper 155.

"LOBBIES"

My reading of history convinces me that most bad government has grown up out of too much government.—John Sharp

Chapter 4   Regulation, Litigation, Lobbies, and COLA

THE INVISIBLE COSTS OF FEDERAL REGULATIONS

The cost of federal regulations passed since the 1960s was purposely made invisible by the old Congress. It didn't affect taxes. It didn't affect purchasing power. It did affect jobs.

1. American goods cost more as manufacturers passed the cost of complying with regulations back to the consumer. Most employers and all retirees had COLA increases, so purchased goods didn't seem to cost more. We began to purchase foreign products at lower prices.

2. Regulations caused an unprecedented rise in COLA above worker productivity, and made our products less competitive. This caused the loss of American jobs.

3. The expense of federal regulations and overspending was hidden by the old Congress by increasing the national debt. The interest on the national debt has increased from 22% of personal federal income tax in 1965 to 57% in 1995. More recently federal agencies such as OSHA have been collecting expanded fines and using the fines to pay for agency operations.

4. Regulatory and litigation costs in the United States are so high that much of our research is being developed into products produced overseas, by foreign competitors.

COLA AND THE ECONOMY—OPPOSITES

An ideal economy is one that automatically rewards employers and employees for creating better quality at less cost. In such a system all workers and business would have common twin goals as a means of higher pay and profit. Congress eliminated both of these goals by means of COLA, in order to pass an unprecedented amount of legislation that would increase living costs far more rapidly than taxpayers would normally accept. Their legislation made COLA the standard for wage increases in contract disputes, and Social Security benefits since 1972. **COLA has nothing to do with productivity or quality**. The economic penalties to households of costly legislation raised the consumer price index and increased COLA. The employer paid the increased cost and passed it back to the consumer at a COLA increased price. This all appeared as a "normal" price increase except that, like not making loan payments, the cost of goods and then the cost of labor ratcheted up another few percent each year until our goods became uncompetitive internationally. The artificial COLA increases and cost of government, laws, and regulations has been a primary cause of our expanding national debt and the interest on it . The major portion of each year's percent COLA should be considered as an equal percent loss in U.S. competitiveness.

In 1936 the consumer price index (CPI) was 78% of the worker productivity index (WPI). Thirty years later CPI was 75% of WPI. Over a 30-year period this accumulated change in worker productivity was 5% higher than COLA. An activist Congress from 1965 to 1995 passed an enormous amount of legislation which increased the cost of living 263% above worker productivity.[1] This difference represents a change of ratio 51 times larger than the previous 30 years. In 1965 the GDP was 78.7% labor cost and is now 84.5% in a $7.1 trillion economy.[2] This 5.8% economic friction alone raises our taxes and cost of goods and services $412 billion each year ($8,240 per support household). It now takes 20% more labor to make our economy run. The percent changes of our GDP are shown for four important sectors of our economy.

Table 6. Loss of Economic Productivity

Sector	1965	1993	Diff. 65-93	% change	Projected 1995
	%	%	%		Amt. in billions
Personal income	78.7	84.5	+5.8	+7.3	+412
Corporate profit	11.6	7.3	-4.3	-37	-305
Social Insurance	4.3	9.2	+4.9	+114	+348
Taxes	9.4	10.7	+1.3	+14	+92

Corporate profit dropped 37% primarily because of lost industries and competitiveness. Total social insurance increased 114%, and half was paid by employers. Taxes were increased only 14%. This increased our debt $4.6 trillion in 30 years.

Lobbies provided campaign contributions to the old Congress in exchange for legislative and regulatory favors. Congressional hearings were purposely stacked to favor special interest views and a massive body of legislation was passed which gradually raised our cost of living far above worker productivity. The accumulated effect over 30 years made our farm and manufactured products uncompetitive worldwide. They will become much less competitive in the future if current laws and regulations remain. We lost many major manufacturing companies, millions of high paying manufacturing jobs and foreign manufacturing markets, and started down the road of heavily subsidizing farm products. The winners were the members of the old Congress who retained their power, special interests, lawyers, and federal bureaucracy. The big losers were all other Americans. If the old Congress deliberately set out to destroy our economy, it could not have done a better job. It simply added to the unproductive side of the economy and took away from the productive side.

If everything that farmers needed to buy over the last 30 years cost half as much (tractors, seed, fertilizer, food, taxes), and everything they produced cost half as much, how much more grain, beef, and pork could farmers have sold overseas? How much less federal assistance would farmers have needed? How many more automobiles, tractors, heavy equipment, airplanes, and computers could U.S. manufacturers have sold to foreign countries if their production costs were cut in half? How many foreign products would have been sold in the United States, if they appeared to cost twice as much? How well off would the labor unions be? How would minorities have fared in a much more robust economy? How many more of the six million unemployed or underemployed college graduates would be working and paying back their loans? Our economy was made uncompetitive by the greed of lobbies and the complicity of the old Congress, lawyers, and federal agencies.

WORKER PRODUCTIVITY AND THE ECONOMY

In 1965 Congress could have justified a law that all worker increases in productivity be matched with increases in pay and health benefits and be called worker productivity index (WPI). It would have been substantiated by historic COLA and worker productivity patterns. National productivity increase would then set Social Security and welfare benefits. This legislation would have focused workers, management, and government on productivity, efficiencies, and improvements as a means of increased wages. Had the assumed WPI legislation been enacted, we would now have a very different economy. All U.S. households would immediately have seen tremendous financial penalties caused when Congress passed new laws and regulations in six areas including regulations; discretionary spending; civil and criminal justice practices and laws; lobby rewards; federal government growth, pay, benefits, and management; and federal mandates on business, states, and local government. The full cost of these bills, laws, and regulations would have caused American taxes and living expenses to rise 263% faster than their productivity in 30 years. Taxpayers would have quickly demanded that Congress rescind much of the legislation it had enacted because the cost was too high for the benefits received. Unfortunately Congress did not enact WPI legislation and COLA has been the basis of wage and entitlement increases. We have continued to recycle this difference which adds to itself year after year just like a very large unpaid loan with rapidly increasing yearly interest, and we have been passing the cost on to our children. The interest on the unpaid loan in 1995 was 57 cents of every personal federal income tax dollar, and it will continue to increase until the new Congress rescinds the most economically detrimental legislation of the last 30 years.

Had the hypothetical WPI legislation passed, workers would have been paid for their productivity. The cost of living, national debt, and wages would be 263% lower than today's, and our economy would be much more robust. Assuming no laws were repealed, this would make all taxes now appear to be 263% higher (about what our grandchildren's taxes may be). Interest rates would be down, homes would cost less, and U.S. goods and services would cost half as much. The national debt would be about one-fourth of the present $5 trillion. Social Security would be fully funded. Foreign products would cost twice as much, and we would purchase very few of these items. Our goods (airplanes, cars, computers, clothes, and farm products), would cost half as much in overseas markets, and our market share would be expanding instead of shrinking. If you realistically assumed at least half of the least beneficial congressional actions would have been repealed because of the triple tax burden, business would be much stronger, new businesses could form more quickly with less legal complications, government would be smaller, and our court system would have more time to deal with criminals.

REGULATIONS AND THE ECONOMY

We are drowning in a sea of regulations. According to Daniel Oliver, former chairman of the Federal Trade Commission, "The cost of regulation to American society exceeds the cost of federal taxation." This cost was $1.37 trillion in 1994 ($27,400 per support household). The *Federal Register*, which reports new and proposed regulations, had 15,000 pages in 1962 and 69,000 pages in 1992. Like carbon monoxide gas, we can neither see nor smell regulations as they anesthetize our economy. They are used by central government to make all decisions about every action of government. Instructions are then passed down so that lower level bureaucrats can make decisions without thinking. An ounce of clear rational thinking does more good than a ton of regulations. Regulation costs accrue to business primarily and are passed on to the consumer in the form of higher prices.

At a conference on regulatory policy in Canada and the United States, Thomas D. Hopkins outlined five types of regulatory costs which, in 1995, will exceed $600 billion. Presently the largest costs are process regulation, amounting to $205 billion ($4,010 per support household) and the paperwork burden on people and businesses that consumes 6.6 billion hours of time according to the Office of Management and Budget. Next largest are environmental regulations, which cost $150 billion per year ($3,000 per support household) and are the fastest growing. The next largest cost is economic transfer regulation that restricts import entry of products and allowable prices and quantities. It costs $130 billion ($2,600 per support household). It transfers costs from and to various segments of society. Next largest is economic regulation, $73 billion transfer costs ($1,460 per support household). These relate to trucking, railroads, gas, oil, communications, and other interstate commerce. The smallest is social regulation, $49 billion ($880 per support household). It is enlightening to note that the federal government budget for social regulation of $12.4 billion ($248 per support household) is four times larger than its budget for economic regulation, $3.12 billion ($62 per support household).[3] That is because the government writes most of these checks directly to support social programs.

Heritage Foundation economists Nancy Bord and William Laffer have pegged total regulatory costs at $1.1 trillion in direct and indirect expenditures. Compare that with the 1992 tax revenue, which totaled slightly more than $1 trillion. Federal regulations and mandates inflate goods, services, and state and local taxes. This inflation was matched by COLA, and the household felt no direct pain.

THE TIP OF THE ICEBERG

According to Hopkins "Since 1988 the number of new regulations has increased sharply. In October 1991 the government reported 59 agencies were at work on 5,000 new regulations covering 67,715 pages. The federal budget hardly budges when a major change is mandated by regulation. For example, when Congress wants new water treatment facilities built, it has two basic choices. It can issue a check or it can issue a regulation. Either way the same bricks and mortar will be used to construct the plant. With a check, the cost is explicit and either federal taxes have to get raised to pay for it or the deficit gets bigger. With a regulation, the cost is hidden in that the federal government doesn't have to pay the bill. The factory owner or local government that must comply with the regulation pays the cost."

The average costs of operating all state and local governments have increased 15% due to the requirements placed on them by federal regulations. The federal government's cost of monitoring regulations for each support household is $332, while the support household's added cost is $12,658, or 38 times more.

This means that the regulatory cost showing up on the federal budget represents only 2.5% of the real cost to the national economy. The tip of an iceberg represents 10% of the total mass of ice. Federal regulatory costs are barely visible and do vast damage to the economy. The economy could save massive amounts of money by simply undoing many regulations and allowing federal regulators to sit in their offices and do nothing; however, it makes more sense to complete the process of reducing unnecessary regulators.

MANY REGULATIONS ARE GOOD

Not all the regulatory legislation passed since the 1960s should be undone. It is fair to say that many regulations are necessary and do a great deal of good. Banking and highway regulations provide safety for our assets and our lives. According to the 1994 Statistical Abstract of the United States, water in our lakes and streams is purer. From 1970 to 1991 lead emissions are down 97%, soot and smoke are down 61%, hydrocarbons are down 38%, and gas mileage is up to 21.7 mpg from 13.5 mpg all in 12 years.[4]

DEREGULATION CAN BE BENEFICIAL

Reducing regulations may be one of the best places to reduce economic waste, improve our economy, add jobs, and reduce the debt. There are positive aspects to deregulation according to a 1992 report from Center for the Study of American Business. The year before the airline industry was deregulated there were 41,000 passenger complaints. In 1992 there were only 5,700, which was seven times less.[5] Customer satisfaction now drives the market. Airline deregulation also lowered airfares 20% and reduced accident rates 48%. The cost of shipping dropped when the trucking industry was partially deregulated. Trucking jobs increased 30%, accidents dropped 40%, and the economy now saves $7.8 billion a year. Further state and national trucking deregulation could reduce economic loss $40 billion ($800 per support household). Appendix A describes a 13% national sales tax that saves $165 billion ($3,300 per support household). Overregulation penalized our households with a 263% increase in our cost of living since 1965.

Existing regulations prevent many useful products from ever reaching the public. Regulations may prevent products from reaching the public for years or cause them to be developed and marketed in foreign countries instead of the United States. Procter and Gamble may start commercial production of Olestra in 1996, 21 years and $200 million after applying to the Food and Drug Administration for approval. It is a substance that can be made to taste and feel like butter, cream, and cooking oil, but it is not digested and processed into body fat. It is a product that can be boiled or frozen and will predictably be in great demand. Other examples of lost jobs and commercial opportunities abound. Some are cited in Chapter 7. Regulations play a major part in our loss of competitiveness. More value must be placed on the good a product has.

A survey by the Health Industry Manufacturers Association concluded that Food and Drug Administration red tape is the main drag on the U.S. medical device field. Restrictive regulations mean that medical device companies are selling their products overseas for as long as three years before they are available to American patients, according to an AP report.

SOCIAL REGULATION

Social regulation deals with product defects, misleading information, health hazards, energy shortages, job and pension concerns, discrimination, and inaccessible facilities. Why do we bother to regulate air quality contaminants to a few parts per million when we allow people to smoke cigarettes with hundreds of times more parts per million of known carcinogens? Why would you require funds to be spent to make all wilderness trails have handicapped access? Why is a job a right unless there is workfare? Why have we allowed the government to borrow $1.3 trillion from the Social Security trust fund? Why is 95% of the cost of polio vaccine liability insurance?[6]

Assume you are a business that wants to hire a hardworking, innovative manager with good communication skills. You interview a 55-year-old white male with a good record as a manager. You interview a 35-year-old white female who is a good communicator. You interview a 40-year-old black male who is a hard worker, and you interview an innovative 30-year-old paraplegic. Can you hire any of these people without incurring a job discrimination lawsuit? If a lawsuit is filed, you only have one chance in four of winning it. These regulations bring additional tort costs. Tort costs will be addressed separately; however, they feed off regulations. During the last 24 years, the number of lawyers has grown eight times faster than the population and they produce nothing. We now have four times more lawyers per 100,000 population than the big seven economic nations. We have five times the cost of tort litigation per 100,000 population than these same countries.[4] Litigation is shredding our economy. There are regulations that require industry to verify that a job applicant is an alien, and other regulations prevent a hospital from asking an expectant mother the same question.

Consider a case of sexual harassment in a corporation. By federal regulations the employer must act immediately to take corrective action. Should the corporation dismiss the harasser, it may be brought to court for regulations against firing employees without first having several other warnings on file. Now the corporation can have two lawsuits filed against it and the corporation will probably lose one. Courts now are holding that an organization will be held financially liable for sexual harassment charges against an employee with no previous complaints, even though the organization has complete harassment prevention programs and harassment reporting procedures. At the same time, these organizations are prohibited from asking at a job interview anything pertaining to criminal records, juvenile records, discrimination, harassment, or information and specific names of people the interviewee worked for previously. Previous employers generally can tell a potential employer very little because they can be brought into court for giving out damaging information about a previous employee.

Mike Royko, a syndicated columnist, recently wrote about Koch Poultry Co. near Chicago, which hires workers to cut, weigh, pack, and freeze chickens. Wages are $4.50 to $6.75 per hour. It is not desirable work and 90% of the workers are Hispanic. Koch does not need to advertise for workers since most people are recommended by present employees. The Chicago EEOC office has come down on them for not hiring enough non-Hispanics (not enough majority white or black members) and that word-of-mouth hiring was inherently discriminatory. EEOC told the company they must set up a $5.2 million fund and take out ads in the newspaper asking any non-Hispanic people who might have applied for a job or were thinking about it to contact the company for a financial settlement. They later dropped the amount to $500,000. Koch's lawyers advised the company to fight it even though it may cost $100,000. EEOC filed the suit. Here we have a company providing regular paychecks to a needy minority group, and hounded by government because it doesn't hire enough nonminorities.

According to John Leo, United Press Syndicate, in 1988 the U.S. Supreme Court ruled that public schools may not expel or remove disruptive, emotionally disturbed children from their classes even to protect others from physical assault without the parent's or a judge's decision. A student in Huntington Beach, California, threw chairs, toppled desks, repeatedly bit and kicked other children and teachers, and disrupted classes by throwing temper tantrums. The father denied his son's violence. The district sued to transfer the boy to a special education class. A county judge allowed it but a federal judge ordered him to stay in class. The teacher went on medical leave and 12 of 31 children in the class were removed by their parents. The laws now require that the placement decisions of a school district be turned over to lawyers and the judicial system all the way to the Supreme Court. The rights of schoolchildren to a chaos-free environment are ignored. More recently a 9-year-old's mother sued for him to be mainstreamed. The boy had broken the jaw of one staff member and three ribs of another. Another high school student urinated on the floor, banged her head against the wall, and tore off her clothes and shredded them when she did not get her way. Should the federal government pass laws and regulations and then regulate and litigate cases like this? The Constitution does not prescribe this type of meddling in local affairs. These costly complexities can be undone by eliminating appropriate laws and regulations. History tells us, and industry has found that you can't run a government or business from the top down by means of regulations. All decisions must be made and finalized at the lowest possible level.

Park Rapids, Minnesota, population 3,000, has a small nursing home. OSHA made an inspection on September 23, 1995, and fined the home $7,200 even though all corrections to the minor deficiencies were made before the OSHA inspector left. The violations were:

1. No ground fault interrupter in a service area and on a refrigerator, $3,000

2. Circuit breaker panel covered by a bulletin board, $900
3. Sewing machine v-belt exposed and dryer hazard, $900
4. Insufficient manual information on (1) communicable diseases and (2) hazardous substances, $2,400

The costs will ultimately be passed on to the residents. OSHA must raise funds with fines to retain staff in the face of general funding cuts. OSHA has become accuser, judge, jury, and beneficiary. Does this seem constitutional, rational, or reasonable?

President Clinton, a lawyer, is now pushing efforts to expand the regulation of fair lending practices. This expansion will create a new class of victims, namely any low income or minority person whose loan request was rejected. Why should the government tell a bank to whom the bank must lend money, and at what rates? If you were a banker, how would you feel?

EEOC is poised to expand guidelines covering workplace harassment. The new guidelines substantially broaden the concept of harassment to include essentially any action that anyone finds offensive. Employer liability will be greatly increased. This power grab is common among federal agencies, and a single claim against a small company could sink it. Previously the laws required proof of hostile environment or interference with work performance. The new standards add or otherwise adversely affect an individual's employment activities. According to Douglas Laycock, professor of constitutional law at the University of Texas School of Law, "These very broad rules can mean anything in the eye of the beholder." The author of *Lost Rights*, James Bovard states that the expense for business to defend itself will exceed the penalties. Currently an employer's average bill for a Title VII case is about $80,000. Unlike a business that must make a profit, the federal bureaucracy can expand laws and regulations, forever creating work for lawyers and federal employees while adding cost to business, taxpayers, and state and local government.

Robert Moran, past chairman of the OSHA Review Committee, who listens to businesses' appeals of rulings said, "There isn't a person on earth who can be certain he is in full compliance with the requirements of this standard in any particular point in time." Regulations cost jobs, bring litigation, create additional friction on the economy, stifle creativity, raise our cost of living, and make our products less competitive. The regulations cited as examples demonstrate a few of the problems and complexities with which our government has burdened business, local and state governments, and ultimately each of us. Regulations usually start out well intended, then become outrageously expensive, and finally cost jobs and drive up the national debt.

We live in an imperfect society. Trying to make it perfect with imperfect regulations is destroying our fragile economy. People work and people die at work. OSHA was enacted in 1970 to help prevent worker deaths with very harsh penalties to business for not following OSHA regulations. The regulations are punitive, extensive, and complex. They and the reference to other standards produce a pile of standards 30 feet high. According to National Safety Council data, Manufacturing Sector, before OSHA, in 1950, the worker death rate was 17 per 100,000 workers. Over the next 20 years, without any regulations, manufacturing companies lowered this rate to nine deaths, a drop of eight. In the 20 years since OSHA was enacted in 1970 the death rate has dropped to six deaths, a drop of three. This is just 38% of the drop in the 20 years before OSHA. For the hundreds of billions of dollars spent on enforcement, litigation, fines, and compliance, there is little compelling argument that industry would not have reached the same level without OSHA. Its regulations have greatly benefited politicians, lawyers, and bureaucrats, but OSHA has closed factories and cost jobs.

PROCESS REGULATION

The OMB reported that the private sector was spending 6.6 billion hours meeting government paperwork requirements and queries related to tax and regulations. The code was written to satisfy lobby interests. A flat tax above a household minimum could reduce up to 80% of personal income tax paperwork and substantial federal payroll,[7] while corporation tax compliance costs ($86 billion) would remain extensive and cumbersome.

A friend convinced me that we now pay the manufacturers' and retailers' FICA contributions and income tax whenever we purchase a product or service. Our purchases consume all but 4% of our disposable personal income. All federal and state corporate and personal income taxes plus inheritance and gift taxes can be replaced with a revised 7.65% FICA and additional 4% employer wage tax, plus a 10% national, and an average 3% state sales tax on all goods and services. Sales taxes are now collected by 46 states who could easily collect them for the federal government. This proposal would make the IRS, state, and local income tax offices obsolete. Individuals would average savings of over $1,400 a year and corporations would save $24 billion a year in tax compliance costs. Workers with wages below $7 to $8 per hour would receive a 4% wage increase or increase the minimum wage above 1995 levels and have no 7.65% FICA deduction. FICA taxes on all wages above this level will be 7.65%. The increase in disposable income will stimulate the economy. Details of this proposal are included in Appendix A.

Paperwork for health care cost reimbursement alone is estimated at $25 billion by Thomas D. Hopkins. Twenty-five years ago radio stations could renew their federal license by filling in the information on a postcard. Regulations now require 1 1/4 pounds of paper to be filled out and sent. "There's a growing feeling among the business community that they're simply being regulated to the point that many of them can't survive," says Thomas Gray, a Washington economist and independent consultant "We're strangling ourselves. We're hurting our standard of living terribly because we're preventing businesses from doing what they can to improve our lives." In a recent national survey by Arthur Andersen & Co., 52% of 100 midsized companies said dealing with government regulation is now their biggest challenge. In contrast, just 20% consider health care their greatest problem.

ENVIRONMENTAL REGULATION

Only 17% of the 1,200 environmental Superfund "contaminated sites" have been cleaned up since 1980, according to the *Washington Post*. This is because the largest amount of money spent to date has been used to pay for government lawyers opposing corporation lawyers. RAND Corporation of Santa Monica, California, estimates that 40% of all Superfund cleanup costs to date have gone to lawyers. Of the nearly $9 billion spent on asbestos litigation and settlements, as of 1992 nearly two-thirds, or $6 billion, has gone to lawyers.[8] Flawed legislation has predictably been a multibillion dollar bonanza for lawyers who lead government and corporations through the minefields of complex codes and regulations. Regulations can reach out and snag anyone. Ross Zimmer of Torrington, Wyoming, is being forced to pay $3,500 for selling a bag of dog chow and a bag of seed to Torrington Hide and Metal. This company site was found by the EPA to be contaminated, and the owners filed bankruptcy. The EPA then sued the five biggest companies who did business with the Hide and Metal Company.[9] They in turn sued anyone who received checks from the company. Others included a children's home and a fire department. These third parties paid $500,000 toward the cleanup cost.

How did federal regulations evolve into such a complicated, unfair method of indiscriminately assessing fines? It was prompted by the special interests who profit from litigation, and an old Congress that made regulations and accepted reelection funds from special interests instead of writing a check and raising taxes. Thomas Root, a lawyer from Golden, Colorado, believes that the government must stop regulating every environmental issue that comes along. He said, "The government is so large and the environmental movement has moved so far and so quickly, people have been crushed in the process."

Author Larry Burkett wrote this about a friend, "Some time ago a business friend said he was locating his business out of the country. His business was providing catalytic converters for automobiles. A part of the manufacturing process required the use of a potent acid catalyst, which was recaptured and used again. He was required by the EPA to install some specific and very expensive equipment to monitor the plant's environment to be sure no workers would be harmed. He did this willingly. Recently he received a bill from the EPA for his share of an environmental cleanup. The company he bought his equipment from failed to meet EPA standards and was required to decontaminate their complex. The foreign company declared bankruptcy and closed. The EPA then sent a portion of the several million dollar cleanup to all people who had done business with the firm. The EPA warned each of the businesses that if they refused to pay their share, amounting to tens of thousands of dollars, they could be held liable for the entire cleanup. "Enough is enough," he told me. "Other countries want my business." He offered his employees a chance to relocate and none took the offer, so 1,300 employees lost their jobs and another industry left the United States.

Silent Spring, the book written by Rachel Carson, ushered in the environmental movement. Saving the earth was like apple pie and motherhood. For over two decades the environmental movement has grown, abated by the legal lobby, federal bureaucrats, and Congress. A recent book, *Trashing the Planet*, written by Dixie Lee Ray, challenges most of the big ticket items of the environmental movement excepting PCBs and some water pollution. Specifically challenged in the book are laws deemed necessary to prevent global warming; prohibit use of nuclear energy, asbestos, Alar, dioxin, DDT, and CFCs such as Freon; and much of the data used to assume these were worldwide environmental problems. The impetus for asbestos laws and regulations came from a 1978 "Draft Summary" released from the National Cancer Institute and the National Institute of Environmental Health and Sciences. To date, no one claims to be the author of this summary. In 1981 two of the foremost epidemiologists studying cancer, Richard Doll and Richard Peto, revealed that the study estimates "were so grossly in error, that no argument based on them, even loosely, should be taken seriously." They further charged the U.S. health agencies of fabricating a politically motivated document, and that scientists should treat the summary as a "contaminant of scientific literature." The EPA regulations and legal precedence necessitated chrysotile asbestos be removed from 45,000 schools by authorized decontamination contractors. This work was not paid for by the federal government. After removal, schools can have airborne contamination 40,000 times higher for years. These laws caused the former industrial giant, the Manville Corporation, to go into bankruptcy. It now appears that the environment would have been safer if hundreds of billions had not been spent to remove the asbestos. At the same time, OSHA is reaffirming that chrysotile asbestos is dangerous, according to an AP report of August 9, 1994. If the other charges in *Trashing the Planet* are correct, elimination of DDT directly caused the deaths of millions of people in Asia and Africa who were not afforded protection from mosquitoes and locusts. These people died needlessly from malaria and hunger. The scientific studies Dixie Lee Ray collected show that PCB, not DDT, makes thin eagle shells. Only 1/500,000 of the ozone hole is due to CFCs—not enough to now make industry spend billions for retooling to use less efficient refrigerants. "As usual," she states, "the government misdiagnosed environmental problems, prescribed the wrong solutions, put industries out of business, gave lawyers more business, reduced jobs, increased our cost of living, and raised our federal, state, and local taxes."

James Bovard, author of *Shakedown*, discovered that if a migrating bird sees a wet spot on your property, federal agents can prohibit you from using your land. Under a bizarre interpretation of the 1972 Clean Water Act known as the "glancing geese" test, the EPA can assert jurisdiction over any land with a wet area that might conceivably be used by passing birds. Environmental regulations are the fastest growing of all regulations and can not be sustained in light of the impending debt. Nature made over 95% of all living organisms extinct. We must be more selective in what we choose to protect. Substantial scientific questions have been raised as to whether some regulations, which are very expensive, do any good at all. The EPA must look carefully at what we fund and mandate. It should exchange information and studies with those who do not scientifically agree with present laws or regulations. It should then recommend how at least 20% of their burden on the economy ($32 billion) can be eliminated.

Our economy is nearer to imminent collapse than even 1% of all living creatures. Over 30 years, the old Congress abused the economy, overspent $4.3 trillion, and left $17.2 trillion of unfunded retirement obligations. The time has come to put our unsustainable economic burdens into perspective. Environmental laws designed to protect endangered species such as wolves and eagles now keep Idaho farmers off their land for the sake of a thumbnail-sized Bruneau Hot Springs snail. Research grants, funding, and litigation continue for many minor species. These species cannot be given the same importance, funding, and protection that we give wolves and eagles. The economic costs of these laws and grants is not sustainable, and must not be passed to future generations, who will be taxed unmercifully.

ECONOMIC TRANSFER REGULATION

The Davis-Bacon Act of 1931 was passed to protect northern construction firms from southern construction firms with lower paid black workers. The law stopped and reversed black employment 25% in the North. The law requires that area prevailing "union" wages be paid for all federal construction projects.[10] Joseph Perkins wrote in a June 1994 column that the Davis-Bacon Act of 1931 requires that federal contractors pay their workers "prevailing wages" pegged to union scale by the Labor Department. This act increases the cost of all federal construction projects as much as 30%. The Congressional Budget Office believes that repeal of the act will save $7.3 billion over five years.

Gregg Easterbrook, author of *A Moment on Earth*, writes that regulations reduced pollution 99% and cars burn 300 fewer gallons of gasoline each year. Perkins wrote that the 1975 corporate average fuel economy (CAFE) regulations requiring gas reduction from car manufacturers have made cars 500 pounds lighter. Economists Robert Crandall of the Brookings Institute and John Graham of the Harvard School of Public Health have estimated that the reduction in weight has caused the additional loss of 2,500 lives and an additional 25,000 serious injuries. If CAFE standards were lifted, manufacturers could save thousands of lives. Should we be saving gasoline or lives? Gasoline is at its lowest price this century in inflation-adjusted dollars. It is time to evaluate the value of a life.

Vancouver, British Columbia, is 150 miles north of Seattle. According to a *Forbes* article printed June 1994, Vancouver has 235 cruise ships yearly that dock there with up to 1,600 tourists each. These cruises generate $100 million of income for Vancouver. Seattle by contrast has a beautiful harbor and books only 12 cruise ships each year. The Jones Act of 1886 blocks foreign flagged ships from sailing between U.S. ports. It also requires the ships be U.S. made and staffed with expensive U.S. crews.[11] This law was passed to protect U.S. shipping. It has now almost destroyed our competitiveness. Repealing the act could create much of Vancouver's prosperity in Seattle, but is opposed by the American Maritime Congress and other trade associations.

Most regulations were created by lobbies haphazardly, and with little relation to cost and benefit. Saving a life should have a fixed value. U.S. Highway Safety Standards require agencies to spend $120,000 to save a life. Nuclear plant safety costs $2.5 billion to save a life. The hazardous waste disposal ban costs $4.1 billion to save a life. Formaldehyde occupational exposure costs $119 billion to save a life.[12] Cancer screening costs $75,000 to save a life and colorectal tests cost $24,976 to save a life, and neither are required. Lobbies paid for 43% of all campaign funds of successful House members and 34% of all campaign funds for successful Senate members. This totals 40% of all congressional contributions.[13] Successful candidates' campaign costs averaged $4 million per senator and $500,000 per representative. Unsuccessful candidates were also supported by lobbies. Elected members of Congress have historically repaid their special interest contributors with favorable legislation.

LOBBIES AND SPECIAL INTERESTS

Lobbies and special interests kept the old Congress in power for 30 years with money and votes in exchange for unprecedented legislative and regulatory favors. The federal government grew, lawyers tripled, and unfunded mandates raised state taxes, crippled businesses, and cost jobs. U.S. lobby costs, estimated to be from $300 billion to $700 billion, are closely tied to federal regulations affecting the economy. One expert, Dr. Stephen Magee, estimates that legal lobbies alone reduce our GNP $660 billion each year. The legal lobby's national contributions reached new highs in the 1992 elections. Sugar beet growers want protection, honeybee and sheep farmers want subsidies, unions want all government projects built using union scale wages, business wants tariff protection, the elderly want social entitlements, and foreign countries want trade concessions. "Lobbies expect to receive more value than they spend on contributions," according to Tom Hopkins at Rochester Institute of Technology. "Much lobby effort is directed at economic regulation which is simply redistribution of wealth from one part of society or the economy to another. Unlike some social and environmental regulation, it is difficult to find substantial benefits for economic regulation." The Center for Study of American Business states, in current dollars, as of 1995 federal regulatory spending had increased elevenfold in the last 25 years. In constant dollars, it has increased threefold.

There are many necessary regulations that need to be preserved and are reasonable and cost-effective. There are many that are not cost-effective and need to be substantially blunted and many more that need to be repealed outright. Reducing the lobby-incited economic penalties of laws and regulations passed by the old Congress must be a major focus of reform. We need give up only one-fourth of all the regulations' least important benefits relating to defensive medicine, product liability insurance, litigation, lobbies, OSHA, the environment, and COLA to substantially reduce over $682 billion of wasted time and capital. This would be an excellent alternative to having our children face an 82% tax of lifetime income, a major depression, and runaway inflation.

A PLAN TO REDUCE COLA

Deregulation changes can best succeed if they accomplish the following:

1. Higher quality and productivity must become the twin goals of government and business. They must become the only basis of financial reward. The United States should replace COLA with a worker productivity index (WPI) and allow all workers and employers to focus on all the things government has required which have made our economy flounder. We can and should quickly undo much of the least productive and least cost-effective legislation and laws passed in the last 30 years and turn inflation into deflation. Deflation by rescission of our artificially inflated economy should reduce the cost of living for years to come. The main purposes of the cuts and changes should be to grow business and jobs while eliminating as much unproductive work as possible.

2. Assess the total costs of all regulations on federal, state, and local government; the national economy; business; COLA; and the taxpayer. We should set the value of human life as in highway safety. We should then terminate all laws and regulations above that amount and start to fund those actions below that amount. We should not be wasting our resources enforcing regulations we cannot pay for when we can spend much less on other lifesaving actions. All regulations should be based on cost-benefit studies.

3. Sever the money connection between Congress and all special interests. Replace it with federal election funding costing $6 per support household per year. Prohibit all funding from outside a legislative district.

4. Reduce the total costs of our present tort litigation system including liability insurance, defensive medicine, and costs to states, cities, business, and the public. Require that prompt mediation, using polygraph, and simplified laws precede all tort litigation (see Chapter 6).

5. Rescind or phase out all federal laws and regulations that are not absolutely necessary.

6. Speed up approval of potential lifesaving medical drugs and devices.

7. Replace all income taxes and the IRS with a sales and progressive FICA tax.

The WPI increase for all workers, retirees, and welfare payments would be very positively affected by a yearly drop of several percent in the cost of living. The cost of living is like an elevator. When the old Congress pressed the up button to benefit special interests with laws and regulations, it left the economy receding below us. The economy will return, and the cost of living will come down when the new Congress brings the elevator down from its ivory tower. We have been on the ivory tower elevator too long. It is all too apparent that you can have regulation or you can have jobs, but you can't possibly have both in our present economic environment. This has been a very painful and instructive lesson for American workers and business. It is a lesson we should never forget.

ROB ROGERS reprinted by permission of United Feature Syndicate, Inc.

Power tends to corrupt and absolute power corrupts absolutely. —Lord Acton

Chapter 5 The Political System

THE FAILED POLITICS OF "SPEND NOW AND PAY LATER"

The road to hell is paved with good intentions. Franklin Roosevelt wanted to provide for the elderly and proposed Social Security, to be financed by those who are employed and their employers, at 1% of earnings and maximum of $30 contribution total. Few lived to be 65 then. In 1935 when Social Security started, the government funded all retirees with a tax of 1% of wages from employee and employer on a maximum of $300 of wages, which provided a maximum of $60 per worker per year.[1] There were 42 workers per Social Security beneficiary in 1945; there were 16.5 workers per beneficiary in 1950; there were 3.3 in 1980; there are 3.2 workers per beneficiary now; and this number will shrink to 2.2 workers after 2025.[2] The Social Security Medicare Board of Trustees reported in April 1995 that "The Health Insurance Trust Fund will be able to pay benefits for only about seven years and is severely out of actuarial balance over the next 75 years." They added, "During the past five years there has been a trend of deterioration in the long-range financial condition of the Social Security and Medicare programs and an acceleration in the projected dates of exhaustion in the related trust funds...The Medicare program is clearly unsustainable in its present form." These reports assume that future taxpayers will repay the $1.4 trillion trust funds borrowed by the old Congress. The 1946 to 1964 baby boom generation (76 million babies) is 30% of our population. They will begin retiring in 2008 and the baby bust generation is too small to support them and also pay back the Social Security trust funds Congress borrowed, without radical changes. All recent budgets of the old Congress projected deficits of $300 billion, including borrowed trust funds, into the next century. It could have been a beautiful program had all the workers first paid into funding until they received their retirement benefits. The trust funds would have earned enough dividends to substantially reduce the national debt and finance our future trust fund needs, if they were invested in the market until needed.

The previous chapter described in detail the damage the old Congress imposed on our economy, due to the massive body of laws and regulations it enacted over 30 years. After World War II, big labor wanted to reduce the power of booming industry in order to have stronger negotiating positions. The old Congress became a willing partner of labor. Over 30 years they enacted every imaginable consumer, health, safety, environment, employment, discrimination, and protection law, and raised taxes for none of them. Industries complied and added these costs to their products, and we artificially imposed inflation. Our goods became more expensive than foreign products, and we lost market share. In the process, the cost of living exploded above worker productivity, industries failed, good jobs were lost forever, and labor suffered most.

President Johnson craved adulation. He pushed a War on Poverty to help single parent and poor families and their children by telling Congress the $500 million cost should pose no problem. Now, 25 years later, his program is $175 billion (350 times higher, and growing).[3] Some families were helped and became productive, but the system for years has been badly abused. It assists teenage girls to leave home, by getting pregnant. It promises them an apartment, frequently in dangerous surroundings, and cash, so long as they don't work. For 20 years the old Congress refused to fix this program or admit it had failed. It has consumed more funds than Congress borrowed from Social Security trust funds.

From 1964 to 1994 the old Congress spent the funds needed to support future retirees on unnecessary projects and programs, in order to obtain the money and votes necessary to reelect over 95% of its members. In 1994 President Clinton forcibly opposed a Balanced Budget Amendment, and Senator Robert Byrd, chairman of the Senate Appropriations Committee, told the senators that they would lose committee assignments and special projects if they voted for the Balanced Budget Amendment.

Business has been required to fully fund any contracted employee retirement programs. The government was exempted until the new Congress passed a law requiring that government must abide by the laws of the country. Part of the unfunded entitlements include federal retiree health and benefit programs. Federal retirees can contribute as little as $7,000 to their retirement program and withdraw over $120,000 plus Medicare. They can then retire at 55 and work briefly under Social Security and draw its benefits also. Federal workers pay for only 20% of their retirement benefits.[4] The federal government pays nothing, and taxpayers fund 80% of their benefits on top of the 50% they pay for their own benefits. In 1984 the Grace Commission estimated that funding of future federal retiree programs would require putting aside an additional $40 billion each year for 40 years ($1.6 trillion).[5] How can our children and grandchildren fund increasing interest on an increasing debt, medical entitlements, and a retirement benefit program for federal government retirees whose benefits are 250% higher than the best blue chip corporations?

HOW DID THE OLD SYSTEM WORK?

Congress funded countless absurd projects in exchange for votes or money, and sent the bill to our children. In 1994 Citizens Against Government Waste pointed out that the $11 billion earthquake relief funds for California were loaded with $3 billion of log rolling unrelated goodies, such as cooperative space ventures between Russia and the United States, costing $112 million; NASA's "space lab" module costing $40 million; $22 million for Senator Robert Byrd (the king of pork) memorial West Virginia dam and locks, plus 500 new employees at an FBI fingerprint lab in West Virginia, previously funded; conversion of a New York post office into a train station costing $10 million; high speed rail research costing $4.5 million; efforts to battle the potato blight in Maine, $1.4 million; and two sugar mills in Hawaii costing $1.3 million. Funding of $78,000 "saved" 16 endangered beetles on a construction site. In 1993 Congress voted to spend $34.6 million for research on screwworms, which have been eradicated in the United States. They voted $11.5 million to modernize a power plant in the Philadelphia Naval Yard targeted to close, and $19.6 million (annually) as a tribute to Tip O' Neill to create jobs in Ireland. Misuse of nonexistent funds is trashing our economy. The new Congress should require an up or down vote, without amendments, for the complete package of recommendations of the bipartisan Citizens Against Government Waste (CAGW), who have spent countless hours tracking and documenting abuse.

Franking privileges, totaling $200,000 per year for representatives and $300,000 for senators, also ensure easy communication with the voters. How can challengers compete with this system? How can an incumbent not be elected? It can only change if voters understand that the present economic system is near collapse and action is necessary. Congress wins funding battles with presidents. In 1994 the president proposed substantially limiting Rural Electrification Administration (REA) subsidies. Glenn English is chairman of the committee that protects REA subsidies. Member REA co-ops contributed $715,000 to congressional candidates supporting REA. As a result REA lost no major funding. If Congress has been making sound decisions for 30 years, based on what's good for the country, why are we so close to bankruptcy?

The old system ensured that 95% of incumbents got reelected—until November 1994. They were privileged; had free travel, junkets, and major election funds paid for by lobbies; a generous salary; and had an outstanding retirement pension. Over 400 congressmen now are paid with these federal pensions. Pensions follow congressmen to prison. National Taxpayers Union estimates show that former Representative John Dowdy has amassed more than $1.1 million in benefits since leaving office for jail in 1970. Dowdy was convicted of perjury. Former representative Cornelius Gallagher, a tax cheat who draws $63,979 a year, will join the congressional cons' millionaire club this year. Former representative John Murphy of Staten Island receives $58,657 a year. He was convicted for accepting $50,000 in the Abscam scandal. Former representative Mario Baggi of the Bronx gets $44,494 a year. He illegally accepted $1.8 million from Wedtech, a defense contractor.

The power of legal lobbies was defined in a small portion of an article in the *Wall Street Journal* by Evans and Novak: "Why are any legislative proposals that would limit damages to a plaintiff automatically beaten down in Congress? A lobbyist who went to see a member of the Senate Democratic leadership about tort reform received this response: 'Let me tell you two things. First, the bill will never pass. Second, we will never kill the bill.' In other words, keeping the possibility of reform alive would assure a steady flow of contributions from worried trial lawyers. And political contributions are a major reason these lawyers have become so powerful."

Power is addictive and extremely corrosive. Congress likes having lobby money as much as lobbies like the power of Congress to fulfill their desires for beneficial legislation. Because the media have focused much attention to lobbies wining, dining, and giving congressmen free exotic vacations, Congress is now considering making these activities illegal; however, they are just the tip of the iceberg compared to the money lobbies give each congressman each year in campaign contributions. Federal judges could never accept money from lobbies or special interests given in the name of freedom of speech. Why does freedom of speech then make it acceptable to bribe Congress? Did these contributions corrupt Congress? Many strong civilizations collapsed because an elite person or group became obsessed with power or greed. Those with power will always be our greatest danger.

POWER AND CORRUPTION

Projects and pork at home created jobs, headlines, and reelection for the old Congress. Did power—over time—induce illegal, unethical, or immoral behavior? Should it be curbed? Many congressmen believe there should be no term limits. Committee chairpersons do not want to be displaced under any circumstances. These chairs attract vast amounts of lobby money. How have they been affected?

Chairman of the Ways and Means, Wilbur Mills, was arrested in a tidal basin with stripper Fanny Fox. He resigned. Chairman of Health and Services, Ted Kennedy, was involved in the death of his female assistant at Chappaquidik. Chairman of the Appropriations Committee, Jim Wright, resigned under fire because of using his power to extort political contributions and other unethical dealings. Majority whip Tony Coelho was also forced to resign because of financial transactions. He is currently advising the Clinton administration. Chairman of the House Ways and Means Committee, Dan Rostenkowski, was indicted for illegal activities related to the house post office scandal. He and his committee are half of the reason we are so far in debt. House Postmaster Robert Rota resigned and pleaded guilty of conspiracy and embezzlement for trading cash for postal vouchers. House Speaker Tom Foley concealed the scandal and became the only House Speaker not re-elected. The Keating five, and particularly Senator Alan Cranston, were involved in trading money for votes on the Senate Banking Committee. Senator Bob Packwood, senior minority member of the Finance Committee was charged with sexual harassment and resigned. The old Senate Appropriations chairman, Robert Byrd, fully understood our country's difficult financial condition; however, his committee and Dan Rostenkowski's had complete financial control. They were opposed to balancing the budget, and presided over spending one-third of a trillion dollars a year more money than income, increasing our federal debt by $4.6 trillion. Senator Byrd literally flooded his senate district with pork, and is frequently referred to as the "King of Pork."

Congressman Rostenkowski was a consummate rent seeker arranging to gather wealth by conferring advantages including tariffs, import quotas, regulations, and tax breaks with Washington's lawyer lobbies. The tax code is the primary instrument of change and the primary place is the House Ways and Means Committee. Rent is what you pay for the use of their resources. He was charged with 17 counts of fraud, obstruction of justice, and abuse of congressional payroll and exchanging post office vouchers for cash, all amounting to almost $700,000. If convicted he could be sentenced to 10 years in prison and fined an additional $250,000. In his committee, he disbursed benefits and demanded loyalty. He expected support and noted defectors and put them in his vision of purgatory. Rostenkowski was once quoted as saying, "If a guy is your enemy, you might as well kick his brains out." Edmund Burke once said, "Power gradually extirpates from the mind every humane and gentle virtue." The Justice Department said in its indictment that Rostenkowski perpetrated an extensive fraud on the American people. Chicago said with their primary votes that they would rather be represented by a powerful politician than a clean one. This is not the form or style of government our founding fathers fought the Revolutionary War for. He was rejected November 8, 1994; however, the lobby system that allowed him to abuse his power is still intact. In June, 1994, the Justice Department had 190 active investigations or litigation cases against Congress and other public officials.[6]

CONGRESS AND FISCAL RESPONSIBILITY

The old Congress legislated special interest funding for their districts and expanded the debt without any plan to repay it. The Bipartisan Commission on Entitlements and Tax Relief estimated we have an additional $14.4 trillion (on top of the $5 trillion debt) of unfunded retirement obligations, such as Social Security, Medicare, Medicaid, and federal retiree benefits, promised to various interest groups. These excessive expenditures for political purposes at a time of relative peace were in the full control of the old Congress. The new Congress must balance the budget and pay down the debt while stimulating the economy.

Thomas Jefferson believed all government debts should be paid for by the generation that incurred them. Alexander Hamilton said of debt, "There ought to be a perpetual, anxious, and increasing effort to reduce that which at any time exists." Andrew Jackson thought that national debt was "A National Curse." There is little doubt that the politicians prior to 1930 would agree that our national debt is a national disgrace and should be sharply reduced. They would agree that our generation should pass the economy along in the same condition we received it, or better, by paying down the debt. They would agree that spending should be reduced, taxes raised, or changes made in our political or social system to accomplish a balanced budget.

Few politicians can resist the gravitational pull of power. George Washington could have been president for life, but declined. One-fourth of the old Congress, from both parties, opposed deficit spending proposals. Senators Phil Gramm and Warren Rudman both worked to balance the budget. Warren Rudman, in his announcement of retirement from the Senate, took politicians to task for the burden they were placing on our children for political gain. Senator Paul Tsongas, when he ran for president, emphasized that we must get our financial house in order and getting it in order should be our first priority. Representative Newt Gingrich and House candidates who signed the Contract with America took a stand against big government and big spending. This clear message was resoundingly approved by voters in 1994.

RESTORE AMERICA'S FUTURE

Congress dislikes raising money for elections, so they are very happy to take any funds available from PACs, unions, foreign lobbies, and business in exchange for support of legislation supporting their various points of view. In 1992 PACs furnished over $95 million of election funds, and 89% went to old Congress incumbents.[7] Almost $250 million were spent on the 1994 nonpresidential elections. Numerous PACs furnish 40% of all Senate and House election contributions.[8] According to the Justice Department, Japan alone invested $60 million for lobbying its interests in 1992. Money is usually accepted when not opposed by the majority of the congressman's constituency. Special interests know that a dollar spent for a favorable vote will be repaid many times over. The American Trial Lawyers Association strategically places its forces and money with the lawyers and lobbies in Congress who actively create additional rights and resist tort and regulatory reform, especially congressional judicial and regulatory committees. One in 10 employed in Washington are lawyers protecting and increasing their turf. Our 860,000 lawyers' political contributions increase support household costs at least $6,000.[9]. The new Congress must quickly close the door on all lobby campaign contributions, before they are seduced by the power of money.

The AP reported in January 1996 that the 13 million member CIO union will target 75 House races this year and boost Democratic candidates. It will spend $35 million and have 2,500 union activists (33 per house district) help in the last six weeks of the campaign. This effort costs each union member only $2.67, and provides $467,000 in campaign contributions to the targeted House districts. Past successful House candidates averaged election costs of $500,000. This move by one union representing 8% of the workforce will provide 93% of all needed election funds and 33 workers to elect House representatives owing full allegiance to the CIO. We must quickly understand that for less than $3 per member, 75 "yes" votes in the House may change to "no" votes.

The new Congress should make all lobby and special interest campaign contributions illegal. We don't need the quantity and quality of congressional advertising we have had in the past, but almost all election campaign funds could be replaced at less than $6 per support household per year if Senate candidates were required to raise $600,000 and House candidates $100,000 in contributions not to exceed $200 per person. Government would then fund $3 million and $300,000 respectively, with total contributions limited to $4 million and $500,000 respectively. Campaign funding should similarly be adopted for presidential and state elections at a $10 cost per support household. Present lobby expenditures are $6,000 per support household.

It is absurd for Congress to believe that only 535 people in our country have the insight to run it and make it flourish. In both houses of Congress, terms should be limited to three in the House and two in the Senate. Old seniority rules frequently drive committee chairpersons to abuse and corruption. Power should be distributed by having committee chairs preside one year only and rotate out. During that year, no special appropriations should go to the chair's district.

Both the Democratic and Republican parties are being polarized by special interest groups. It is difficult to find and keep centrist politicians because of the thrust of special interest groups and their money to control the party platforms. The result is that in both major parties, candidates are committed to special interests contrary to our country's centrist majority. Many of these centrists just don't vote or vote and hold their nose and their breath. It is time that every special interest and lobby group look at the benefits of national mediation with a referendum on two opposing proposals.

Opposing special interest views, such as term limits, abortion, and media excess, are by nature polarized and frequently confrontational. National referendums will necessitate moderation of extreme views in order to receive over 50% of the vote and become law (which can be overturned by the Supreme Court). The national referendum should become a constitutional amendment if passed in 75% of the states. This natural mediation process should begin when a special interest group formulates a final proposal and presents it to the House of Representatives along with the signatures of 20% of the number of registered voters in the last election. The opposition must also prepare an alternative proposal within nine months. The referendum will then be held at the next national election. This moderation process will make both parties less subject to strong single interest voters and more responsive to our national economy and society.

Can we continue to afford confrontation, considering our financial and economic problems? We have opponents fighting over who steers the federal car, moving 80 miles per hour with a jammed accelerator, approaching a dangerous fork in the road. Wasted resources of people and money must end so we can get our economic car under control. We can balance the budget, cut our debt in half in 10 years, and maximize life, liberty, and the pursuit of happiness for all. Most of the benefits will come from revising our concepts relating to centralized versus smaller decentralized government. History will prove the greatest decentralization and the least government interference possible will deliver the greatest benefits at the least cost.

Of Athenians: In the end, more than they wanted freedom, they wanted security. They wanted a comfortable life and they lost it all—security, comfort, and freedom. When the Athenians finally wanted not to give to society, but society to give to them, when the freedom they wished for most was freedom from responsibility, then Athens ceased to be free. —General Omar N. Bradley

To see what is right and not do it is want of courage. —Confucius

Politics is the art of looking for trouble, finding it, misdiagnosing it, and then mis-applying the wrong remedies. —Groucho Marx

Doctors purge the body, preachers the conscience, and lawyers the purse. —German proverb

Chapter 6. Confrontation, Polarization, Mediation, and the Legal System

A FLAWED TORT SYSTEM

The United States has 26 times more lawyers per million people than Japan.[1] Some years back, two planes nosed into the ocean at the end of their runways and both planes had several fatalities and other injuries. The airliners went down in Tokyo Bay and Boston Harbor. The day after the plane went down in Tokyo Bay, the president of Japan Airlines apologized to the families of the deceased and made settlements with them. The airliner that went into Boston Harbor was in litigation for 10 years and the attorneys from both sides got over 40% of the total settlement costs plus court expenses while the families waited for years. Which system of law is most efficient? effective? humane? Why don't we have it? What organization prevents us from having quick and inexpensive justice other countries have?

Our present legal system, laws, procedures, and costs deal with exaggeration of claims, confrontation, complications, and technicalities. The resulting polarization of participants in a dispute becomes extremely expensive. Frequently, judgments are technically correct but do not render simple justice.

Breast implant manufacturers have been battling a class action suit filed by lawyers representing 400,000 women with implants. The manufacturers claimed no fault, but offered $4 billion to settle, because there were no major studies showing no harm. The lawyers will receive over $1 billion. In June 1995 the *New England Journal of Medicine* published a Harvard Medical School study of 87,501 nurses, 1,183 of whom had breast implants.[2] The study found no association between the implants and connective tissue diseases, the major complaint of the suits. Chemical companies and manufacturers of materials used to make artificial blood vessels and other implants intend to stop production because of potential lawsuits. Doctors say the trend could make lifesaving implants difficult or impossible to obtain. Already 100 equipment companies are having supply problems. Manufacturing giants such as DuPont and Dow are dropping the medical business because of the high risk of being dragged into lawsuits by ultimate customers claiming defective products. Electronics companies and manufacturers of lithium batteries have the same problem. A warning by the manufacturer of basic products that they have not been tested for medical applications is no longer considered as insurance against litigation by attorneys looking for "deep pockets."[3] Medical costs per capita in the United States climbed $2,400 (3.5 times) in inflation-adjusted dollars from 1968 to 1993, approximately the same time that lawyers' growth increased 13 times faster than U.S. population growth. This also caused law school graduates in 1994 to average salaries of $74,560 while all other graduate salaries averaged $32,629.[4] Health costs per car built in the United States are now $500 higher than health costs per car built in Japan.[5] Litigation adds $3,000 to the cost of a $15,000 pacemaker. It adds $20 to the cost of an $80 ladder. The present cost of polio vaccine is 5% serum and profit and 95% product liability insurance. The cost of defensive medicine in the United States is 20% of all physician expenditures in our $1 trillion health care system. This defense is necessary because the laws of our country now seem to say that every doctor must make a "perfect" decision for every procedure and prescription every time. Should any baby born or any operation or diagnosis not be perfect, the doctor will need every possible test, observation, and piece of data to overcome the plaintiff's aggressive trial attorney and expert witnesses. A Harvard study showed that for every baby born in Florida, $1,100 of the doctor's fee was for malpractice insurance. Is it any wonder why the cost of drugs and health care is much less in other countries?

THE LEGAL LOBBY AND POLITICS

Lawyer lobbyist groups raised record amounts for the November 1992 elections. It was announced that President Clinton was opposed to tort reform. At an American Bar Association forum, Ron Brown, the president's chief of staff, said regarding the election, "I'm here to tell you the lawyers won."[6] A year earlier, 59 federal agencies drafted 5,000 new regulations comprising 69,000 pages. These new litigation possibilities will provide full employment for trial lawyers for many years to come, and this is a major source of our country's outrageously high legal costs. In 1995 ABA president George Bushnell described Congressional Republicans as "reptilian bastards."

America's most powerful lobby is the Association of Trial Lawyers of America. It contributes heavily to congressmen who create additional rights and resist tort reform. Their contributions now cost the support household at least $6,500 a year. For almost 10 years, Congress has considered product liability reform. According to the *Washington Post*, Joseph Califano, former HEW director said, "Congress dances around the medical malpractice protection racket for fear of alienating the Association of Trial Lawyers of America...in the Beltway bubble, the disgust of the American people with lawyers, and the malpractice system isn't heard above the clatter of political contributions." In 1994 liability reform passed through the Senate Commerce Committee 16-4. On the Senate floor a filibuster ensued. The Association of Trial Lawyers of America were behind the filibuster and the bill did not go through. It should be noted that over 60% of the Senate members were lawyers. There was a time when turn of the century statesman Elihu Root would tell would-be clients with an urge to litigate, "that they were damned fools and should stop."[7] Author Glendon observed that lawyers are "rapidly shedding the habits and restraints that once made the bench and the bar pillars of the democratic experiment." Today, lawyers are connoisseurs of conflict, maximizing billable hours. The result of laws and regulations passed over the last 30 years by Congress is painfully obvious. By the best available estimate of RAND Corporation, fully 40 cents of every dollar spent on Superfund cleanup since 1980 has not gone toward cleanup, but to pay lawyers' fees and other costs of litigation. The government and private industry spend over $5 billion a year. The insurance industry and its clients spend over $500 million annually wrangling over liability for these cleanups according to the House Banking, Finance, and Urban Affairs Committee.

LAWYERS AND JUSTICE

Lawyers and laws grow, become more complex, and resist change. The combined efforts of the legal lobby and the old Congress are the major reason American workers have become so uncompetitive with the rest of the world. Lawyers funded the old Congress and were rewarded with an unprecedented body of laws and regulations to litigate and thrive. The laws passed and the ensuing litigation quickly drove our cost of goods up 263% above worker productivity. From 1970 to 1980, the number of lawyers grew 13 times faster than the U.S. population. Business became uncompetitive internationally and jobs fell like leaves in fall. Cash stopped flowing into our country, while jobs and cash began to flow out. Interest on the national debt accelerated, and taxes were not raised to cover the loss.

Our legal system has changed freedom of speech to become freedom of expression no matter how much it offends others' pursuit of happiness. It has changed the unshakeable belief of our forefathers in God, and their expression of this faith on coin and buildings, to a ban on prayers in schools.

America has little respect for lawyers. According to West Publishing/National Law Journal survey, lawyers' images have worsened. Surveys showed 73% said there are too many lawyers, up from 55% in 1986. It found that groups most likely to deal with lawyers had the lowest opinion of them. More than four out of five did not think they are caring and compassionate. Only 22% called lawyers honest and ethical, while 59% called lawyers greedy. A 1993 Gallup poll on integrity placed lawyers among the lowest ranked along with TV talk show hosts, car salesmen, and advertising practitioners. They had little respect for lawyers in England when Shakespeare's Falstaff said, "Let's kill all the lawyers" in the play *Henry VIII*. At that time the lawyers just had their hands in others' pockets. Now they have their hands on our economy.

ANTIQUATED PRACTICE IN CONTEMPORARY TIMES

The legal system works like farming with horses instead of modern machinery; it is very slow, expensive, and outdated. It doesn't fit all situations and frequently true justice is not achieved because of old precedents of an ancient environment. Widespread technicalities in the law, built up over centuries, allow injustice to continue. There is too much emphasis on criminal rights and protection and too little emphasis on society and victim's rights. The general public overwhelmingly supports turning society's rights and criminal rights upside down. In most democratic countries, society's rights take precedence over criminal rights. Our Constitution calls for life, liberty, and the pursuit of happiness. To achieve this we must include permission to do polygraph, DNA, alcohol, and drug tests to verify information, protect society, and find truth. The CIA and FBI regularly use polygraph testing to determine deception. Susan Smith, who drowned her children, failed the test three times. We should also require quick mediation, restitution of damages, and limiting appeals to the difference between parties.

In Kalamazoo, Michigan, the Upjohn Co., a major pharmaceuticals firm, was named by the Environmental Protection Agency as the party responsible for the $20 million cost of cleaning up a toxic landfill. Hoping to spread the cost among other polluters, Upjohn wrote letters threatening to sue 741 parties that had dumped trash in the landfill. They ranged from Flipse's Flower Shop to the Milwood Little League. Even the mother of Upjohn president William Parfet couldn't escape the company's dragnet. Martha Parfet, chairwoman of Gilmore Bros. department store in downtown Kalamazoo, received a letter from Upjohn notifying her that the trash the store had put out on the curb could make it liable for a share of the cleanup.

ENVIRONMENTAL PRACTICE

The *Los Angeles Times* reported in July 1994 in regard to the case of the Hardage landfill in Criner, Oklahoma, attorneys for a group of 350 companies held responsible for the cleanup stretched across the nation and read like a "Who's Who" of Superfund law, according to one participant. The cleanup itself was expected to cost $70 million. But over nearly a decade, lawyers earned more than $45 million in legal fees in the case and several suits are still unresolved.

In cases such as these, the EPA now determines the largest and most visible polluters of a Superfund site and splits the cleanup bill among them. Those enterprises typically turn around and sue many others in hopes of spreading the cost and recovering some of their own expenditures. The result, said Rep. Al Swift of Washington, a key proponent of Superfund reform, is a feeding frenzy of litigation that cascades down the corporate food chain.

AND VICTIMS FOR ALL

The laws passed by Congress have made victims of almost everybody by age, sex, national origin, race, religion, harassment, unfair dismissal, reverse discrimination, and disabilities, to name a few. On May 16, 1994, ABC reported that the Disabilities Act of 1992 had already produced 88,000 lawsuits all claiming damages, including the following. A 340-pound woman claimed a theater's seats were uncomfortable and they would not allow her to bring her own chair. A paraplegic skier sued a ski resort for having one of its many chairlifts unavailable to her to enjoy the view and ski those few slopes. It is hard not to see the connection of big lawyers to big pockets by means of big damage awards through discrimination, pain, and suffering. Less than one-fourth of 1% of our population receives payment totaling half of the total amount of all the settlements and judgments of all the litigation in this country. These privileged people are called lawyers. The friction they create on our economy is dragging us toward bankruptcy.

Navy lieutenant Paula Coughlin was awarded $1.6 million in compensatory damages and $5 million in punitive damages from the Las Vegas Hilton and its parent company. She was groped and fondled by a gauntlet of navy men in the now famous Tailhook incident. Defense witnesses said Coughlin was a drunk and willing participant in the festivities. Payments were made by none of the gropers and fondlers, but by the hotel who she claimed failed to provide adequate protection. The hotel testified that during 19 years of Tailhook conventions involving thousands and thousands of people only one previous complaint in 1988 was ever filed. The hotel claimed, "the law does not charge a hotel proprietor with knowing that which is not reasonably foreseeable."

A dental patient with AIDS, Harrison Totten, was told by the Castle Dental Center in Houston, Texas, that they would no longer treat him. He and his lawyer sued for violation of the Americans with Disabilities Act. The court held that testing positive for HIV and having AIDS are considered disabilities under the act and ordered Totten to be paid $100,000.

Beverly Schnell, a middle-aged woman, lived near Milwaukee in a house that needed work and had vacant space on the second floor. She placed an ad stating, "Apartment for rent, one bedroom, electric included, mature Christian handyman." She was taken to court for violating Wisconsin's fair housing law because handyman is sex discrimination and Christian is religious discrimination. She lost and was ordered to pay the housing council "reasonable" attorney fees of $8,000.[8]

Martin Siegel, named in a $2.75 billion inside trading suit, knew that his $717,000 Florida beachfront home could not be included in any settlement because of bankruptcy laws. The same was true of attorney Bowie Kuhn's $764,000 house in Florida when his firm was going through bankruptcy proceedings.[9] The creditors were penalized by a century-old bankruptcy law exempting a multimillion dollar home from restitution because a cabin shelter, needed for survival on the prairie, was exempted years ago.

SUE THE DEEPEST POCKETS

There is presently a $550 million suit pending regarding the December 1988 Pan Am Flight 103 airline crash in Lockerbie, Scotland. They are not suing the terrorist or the country that sponsored them. They are not suing the airline, which is now out of business. They are suing the airline's insurance company and believe that if they can prove that at least one company employee failed to take some action that could possibly have prevented the passengers' death, they will win. Should the lawsuit succeed, the attorneys' fees, expenses, and investigation costs will exceed $200 million. Should the lawsuit fail, neither the passengers' families nor their attorney will receive anything. Should a corporation be held liable for the imperfect actions of an employee? Should all employees be required to act perfectly all the time to keep their job? Should lawyers? Does our legal system serve society or itself? Mark Zwyenburg died in the crash. Six years later, his parents got a notice that the IRS wanted payment of $6,484,339.39. The IRS assumed Mark's estate will receive $11 million. No payouts have yet been made. If a settlement is made on this basis, the lawyers for Mark's estate will receive $4,400,000. It is easy to see how lawyers and the government always win, using current laws.

Our legal system dictates that defendants admit nothing. Plaintiffs accuse everyone possible and let the innocent crawl away. This system is antiquated, and is five times more expensive per person than other big seven nations (Canada, England, Germany, France, Italy, and Japan).[10] A much better tort system would be to change our laws and match their costs. With such change, our support households will save over $2,500 per year in tort costs alone. Had all the people who died in the Lockerbie crash died of natural causes, stroke, heart attack, cancer, AIDS, or drowning, their families would have also had pain, suffering, and financial problems. Families should have some minimal health, life, and / or disability insurance in case of death of a wage earner by natural causes. It should be the responsibility of each family to decide the amount and provide insurance protection. Why not terminate our unnecessary and expensive litigation, huge awards, and resulting high liability insurance costs and free thousands of dollars to save, invest, or purchase insurance? Each household can then afford to protect itself from all uncertainties, instead of a few.

LAWYERS AND ECONOMIC GROWTH

Dr. Stephen P. Magee, professor of finance at the University of Texas claims that the country's lawyers are dampening the country's gross national product by 10%; this would now be over $700 billion a year, or $14,000 per support household. He says lawyers are like the knights of old. You can use them to plunder other people's stuff. They bring 18 million new suits through the system each year. They have a vested interest in seeing that suits are not settled quickly or cheaply. The United States spends 10 times the average of other major industrial nations on personal injury claims, 40 times the average on malpractice claims, and 100 times the average on product liability claims, says Walter Olson, author of *The Litigation Explosion*. Another study showed that U.S. tort costs alone are 2.6% of our GDP ($182 billion in 1995), or five times the average of other major industrial countries.[11] As a result, foreign business liability insurance policies are 5% of ours and U.S. liability insurance is 5% of the cost of an automobile, 25% of the cost of a tour bus ride, and 95% of the cost of flu vaccine. The last study shows legal judgments alone account for 2.3% of our GDP ($160 billion in 1995). The big winners are plaintiff lawyers, who make nearly $20 billion skimming 30% to 40% of court judgments as their fee.[12]

Professor Magee also suggests that loss of money to a person armed with a weapon is little different than loss of money to a person armed with an attorney. He contends that in a 25-year study (shown below) of real GNP growth compared to lawyers as a percent of white collar workers, the United States has the highest percent of lawyers and the least growth of our major trading partners. Since 1985 the arrow shows real GDP has dropped 13% as lawyers increased 17%. New York has the highest percent of lawyers in large cities, and corporations there are leaving in droves. His studies show that beyond 2.3% of white collar workers, the legal profession subtracts $660 billion (in 1990 dollars) from the U.S. GNP each year. Much could be gained by rolling back laws, regulations, and precedents to a simple common law, which every person would know by heart, and administer it with little possibility of being overturned. The core of these common laws should have no more than 12 items, and these common laws should supersede all existing laws. They would generally not require lawyers to represent clients. These are suggested at the end of this chapter.

The Negative Effect of Lawyers on Economic Activity

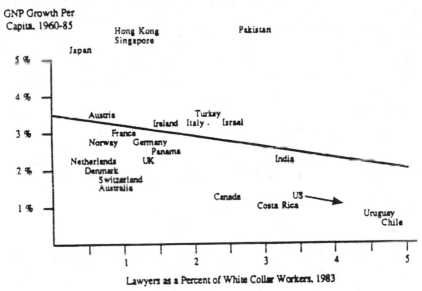

Lawyers as a Percent of White Collar Workers, 1983

UNAFFORDABLE AND IMPRACTICAL

Compared to Great Britain, a country of similar common law heritage, the overall tort claims in the United States cost our economy an additional $120 billion per year by one estimate to $660 billion by another. This costs the support household $2,500 to $13,200 per year. At this rate, had we been able to correct our tort system in 1970, we would have reduced cost of living to half the present level and eliminated most of our national debt. The number of lawyers increased 13 times faster than the population from 1970 to 1980.[13] This increase is a direct result of the congressionally-mandated explosion of laws and regulations.

Mike Scanlon, spokesman for the American Bar Association, was quoted as saying, "Justice in the U.S. takes too long, costs too much, and is virtually inaccessible and unaffordable for too many Americans...Our courts are grossly overburdened and woefully underfunded...The justice system is being asked to resolve complex societal problems it was not designed to handle."[14] Henry Manne Dean of the George Mason University Law School recently said, "We've almost eached the point where as we go through life, we have to have a lawyer at our side to do anything."[15]

Every day our economy is assaulted by the laws and regulations promoted and lobbied by the Association of Trial Lawyers of America. The lawyers purchased these additional rights to litigate with millions of dollars of election campaign funds to national and state judicial and legislative candidates. Japan has many times more engineers than lawyers. We have the reverse. Whose productivity is greater? Who is the world's largest debtor nation? Who has more crime? Why?

Lawyer lobbies since 1965 have turned our nation's easily understood laws into a minefield of costly and conflicting laws and regulations. The result is an immense hidden tax. Once the high costs of confrontation and litigation to the support household ($6,000 to $14,000 per year) are understood, the advantages and efficiency of mediation are apparent. It should always be easier—and required—to mediate than to confront, litigate, or protest.

Criminal Justice System

THE COST OF CRIME

Crime, drugs, and violence cost us $250 billion, or $5,000 per support household, according to a recent network study, and $150 billion[16] partial cost by another study. Crime has experienced unprecedented growth in recent years according to a U.S. Department of Justice study. All violent crime (murder, rape, robbery, and aggravated assault) has increased over 450%[17] from 1960 to 1990.[18] Juvenile delinquency cases involving weapons violations grew by 86% between 1988 and 1992.[19] Inner cities have become very dangerous places in which to live. The legal, penal, and court system has not substantially reversed these trends, and they cost society more each year. It is long past time to change our systems and practices. The focus of the changes should move from criminal rights to victims' and society's rights. Present laws and precedents allow people who commit crimes to escape punishment. Society can be much better served with less complex laws and more assurance that criminals will spend more time in jail working.

In June 1994 Molly Ivins, columnist for the *Fort Worth Star Telegram*, and Dan Rather were on a four-hour panel with several nationally renowned lawyers, including the president's lawyer. She offered several comments: "What struck me about all three distinguished members of the defense bar was, finally, not the skill with which they defended their calling but the sorrow with which they regard its current state. In fact, there were even undertones of anguish. Some phrases they used were, 'As our society becomes increasingly complex and you practically need a lawyer to go to the bathroom.' 'We have to blame the lawmakers—Congress churning out endless laws, legislatures making endless regulations. Except, of course, lawmaking bodies consist mostly of lawyers.' But no one argued with the observation that perjured testimony is just not that unusual and that most of it comes from cops."

According to *Issues* by Heritage Foundation, crime now really pays. Only half of the burglaries in the United States are reported. Only 14% result in arrest. Only 87% of those arrested are prosecuted. Only 79% of those prosecuted are convicted and only 25% of those convicted go to prison or serve time in jail. Of all burglaries committed, only 1.2% result in prison sentences, and two thirds of those sentenced will be back in court again. While they are free, a 1982 Rand Corp. study estimated, each will cost society $430,000 per year. Another 1990 study estimated this cost between $172,000 and $2,364,000 per year while out of prison. In most states (37) the federal courts have ordered a reduction of prison overcrowding, and prisoners are released early after serving only an average of 27% of their sentence. Considering that it costs an average of $25,000 to incarcerate a prisoner for a year, it has been very foolish of us to be caught short of prison space.

Crime pays; lobbies, lawyers, and politicians win; and the public loses jobs and pays all the costs. For all its costs, the present legal system has not improved the quality of justice. Expert witnesses regularly lie under oath for money. Every prosecuting attorney knows which "experts" will say what and for how much.

The Menendez brothers provide ample proof that money can beat the legal system. Their lawyers spent the parents' entire estate valued at $14 million[20] in order to avoid the death penalty. Their attorneys are now filing appeals in the case and billing the county because the brothers are now without funds. Consider how much money lawyers made, and Los Angeles county spent, to prosecute the Menendez brothers and O.J. Simpson. Despite the $8 million spent by the prosecution, defense, and a year of lockup costs, only O.J. knows whether he killed Nicole. Required polygraph tests of Simpson and Mark Fuhrman would probably have uncovered the truth in a few days. If Fuhrman lied, he should be prosecuted for tampering with evidence. If Simpson was truthful, he had to spend a year in jail for nothing and millions to unnecessarily defend himself. Does the present system benefit moneyed clients, or lawyers, or both? Does this benefit society? It is past time to put our slow, antiquated, expensive, and sometimes unjust criminal justice system to rest and exchange it for one whose sole purpose is to search for truth.

THE COST OF APPEALS

John Gacy buried the bodies of 27 men and boys under the crawl space in his house. They were found in December 1978. He received 12 death sentences in March 1980, and execution was set for June 2, 1980. His court-appointed lawyer then filed legal appeals continuously. In 14 years his lawyers were paid $154,000, while the state of Illinois continued to pay for his costly incarceration on death row. Gacy was executed May 10, 1994.[21]

Lamont Griswold crashed into his former wife's apartment and stabbed her 11 times with a butcher knife, severely injuring her and destroying her voice box. He was sent to prison for 25 years. From prison he has filed lawsuits over the validity of their divorce and child visitation rights. He has a court-appointed attorney while she has had to pay over $7,000 in legal fees. When Griswold was asked when he was going to stop filing suits, he said, "NEVER."[22]

TECHNICALITIES AND JUSTICE.

Stanley Carter Liggins was convicted of murder, willful injury, sexual abuse, and kidnapping in the death of nine-year-old Jennifer Ann Lewis of Rock Island, Illinois. Her badly burned body was found in a field near a Davenport, Iowa, school in September 1990. She had been strangled, raped, and her body was set on fire after she was killed, court records said. But in its ruling in November 1994, the Iowa Supreme Court said that evidence introduced at Liggins' trial in Scott County showing he had sold cocaine was " inherently prejudicial." The court ordered that Liggins get a new trial on the murder charge but reversed the kidnapping, sexual abuse, and willful injury convictions and didn't send them back for another trial. In its ruling, the Supreme Court said, "There is no presumption or inference that the assault, sexual abuse, or kidnapping occurred in Iowa." The charges are gone from Liggins' record and he will not face them again. "It makes me mad," Representative Steve Grubbs said, "People in Davenport are just stunned by the Supreme Court decision, that this guy could be back on the street. Those of us with children are just furious. The court does not question whether Liggins actually kidnapped Jennifer Lewis, the question is whether her death occurred in Iowa."[23]

An AP report from Norwich, New York, said that 14-year-old April M. Dell'Olio, who stabbed her boyfriend to death, was ordered to undergo five years of outpatient therapy without serving jail time. A jury found her actions were caused by a mental disease or defect and cleared her of her murder and manslaughter charges. She admitted that she repeatedly stabbed her boyfriend. Prosecutors claimed it was because he wanted to break up with her.

Joseph F. Consolo had been drinking and was driving down the road with his tire shredded and sparks were flying from the rim. The police pulled him over and he swore at them and drove off. After a mile long chase, Consolo jumped from his moving car, fell to the ground, resisted arrest, and the police finally arrested and booked him. More than a year later, Consolo, armed with a lawyer, sued the city and police, claiming they dragged him from his truck and kicked him repeatedly as he lay on the ground. One witness said she saw no beating by the police. The jury agreed that Consolo had not been beaten; however, they found the police were "deliberately indifferent" to Consolo's injuries, and awarded him $90,000. The jurors were not allowed to hear Consolo's 13-year record including convictions for larceny, malicious destruction of property, and leaving the scene of a personal injury accident.[24]

New York Times reporter Ashley Dunn wrote in 1992 that an inmate in the correctional facility near Syracuse, New York, filed a million dollar lawsuit claiming cruel and unusual punishment for incidents stemming from a guard's refusal to refrigerate a prisoner's ice cream. Prison suits have grown from just a few hundred to more than 33,000 last year, about 15% of all federal suits, burdening courts and costing taxpayers millions in legal fees. About 97% are dismissed before trial. However the attorney general estimated it takes 20% of his department's resources to defend against these suits. "These suits are burying us," he said. Rejected appeals should be paid by the prisoner by means of added work time while in detention.

CRIMINAL JUSTICE AROUND THE WORLD

China, the country that we believe has a human rights problem, has a population four times larger than the United States, but has substantially fewer prison inmates than we do. They have four times fewer police officers per 10,000 population. They have one-fourth the trials we have and they have 30 times fewer acquittals. The rate of recidivism in the United States is 69%, England 60%, Australia 60% to 70%, and in China the rate is 4.7%.

Robert Elegant's article in *Parade* (October 30, 1988) said that American consul Peter Prahar left his hotel in the People's Republic of China. While walking, a thief snatched his briefcase. Prahar shouted, "Zei, Zei!" (Thief, Thief!). When the thief was 50 feet away, the crowded street boiled around the thief and soon a large crowd, the thief, and consul were on their way to the police station. The evidence and contents of the briefcase—a sandwich—was recorded along with two additional wristwatches in his pockets. He was a repeat offender, an insult and a challenge to the Chinese justice system. This crime would require at least a five-year sentence or death. Judges are inclined to limit the damage to society by having habitual criminals shot. Peter Prahar managed a Radio Shack outlet in the United States before joining the foreign service. Once he caught a thief and went directly to the police station with him. When they booked him, they found he had 79 previous convictions and then they released the thief on his own recognizance.

There are several reasons for China's low crime rate. First, many cases never go to court, because of reconciliation and mediation committees. Social unity is the result and the reason their system works. All Chinese hold the same ideas, beliefs, and values regarding proper behavior and crimes. The Chinese strive to avoid conflict and they have little use for lawyers. Street committees watch their neighborhoods closely and strive to protect their neighborhoods by handling criminal cases themselves. They believe that most criminals can be reclaimed and turned into useful citizens. Their Confucian background makes them believe all people are innately good. They train inmates in trades, they continue to counsel them on sincere repentance, and when they truly reform, they are released. Once reformed, the street committees find them jobs. While in prison they make socks, shoes, towels, and also work at spinning machines, stamp presses, and machine tools. They are frequently given death sentences for second offense theft, but it is postponed two years. Sincere repentance accepted by accomplished interrogators can cancel the death sentence. It is not smart for a young Chinese to show off by committing crime. Can we learn anything from the Chinese? Their society uniformly believes society is to be protected at the law breaker's expense. Harsh penalties work well when mixed with continuous, extensive communicating of the necessity to repent. Our system regularly frees criminals on technicalities. We free criminals who have not repented or release them on their own recognizance, and they commit more crimes. Why not harsher sentences with freedom only after repentance and / or with restitution? Our criminals sentenced to death continue to file appeals 10 years later. Why? Most of our legal system is based on protecting the accused's rights while filling lawyers' wallets. With our present criminal justice overload, many more people are being killed, injured, and robbed yearly because of this protection than there would be if the criminal's rights were curbed and they were promptly prosecuted.

Singapore has a similar public protection policy. Selling drugs carries a life imprisonment sentence. Michael Fay discovered Asian rim countries do not tolerate vandalism. Defacing a car was punished by two months in jail and four strikes with a split bamboo rod by a martial arts instructor. There are almost no lawbreakers in Singapore. In Great Britain, new laws give police new stop-and-search powers, make trespass a criminal rather than civil matter, and allow police to take DNA samples. The new laws also restrict the right to silence by allowing judges and juries to draw inferences from the subject's silence. German courts try murder cases in front of judges, not a jury. The judges pursue any perjury testimony with heavy penalties. France appoints a neutral fact finder for anyone accused of a crime. His purpose is to question the accused and determine if charges should be made. He interrogates and follows up leads, witnesses, and alibis, and then makes a recommendation. Only then does the accused have an attorney.

WE MUST FIND A BETTER WAY

It is relatively easy to understand the reason our legal system is so expensive, dysfunctional, unfair, and unsafe. It is more difficult to recommend legislative changes with a proper mix of carrots and sticks than to now make a substantial positive change in the system. Society's rights must come before criminal rights in all cases. Laws, in particular, should give the public life, liberty, and the pursuit of happiness. Instead, our streets are not safe. Twenty-year-olds stand a better chance of death by violence than they did during World War II. The old Congress and lawyers in 35 years have constructed the most expensive, slow, confrontational, antiquated legal system in the world for their mutual benefit.

MEDIATION OR LITIGATION

America doesn't understand the advantages and benefits of mediation. It's quick, inexpensive, and final. It draws factions or parties together, instead of apart. Our founders intended quick, inexpensive justice. England, China, and Japan believe in it. Litigation and confrontation, for the last 25 years, have been dangerously shredding our economy. Lawyers, politicians, and the media profit from confrontation. Senator Alan Simpson, who has served for 17 years, said, "The media is more interested in conflict and controversy than clarity."[25] It is against their best interests to mediate. Their livelihood demands that mediation must never replace litigation. No-fault auto insurance is aggressively opposed by lawyers. John Leo commented, "Tort litigation is a lucrative, lawyer-driven enterprise that drains the pockets of all Americans." Legal lobbies are very powerful and economically enhanced, but a very small percent of our voters. Changing our tort and criminal justice system can save our economy $120 to $700 billion a year.

No other country in the world tolerates the legal costs we consider "normal." Our present confrontational political and legal system has not produced a safe society. Lawyers and the judicial system, by one estimate, cost 50% to 70% of all tort judgments, five times[26] higher than the average of all other G-7 nations. Its inefficiencies seriously affect our economy. The direct cost is serious and the indirect costs are overwhelming. It is time to change our political system, our attitudes, our education system, and our laws.

Mediation of disputes has been available through the American Arbitration Association for years; however, both parties must agree. Dubuque County, in Iowa, has been using volunteer mediators for small claims (under $4,000) to unclog the courts, reduce costs to the county and parties, and obtain quick and final resolution of disputes. Mediation is agreed to by 75% of the parties, costs nothing, and takes less than an hour within two weeks. Laws should be changed to require mediation for all disputes, and it should be necessary for both parties to agree to litigation.

NATIONAL MEDIATION

We have a house divided on many other issues, such as a balanced budget, the spotted owl, term limits, media excesses, abortion, and political issues. It should be possible to hold opposing views without disrupting society. Opposing interests spend billions of dollars and billions of hours disrupting society with only meager or no rewards. Is it not time to find a way to have those with opposing views sit down and mediate until they each have two proposals to present to America which will be settled by a national referendum? Imagine, if you will, that the United States has a 30% Hindu population. Hindus believe that cows are sacred. Hindus all over the country are boycotting McDonalds, and picketing meat packing companies and grocery stores to prevent the killing of cows. There are riots, Hindus are being injured, and police all over the country are working overtime to keep up their regular duties and keep the protests under control. If we are a country that accepts other races, religions, and ideas, what should we do? Why not mediate a solution proposing that advertising beef products and media reports of processing beef be prohibited? This is similar to our laws regarding alcohol and tobacco. This would prevent "in your face" distress to Hindus. Freedom of speech needs to end where pursuit of happiness starts for another person. Hindus would also be mediated to accept that the majority of our country does not believe cows are sacred, and to allow them to eat beef undisturbed. A national referendum process will allow natural mediation to permanently resolve these problems. This is the only reasonable path to resolving our present divisions. The current waste of time and resources of polarized groups is unproductive, disruptive, and will only sap our strength. Mediation will always be a better solution than polarization as presently practiced in the courts, in the Congress, on the job, and in the streets.

There are numerous national polarized positions that can be mediated peacefully and quietly. Mediation should involve a search for middle ground instead of preaching the rightness of one position or the wrongness of another. We are all born into social, racial, religious, and political thought processes. Our parents and friends have wired these thought processes into our minds. Most people cannot, and will not, change. Problems needing national mediation are abortion, term limits, curtailing sex and violence in the media or unrestricted free expression, and adopting mediation in place of litigation.

57

Mediation of national issues should require that protagonists define their proposal as simply as possible, along with costs and benefits. The Congressional Budget Office will verify proposal accuracy, and the American voter will decide which proposal will become the law of the land. Opposing sides will find themselves closer to the center, because it must appeal to the majority, and because the decision will be final. Doesn't this make more sense than dissipating our energies and money year after year in a conflict that is never resolved?

Mandatory mediation should replace all civil, and some criminal, litigation and most should not necessitate lawyers. Parties in dispute will first be required to try to resolve their problem without mediation, and list all items in dispute if they fail. Whenever possible, contemporary means of determining the truth, and responsibility must be used. Polygraph tests will be used as necessary. Mediators can quickly dispense simple justice (not jackpot awards) based on understandable, fundamental justice principles, as our founders originally intended. These principles will define conduct required for all citizens and corporations. All above age 10 will know and understand these common law principles, which take precedence over all existing laws, precedents, and regulations.

COMMON LAW PRINCIPLES:

1. The world is not perfect. Mediators shall not judge against perfect standards.
2. You must always tell the truth. Failure to respond to questions may be considered hiding the truth. Penalties will double if you lie. All tests (DNA, polygraph, alcohol, blood, and others) are permitted to discover truth or protect society.
3. You are responsible for your actions from age 10, as they affect you, society, and the environment. Your records will be public. You are responsible to keep your word.
4. You must do no harm to society, persons, or property, mentally or physically. Penalties for committing a crime with a lethal weapon will be doubled.
5. Restitution must be provided in proportion to your responsibility. Judgments can reach all assets except necessary possessions and some transportation.
6. Your rights end where another person's start. Society's rights (majority rights) come first. We all have the right to life, liberty, and the pursuit of happiness.
7. You must obey all civil laws (driving, building, health, smoking, etc.).
8. Jail or prison is a place of full-time work, education, and repentance. No unrepentant or dangerous prisoners will be released. Released prisoners must remain employed one year.

MEDIATION PRINCIPLES

Mediation must be conducted by persons without conflict of interest. Mediation costs shall not exceed 10% of settlement value. Both sides must present testimony prior to making a judgment; both sides must submit a written proposal of settlement. The mediator/s will select one settlement by vote. Mediators will assign court costs. Any appeal after mediation must be between the values in the proposals of the parties. The party appealing must pay all court and legal fees, if the appeal loses. Mediation cannot be overturned by higher courts if it conforms to common law principles. Some guideline limits will guide mediators on awards of damage or loss, similar to criminal sentence times. Mediation sessions will be videotaped. Participants must fill out questionnaires just before and after the settlement announcement, relating to the fairness of the mediator/s. Mediator/s with consistent unfair ratings will be replaced. Each mediator will write up his individual decision. If three mediators don't unanimously agree, they may mediate their differences. Crimes require mediator unanimity, or the case must go to trial. Mediation should start as soon as possible after a request is received but not later than two weeks. Justice can be swift, easy, inexpensive, and fair. All families will notice a substantial drop in the cost of living and taxes.

ADDITIONAL CRIMINAL JUSTICE PRINCIPLES

Criminal justice should be 99% a search for truth. Disputed accusations and alibis of accusers, the accused, and witnesses must be individually videotaped with simultaneous polygraph testing. A mediator will be present at all interrogations to ensure fair treatment of the accused. The accused must be charged within 24 hours. Mediators will be subject to polygraph testing yearly regarding race, social, and other issues. Cases involving death or sentences over one year will be tried in criminal court, using common law and criminal justice principles. The following principle is added for suspects.

Upon apprehension of a suspect, the police will add the following to Miranda: "You will be required to answer questions truthfully. If you do not tell the truth, any sentence will be doubled. Failure to answer questions may be considered as hiding the truth."

CONSTRUCTING HOUSING FOR CRIMINALS

A plan must be developed to house additional prisoners in or out of state, utilizing abandoned industries and military bases. Prisoners should be used to make improvements and learn construction skills. Once housed, prisoners should work and develop a skill or trade. In Alaska, prisoners build caskets. We have more prisoners than any nation in the world, and 67% return to jail again. This is a testament to the ineffectiveness of our criminal justice system. During the last 14 years, 46% of our prisoners have been black. This percent is now rising slightly. We have too few jail facilities and let too many unrepentant criminals back onto the streets after serving too little time and learning from other prisoners how to be a better criminal. It is time to make crime less attractive.

Once sentenced, those prisoners who want to reform and change their lives should be separated from those who don't want to change. Reform prisoners should be given priority rehabilitation counseling. They should be considered as alcoholics now ready to quit alcohol. These prisoners should be placed in peer groups of eight to twelve. They should take responsibility for their actions, verbally confess frequently, and relate what they are doing to set their lives straight. Education and work training courses should be available to these prisoners.

Why not utilize nonviolent prisoners to construct and build detention facilities or convert former military bases and abandoned industries for detention use? Nonviolent prisoners could be used for road repair, vehicle maintenance, and data entry for government agencies. These would provide prisoners with trade skills and perform useful work. Every potential criminal should know that society has resolved to keep crime off the streets and enough detention facilities will be built for every criminal to serve a full sentence. Each prisoner's sentence should be counted in terms of full weeks of work. Every crime costs society something and every prisoner should work. The Thirteenth Amendment clearly states that slavery and involuntary servitude is allowed as punishment for a crime. Government payments for housing, food stamps, SSI, and other support must be terminated until release. Rejected frivolous appeals should be paid for by adding work time to the sentence. Restitution for losses should then be the norm. We must then counsel and train all prisoners ready to change their lifestyles. They should be released into workfare or regular jobs only if they repent and agree to any restitution. Provide business a financial incentive to hire and further train these new workers.

The aim of all business is service for a profit, at risk. -Peter Cooper

Chapter 7. Business, Congress, COLA, and Jobs

SMALL BUSINESS

Small businesses have a very difficult time with federal regulations. OSHA and all standards referenced by the code are impossible for a small new business to comprehend. EPA and EEOC have more regulations to be complied with. Laws regarding discrimination and harassment can turn a job interview into a jury trial. Most U.S. workers are employed by small business and 80% of these businesses have six or fewer employees. It is impossible for them to deal with all the requirements of all the regulations without hiring a lawyer (who produces nothing). Small business is the primary generator of new jobs, and can face a $25,000 fine from OSHA for noncompliance, or a major court fight for hiring discrimination, from almost anyone except white males. A hypothetical example follows:

A small foundry, in business since 1897, employed 30 people and gave COLA raises. From 1960 to 1970, the owner invested $70,000 a year in modern equipment to keep competitive. In 1970 OSHA required him to install a bag house costing $1,000,000 to reduce airborne emissions. The 14-year investment would require interest and principal payments of $110,000 a year. He raised prices 20% above COLA to fund the costs. Most smaller competitors went out of business and he picked up some of their clients. In 1973 an EEOC official notified him that he employed too many Hispanics and not enough blacks. They assigned him a penalty of $500,000. He hired an attorney and won a two-year court battle. The attorney cost $80,000. He raised prices and lost parts sales to a major equipment manufacturer due to lower overseas prices. In 1979 OSHA informed the company that silicone (sand), used in casting, is a hazardous material and must be disposed of as such. This increased output costs 10%. He raised prices 10%. In 1984 a handicapped person answering a help wanted ad couldn't get up the entrance stairs. Soon EEOC notified the owner that his plant had no ramps, toilets, or drinking fountains for the handicapped. Casting is heavy work and he had never considered hiring the handicapped. A lawsuit was filed. A major farm implements customer filed for bankruptcy and canceled all orders. The foundry owner called it quits too. The overseas and larger foundries got his business.

In looking at the reasons his company failed, he was amazed to find that in his grandfather's time and in his father's time, worker productivity and the cost of living rose identically. In his time, since 1965, the cost of living rose 263% above worker productivity. Labor was 85% of his cost, so everything he and his customers produced cost twice as much as international competitors due to labor costs alone. The other government-imposed mandates and legal costs kept his company from investing in new equipment and being competitive. His paid-for, clean air foundry stands idle, along with three generations of investment capital.

THE INTERNATIONAL BUSINESS ENVIRONMENT
Modern business and industry are in a struggle to survive. They are competing in a world market with corporations and governments having different rules and systems. Winners individually or in cartels may forever reap the benefits of a permanent monopoly. Losers will lose the value of their assets and jobs associated directly or indirectly with them. It is similar to a real war in strategy and tactics. It is similar to a wolf pack whose dominant male is the biggest, smartest, most aggressive wolf. He eats first, he eats all he wants, and he settles all disputes. The smallest, timid wolf is the last to eat and the first to die. The pack as a whole lives on if it is efficient and effective. Nature has created a system known as "survival of the fittest" which has produced our environment. It requires all living things to adapt to changing environments and compete or become extinct. Over 95% of all known living things are now extinct.

Our economy doesn't perform as it did 40 years ago. At the end of World War II, almost all industries in Europe, Russia, and Asia were destroyed except Sweden. All these countries had to rebuild destroyed homes, roads, and utilities first. Only the United States, Canada, and Sweden were intact in 1945. We could manufacture almost any product, with or without defects, and sell it at a good profit. Our environment was a vast market with no competitors. For the next 25 years, we believed prosperity would never end. Business earned record profits, and record taxes supported our government programs. The Social Security system and the federal government also had a surplus some years. A rising debt was not a problem. Reality was near at hand.

In 1991 the Council on Competitiveness found the United States "weak or losing badly in one third of 94 critical technologies driving the U.S. economy." Many industries are now improving. The remaining portions of our economy are not increasing their productivity, and government laws and regulations act as a brake. Both raise our cost of living. John Stern, vice president of the American Electronics Association, said in 1993, "The top 100 U.S. electronic companies eliminated 480,000 jobs. They will not be able to lead a middle class life in the leftover jobs in the service industry." In 1992 the labor force, in selected important export industries, dropped to the following percent of 1979 levels as percentages of the 1992 population: primary metal industries, 49%; blast furnaces/basic steel products, 39%; fabricated steel products, 68%; industrial machinery, 67%; electronic and other equipment, 75%; telephone and telegraph equipment, 56%; and motor vehicle and equipment, 72%.[1] Many of these industries fell from 1971 to 1981, when the cost of living first rose 74% above worker productivity.[2] This made U.S. manufactured goods cost 61% more (labor is 82% of U.S. GDP) and they became uncompetitive. Nature and economies are subject to a natural selection process. They must respond to changing environments or perish.

THE THIRD WAVE
The United States is in the third wave information age, and we are staying ahead of the innovation curve. We understand communications, computers, and networking better than any other country. Fiberoptic cable now connects most of the world, and corporations can inexpensively do data entry, computer programming, and engineering all over the world. Texas Instruments is designing sophisticated computer chips in India. Motorola set up computer programming and equipment design centers in China, India, Singapore, Hong Kong, Taiwan, and Australia. American banks process some statements overseas. First-rate experienced computer programmers in India who speak English work for $1,200 to $1,500 per month. Equally qualified U.S. programmers work for $4,000 to $6,000 per month because our cost of living has increased 263% above our productivity. Our workers would have been more competitive with wages of $1,500 to $2,344 (263% lower). More and more U.S. jobs will be lost as computer work is done overseas. It is impossible to stop this export of U.S. jobs unless and until we do those things necessary to quickly (by 3% a year) bring down the cost of living 30%.

U.S. corporations invested at least $4.5 billion into eight foreign countries in 1992. They now total $19.6 billion. The major beneficiaries of these increasing investments are Brazil, Mexico, and Singapore. Before Great Britain corrected its deficit, British investments moved overseas. Many came here. Once here, the investments never returned to Great Britain.

Until we realize how we became uncompetitive, we will not understand why our money, industries, and jobs are going overseas. Once we understand how the old Congress changed the economic environment for three decades, our economic problems will become crystal clear.

61

A FOCUS ON LAWS AND REGULATIONS
EPA regulations were a triple shot at industry. PCBs and other substances were used for decades before they were known to harm the environment. Owners of contaminated land were required to clean it up. It did not matter if owners were not aware they used contaminants or that they had no part of contaminating it. Is this legislation fair? Suppose Congress makes lobby contributions illegal in 1997. Should they then collect all funds illegally given to Congress prior to 1997? Congress next required that litigation be used to resolve any disputes as to who caused the pollution. Lawyers have now claimed 40% of all Superfund cleanup funds expended to date. Their revenue is a major cost to industry and cleans nothing. Industry has borrowed funds at bank and bond rates, and reduced needed R&D funds. Congress meanwhile provided grants covering three-fourths of the cost of city sewage treatment plants, added these costs onto our economy, increased COLA, and sent the bill to our children by increasing the national debt. All federal regulatory agencies plus litigation costs have been increasing the cost of our export goods to the detriment of industry. If the federal government had planned to reduce exports, industries, and jobs in the United States, it couldn't have done a better job.

An artificial blood manufacturing plant will soon start construction in Germany. It has many applications for safe and available blood supplies, particularly regarding AIDS and the military. The process patent was developed in Iowa. It has already been approved for use in Germany; however, it is not expected to be approved in the United States for years. By the time U.S. approval is given, the German plant will have had a several-year manufacturing and marketing jump on any possible U.S. competitor. Litigation of any possible future alleged blood problem may prevent any U.S. company from starting production and marketing the product.

In 1994 a Minneapolis steel fabricator purchased an immense $3 million Japanese steel cutting device which is computer driven and uses a laser to precisely cut heavy steel plate to very fine tolerances. Both laser and computer technologies were invented in the United States. The U.S. entrepreneurs have reasonable concerns about any possible work-related injury caused by the manufacturer. A suit against a Japanese product sold in Japan would have to be litigated in a Japanese court with no chance of an award. Our laws penalize product development and exports.

GOVERNMENT POLICIES OF THE UNITED STATES AND JAPAN
The old Congress pursued a 30-year policy that the public must be protected from the excesses of business. This policy helped the politicians hold power. Unbridled deficit spending raised interest on the national debt exponentially. The laws and regulations made all business and industry more difficult, time-consuming, and litigious. These added bills, laws, and regulations have raised the cost of living 263% above worker productivity, and made foreign products appear to cost half as much, while making our products uncompetitive in foreign markets. The increased COLA over productivity was 51 times greater than the previous 30 years. The legal profession grew 13 times faster than the population from 1970 to 1980. The United States lost millions of valuable jobs, mostly to Japan. As a result our economy has been hemorrhaging money, industries, and jobs. Our trade surpluses ran out in 1976 and our total trade imbalance since then is $1.5 trillion. This amounts to $2.2 trillion in current 1995 dollars, a substantial portion of the national debt. AP reported as of October 1995 the trade deficit "is running at an annual rate of $165 billion, putting the country on track for the worst trading performance in history, surpassing the old mark of $152 billion set in 1987."[3]

The government is the major beneficiary of all corporations. Consider, when a corporation decides to build a new plant, the construction costs of the plant are all taxed first. Every brick and piece of steel started out as clay and iron ore in the ground. They were dug out with machines, which also had to be purchased and required labor to produce. Labor provided 15.3% FICA tax plus 25% income tax to the government. The clay and ore were then processed into bricks and steel with more labor. Clay and iron ore in the ground represent less than 10% of the final costs of bricks and steel finished on the job. Engineering and construction costs all add over 40% tax revenues to the government. After the plant is operating, everything manufactured is taxed by the government. Finally, any profit the corporation has is taxed usually at 25% to 39.5%. Should the corporation become obsolete or insolvent, that government revenue stream is forever lost. Our gross domestic product (GDP), which is the sum total of all U.S. goods and services, is 84.5% labor. The government will also be stressed beyond recovery with another depression. When unemployment passes 20%, workers will need benefits, businesses will slow down and pay higher unemployment rates, take write-offs, and generally show losses; and stockholders will sell stocks at a loss and take their losses off of income.

Belatedly, the old Congress recognized that industry was needed to support our economy and it began a corporate welfare program, which now costs $82 billion to do for business what it should do for itself. Again, this is like driving a car with one foot on the accelerator and the other on the brake. It is painfully wasteful, and adds friction on small business. Manufacturing alone in our economy has increased its productivity 30% in the last 10 years while the entire economy, government and private, improved its productivity only 0.7% per year.[4] Manufacturing has made this progress in the last 10 years while an immense burden of federal regulations, fines, and an explosion of litigation has penalized manufacturing growth, profits, and R&D. Manufacturing jobs that compete internationally, such as metals, electronics, cars, and construction equipment, now comprise only 7% of all U.S. jobs. In 1970 they comprised 13%. This is a drop of 47% of our primary capability to balance our trade deficit.[5] The only other means of obtaining a trade balance is the sale of timber, mineral, oil, and farm products.

Japan has become a superpower because it understands that industries alone support their economy. Government then protects its industries by making it difficult for any country to introduce a product into their country. In 1950 all major Japanese corporations fully committed to produce quality products, install high production equipment, and increase market share. Japan's unions and management have twin goals of striving for ever more quality and efficiency. Their workers now average 33 suggestions a year on improving quality or efficiency, and most are accepted and implemented. Our workers rarely make suggestions and few are adopted. Japan believes that if all corporations strive for quality, there is no need for consumer protection. Japan believes lawyers' fees represent unnecessary economic waste. In the United States, 50% of all judgments and settlements go to lawyers and the court system. Japan, a country half our size, has less than 20,000 lawyers and we have 880,000. Japan spends more on R&D. In 1978 the four corporations receiving the most patents in the United States were American. In 1990 the four corporations with the most patents were Japanese.

For over 20 years, Japan's worker productivity has been twice their cost of living. Our worker productivity is 260% lower than the cost of living. This makes their productivity five times greater than ours. We then have a negative trade balance with Japan brought on by excessive laws, precedents, regulations, and waste. In reality our workers have received $20,000 a year more pay than their productivity has generated since 1965. Japan is a country half our size and had 52% of our manufacturing capacity in 1980. In 1990 their capacity grew to 78% of ours. Japan in 10 years added 50% more output and jobs while we lost both.

We lost 14% of our manufacturing jobs from 1979 to 1992, while our population grew 12%. This is really a 16% drop when adjusted for population growth. Japan gained the jobs we lost with a better strategic economic plan. Japan's economy has run a trade surplus with the United States and the rest of the world for decades. Beginning in the 1970s at least 30% of the U.S. decline in manufacturing productivity was due to EPA and OSHA and the legal system.[6]

Japan trusted in quality and productivity, and we trusted in laws and regulations. Time is running out. A few examples may help us understand what happened to business and industry, and what creative solutions and changes are necessary to become effective.

JOHN DEERE is a company that started out manufacturing agricultural equipment in the early 1800s and diversified into construction, forestry equipment, lawn tractors, chain saws, and other manufactured products. Our economy and farm income slumped by 1981 and Deere had a great deal of surplus inventory. Production slowed down and layoffs were required. Union and federal regulations required firings be by seniority of employment with the last hired being the first fired. In the Dubuque, Iowa, Deere Works, the total employees dropped from over 7,000 to under 3,000 by 1991. During that time union membership dropped from 6,400 to 2,000. In 1996 the plant had 1,686 weekly employees and 831 salaried employees, a drop of 271%. Computers and labor-saving equipment were purchased in efforts to become more efficient. Management and engineering staffs were given more and more work to do to compensate for the necessary layoffs. Necessity is the mother of invention, and the administration streamlined operations, eliminated many layers of management, and engineering became more efficient and effective. Many parts, components, and subassemblies were outsourced to small manufacturing companies working very efficiently and effectively at much lower wages and overhead. These employees replaced United Auto Workers. Deere now also sells Hitachi tractors with some Deere and American parts and the Deere logo. Deere is now considered a strong company.

Deere is one of five manufacturers of backhoes in the world. All five are now losing money on backhoes. It is much like a standoff near the end of World War I when the two sides in barbed wire and muddy trenches endured bombardment and casualties day after day without advancing an inch. If the parent company of any of the five can no longer support these losses, that company will lose the value of its backhoe plant, the workers will lose their jobs, and the government will lose the tax base of the workers, the corporation, and the FICA for the workers. The other four companies will then gain market share. The country whose company quits will lose the income stream from corporate and stockholder write-offs, FICA, and income tax revenues of the business and workers. Merchants, hotels, travel agencies, and all the people and industries who feed off the corporation will reduce or end their income stream to the government.

What does this tell us? Market economies determine overall production and number of jobs. Downturns necessitate cost cutting. Management and engineering put in more hours of effort for the same pay and streamlined processes. Union jobs were replaced by outsource jobs in order to remain competitive. All management, engineering, and union people under age 30 were discriminated against due to seniority rules imposed by unions and government. Without those rules, the most effective employees could have been retained, instead of the oldest. There are few employees under 40 now working in this plant. Worldwide competition is still fierce and undecided. Corporations need to remain financially strong to compete internationally. Government-imposed regulations with COLA have made U.S. labor costs 263% less competitive. Loss of competitiveness quickly translates to loss of jobs.

CHRYSLER CORPORATION—The Dodge brothers made engines for Henry Ford when Ford restarted his automobile company. Chrysler, like all domestic auto manufacturers in 1950, was an old-line manufacturing company that had a good reputation and earned a good profit. Its designers cosmetically changed styles regularly. Chrysler had a standard adversarial relationship with its unions. Neither workers nor management was focused on improving quality or efficiency. It considered other domestic manufacturers to be the competition. Europe introduced VW "bugs," and Japan produced mini cars which rapidly gained market share on initial cost, low operating cost, reliability, and customer satisfaction. Small foreign autos got a foothold with dealerships and then expanded. Then came the first oil crisis in the 1970s with gas lines at service stations. The small car market took off. Chrysler found itself with a stable of 1950 gas-guzzling cars in a 1977 environment. It had enough losses in recent years to be in great financial difficulty. On November 2, 1978, the *Detroit Free Press* had two headlines: "Chrysler Losses are the Worst Ever" and "Lee Iacocca Joins Chrysler." Iacocca soon found himself on a sinking ship and like a survivor, he directed a classic turnaround. Chrysler unlike GM did not have the financial resources to make even one major mistake. Iacocca asked the government for a $1 billion loan guarantee. The United States had a deficit economy and there was little assurance at the time that the government would not be throwing good money after bad. The government report showed that if Chrysler went under, it would cost the country $16 billion in unemployment, welfare, and other expenses and write-offs. Congress approved the loan guarantee. Thousands of jobs were cut. Workers were asked to reduce pay and work more effectively in exchange for a share in profits.

More and more components were outsourced at lower costs. Chrysler now outsources 70% of its product. Totally new thinking was evolved for the design and manufacture of new models. Chrysler is again a well-respected American car manufacturer. Equally important in the rise of Chrysler is the fact that the Japanese yen increased 400% in value against the dollar from 1970 to 1995. This helped level the labor costs and the playing field.

What does this tell us? The relative value of the dollar against other currencies is a major factor in being competitive. A company or a country that has lost its economic strength has fewer and fewer options. Outsourcing saved manufacturing costs and equipment expense. It transferred jobs to outsource manufacturers with lower labor costs. It is devastating to get behind the competition. The government had to decide on whether to gamble on a major company or not. Tremendous costs can be passed on to all taxpayers when a major industry fails. It is very difficult to compete against lower wages, which are a major component of price. Workers will work harder and smarter when their jobs are at stake and they share profits.

IBM is one of the most respected manufacturers of quality high-tech products. In 1986 it employed 406,396 people. A number of innovative U.S. microcomputer manufacturers quickly stepped into the microcomputer market. Many Asian rim countries had national goals of manufacturing quality computers. Some had labor costs less than a dollar per hour and few or no benefits. Market conditions changed for IBM, and normal (blue chip) profits turned into massive losses, which amounted to annual losses of almost $16 billion during three years. This is an average loss of $17,000 for each employee for three years. By 1994 IBM employed 256,207 people and planned to cut an additional 35,000 workers over the next two years.[7] Much of IBM's competition will continue to be small nimble competitors.

<u>What does this tell us?</u> The bluest of blue chip corporations can become unprofitable very quickly even in high-tech markets. An unprofitable corporation must make changes, in IBM's case, laying off almost half of its workforce. Making this big corporation profitable is in the best interest of the federal government. The federal government has done little to become more efficient and effective. It needs to take lessons from IBM.

INTEL was the world leader in inventing, patenting, and producing computer chips. Other U.S. manufacturers, including IBM, made chips. Japan targeted computer chips as strategic to their economy. Japan copied our manufacturing systems, applied intense technical and engineering R&D, reengineered manufacturing breakthroughs, worked more intensely in quality management, and produced a product of better quality and less cost than U.S. manufacturers. Computer manufacturers liked the price and quality. They abandoned many American manufacturers. Japan's NEC became the top producer. The government made a temporary agreement restricting the amount of chips Japan could ship to the United States. This, however, did not affect world markets and our chip manufacturers' share continued to drop. In 1988 the government agreed to support the computer chip industry by developing a new hybrid, and abandoning the old concept of monopoly. A consortium was formed by Intel, IBM, other chip manufacturers, and the government. Government matched corporate contributions of $1 billion dollars and advanced our engineering, technology, patents, and processing in order to surpass Japan's processes. This consortium and the weakness of the dollar leveled the playing field. Intel focused on the more difficult microprocessor products. Since 1987 Intel has turned a loss of $203 million into a $2 billion plus profit, and is now the top producer of microprocessor chips.[8]

<u>What does this tell us?</u> When Japan targets an industry, it plans to dominate the market. If you don't invest enough in R&D, you will lose market share. It is difficult for our corporations to compete with a nation that helps finance corporate R&D of a product and then has government market and protection. The loss of a strategic industry like computer chips would ultimately be disastrous for us. Quality and price are absolutes in market share. The government abandoned a sacred cow (monopoly) in an emergency and it worked. Joint research and development is less costly, and much more effective, in producing goods in the world market. The government should rewrite antimonopoly laws regarding basic research and allow our corporations to compete with international competitors. International monopolies are more threatening than national monopolies, and monopoly laws must change. The poor alternative is to periodically fund industries in trouble or let them go under.

MICROSOFT CORPORATION was founded by Bill Gates, a college dropout, in the late 1970s. Microsoft is the computer software firm that wrote the disk operating system (DOS) codes necessary to operate all IBM-compatible microcomputer systems. It retains the patent and continually improves the operating system. Microsoft directs much of its efforts toward creating new innovations in the computer industry. Microsoft is now a $2 billion company. In 1993 Microsoft surpassed the stock value of General Motors, the nation's oldest, largest manufacturing company, worth $125 billion. Microsoft's only asset is its patent on DOS plus a work environment that fosters imagination, innovation, and creativity. General Motors deals more with manufacturing and process. Microsoft spends a much higher percent of its income for R&D than General Motors.

<u>What does this tell us?</u> Gaining patents and developing new technology is of vital importance. Corporations working on the cutting edge of technology with highly educated, creative, and imaginative workers, and little organizational baggage, will be more successful than big, reliable, old-line companies.

MOTOROLA is an old-line corporation that used to manufacture radios and television sets. It now produces a variety of quality electronic products from microprocessors to radio telephones all over the world. In 1988 it received the Malcolm Baldridge Quality Award, the most prestigious industrial award for quality. In 1991 plaintiffs' lawyers learned Motorola and other electronics and semiconductor manufacturers had dumped industrial solvents in the ground near Phoenix for over 30 years. One solvent, trichloroethylene (TCE), an industrial degreaser found in household products, regulators believe **may be** a carcinogen. Groundwater near three Phoenix area plants contained traces of TCE. Motorola spent $50 million treating and trying to stop the spread of these traces. Motorola has an insurance policy with Zurich-American Insurance Co. covering environmental damage for $20 million plus legal fees. Motorola has been billed for $15.2 million for legal work done by 180 lawyers. The insurance company has filed suit against Motorola disallowing payment of half of the law firm fees. Maricopa County seeks medical monitoring of 700,000 residents, and 45,000 residents seek compensation for allegedly reduced property values. Motorola claims TCE was in such wide use in disinfectants, furniture polish, fabric softeners, window cleaners, rug shampoos, and air fresheners that if the chemical is a carcinogen, it would be difficult to assess blame. The lawyers are now taking their first dispositions and no end of litigation is in sight.[9]

<u>What does this tell us?</u> Environmental laws blindsided industry by requiring extensive insurance and legal expense for harm done by materials long before they were known to be harmful. In our present environment, costly problems for industries may arise without warning. Is it any wonder Motorola and other manufacturers are looking at plants in other countries?

PIPER AND BEECHCRAFT are the most recognized names in civilian aircraft in the world, and the people who fly these planes praise their quality, durability, and handling. They became the world leaders in civilian aircraft after World War II. Their prices were reasonable and the planes lasted forever. Virtually no flyable planes are junked while on the ground. The National Transportation Safety Board investigated 203 crashes of Beech aircraft from 1989 to 1992 and concluded every one was caused by weather, faulty maintenance, pilot error, or air traffic control. Plaintiffs' attorneys claimed all 203 were primarily caused by the manufacturing faults. Each of these 203 cases cost Beech an average of over $500,000 to defend. They could be required to defend almost every plane they ever built. Beechcraft stopped production of all civilian aircraft due to massive unwarranted litigation. This right to sue also caused the loss of 18,000 aviation industry jobs since 1980 when Beechcraft stopped making small aircraft. It has caused Beech terrible hardships because our laws allow anyone to be sued with no penalty to the accuser, if they are found innocent. Our aircraft industry in 1994 obtained tort relief for aircraft over 15 years old, but no relief from being accused during the first 15 years.

<u>What does this tell us?</u> Manufacturing a reliable, affordable, useful product is not enough to protect a manufacturing company from going under. The tort system distorts justice by preying on corporations with deep pockets. Excessive litigation and the assumption that a product must perform perfectly forever is the root cause of Beechcraft and Piper's impossible financial difficulties. Attorneys have everything to gain and nothing to lose in suing corporations with deep pockets. This practice hurts every individual and business by driving up prices and forcing a reliable U.S. business to quit. Tort laws should be changed to require mediation. The public should assume risks of flying, driving a car, and participating in sports to name a very few. Each family should self-insure these risks. It will save each support household $2,500 a year. Laws should be changed to pay the legal costs of a company, or individual, wrongly sued.

CATERPILLAR—the multibillion dollar worldwide heavy construction equipment manufacturer was one of a kind at the end of World War II. By 1973 Komatsu, a Japanese corporation, had gained substantial market share. The oil crisis was upon the world and demand for heavy construction slowed down. In the early 1980s, Caterpillar lost $1.5 billion, cutting prices below cost to meet competitors' prices. Labor cost at Komatsu was less than half that of Caterpillar. From 1979 to 1991, UAW workers dropped from 40,500 to 15,100 and are now only 28% of all Caterpillar workers. Caterpillar laid off 2,000 (31%)[10] of its workers and became more efficient by spending $1.8 billion on robots and other high-tech,. labor-saving tools. This increased worker productivity dramatically. Much of the lost production was made up in overseas plants. In 1992 agreement was not reached with United Auto Workers and a strike was called. Caterpillar advertised for replacements. The number of applications of experienced replacements was very high. Caterpillar announced they would hire applicants as permanent replacements if the last offer wasn't accepted. The union worked briefly and vowed to do nothing more than the contract called for, then workers went on strike again. After a 17-month strike the national UAW called the strike off and told the workers to go back to work. Because of the loss of so many manufacturing jobs, there were eight times fewer strikes in 1995 than 1977.

What does this tell us? International competition with quality corporations is intense. The cost of living increases caused by the old Congress have caused many good companies to become uncompetitive. U.S. manufacturing processes and workers have not kept up with Japan. There is a surplus of unemployed heavy equipment workers. The work attitude since the strike will be no match in the world market against Komatsu whose employees all search to improve quality and efficiency. International corporations can, and will, move work overseas permanently when the business environment becomes adverse. Labor and management must find a way to improve quality and reduce cost. They must change soon or we will lose Caterpillar and other industries who have adversarial relationships with their workforces. There are fewer strikes now in the United States and they are less effective.

WAL-MART—Sam Walton started work with JC Penney, in Des Moines, Iowa. JC Penney called his employees "associates" and expected them to follow the Penney idea. The Penny idea was:

1. To serve the public, as nearly as we can, to its complete satisfaction.
2. To expect for the service we render a fair remuneration and not all the profit the traffic will bear.
3. To do all in our power to pack the customer's dollar full of value, quality, and satisfaction.
4. To continue to train ourselves and our associates so that the service we give will be more and more intelligently performed.
5. To improve constantly the human factor in our business.
6. To reward men and women in our organization through participation in what the business produces.
7. To test our every policy, method, and act in this wise: "Does it square with what is right and just?"

In 1950 Sam Walton bought his second store (the lease had no renewal option on his first store) in Bentonville, Arkansas. Sam Walton had an overriding something in him that caused him to improve every day. His basic strategy was the same as JC Penney's idea; however, rather than compete head-to-head with them in large cities, he chose to merchandise substantially different products in smaller rural towns. He expected his associates to do it, try it, fix it, and tell of all successes. As he opened new stores, these innovations were passed on. Innovation was expected by Sam Walton and he rewarded success. All employees were associates and stockholders. Wal-Mart developed the lowest administrative overhead and best volume purchasing in the industry. Small town stores with similar products found it impossible to compete with Wal-Mart price, quality, and service. By 1988 Wal-Mart's profits were 60% higher than Sears, the largest retailer in the world. By 1993 they exceeded Sears' total sales volume also.

What does this tell us? Sam Walton beat the best merchandising minds in the world when he started in 1950 with $55,000 and associates who believed in innovation, quality, minimum overhead, treating people fairly, and low prices. Few of these objectives belong to the federal government. Wal-Mart has put many small retail stores out of business, but it reduces the cost of goods and our cost of living. Environments change. The most efficient quality systems will always win. Proper motivators might change the federal bureaucracy.

HYUNDAI AND KOREA—David Halberstam described the rise of Korea's industrial capacity in his book *The Reckoning*. Hyundai is Korea's largest corporation. It is part family owned and part state supported. The state, like Japan, only allows certain firms to compete with it. In 1984 the first primitive cars entered Canada, and 80,000 were sold. In 1986 U.S. sales were almost 150,000 cars. In 1986 Japanese wages were nearing ours; however, Korean salaries were about $3 an hour in heavy industry. The Japanese brutally occupied Korea from 1910 to 1945. Koreans hate the Japanese who consider Koreans inferior. The Koreans in 1950 had a burning desire to move their country from the Stone Age to Japan's leading competitor in a generation. In the early days, workers toiled seven days a week and ten hours a day. The government severely restricted leisure, domestic consumption, and dissent. College students waited in lines at 4:00 A.M. to get into libraries during exam week. By 5:00 A.M. all seats were taken. In the 1980s Park Jin Kean was a foreman on Hyundai's final assembly line. He worked six 12-hour shifts per week for $9,600 per year, and his wife and two children managed to save $6,000 per year. He was proud to be a foreman at Hyundai. He would have been happy to know that, in 1983 when Japanese steel mills were working at 60% of capacity, a Japanese labor union executive said, "I keep telling the Koreans that they have to get their wages up because what they are doing now is destructive to everyone." Hyundai's president, managers, and workers enjoy referring to the Japanese as "the lazy Asians." Michio Nagai, a former Japanese minister of education, observed, "there are few national forces more powerful than the belief that things could get a great deal better within the span of one's lifetime."[11] It must also be said that the opposite is an equally powerful force.

What does this tell us? Korea is potentially a greater industrial competitor than Japan. Properly channeled, being an underdog is a high incentive to excel. One of the greatest positive or negative forces in a nation is a belief that things can get a great deal better or worse. Restricted leisure and consumption produced high savings. Education was considered the path to a good job and was taken very seriously. China, with the largest population in the world, is where Korea was 20 years ago, and has even higher potential to reduce the prices of manufactured goods.

IN A NUTSHELL

The business and manufacturing communities are the heart of our economy. Almost all federal revenues are gained from taxes on the business, stockholders, business suppliers, and workers of the suppliers, and personal and FICA taxes on workers. These taxes, on almost every successful business, amount to substantially more than all profit for the business.

Entrepreneurs, with new ideas of building a better mousetrap, constantly spring up. Most of these small businesses fail but those start-ups that succeed generate most of the new jobs in our economy each year. The environment for business has become much more difficult in the last 30 years. The success or failure of business operates very much like the laws of nature, where the fittest survive by adapting to change. A hostile environment, over time, causes extinction.

Business must be honest to succeed. The general public, according to a recent survey, reported 57% of those surveyed said it was sometimes, or always, all right to say nothing when you receive too much change when making a transaction. No business would make such a decision. Business was continually attacked by the old Congress, as a threat to the public which must be thoroughly regulated. Regulations by their very nature do not adapt to change. A hundred pages of regulations will become a thousand in 10 years, and will be managed by three times as many regulators. Continuous pressure from the American Trial Lawyers Association for more litigation base has produced an avalanche of burdensome laws and regulations. These laws and regulations are so extensive they frequently conflict with themselves, as well as state, county, and city laws and regulations. Finally, these laws and regulations carry large penalties which ignore due process of law. One of the most massive regulations is OSHA. As mentioned earlier, we have spent billions of dollars on OSHA only to find the rate of workers' lives saved slowed down to 38% of the rate before OSHA. Should a worker know the regulations and choose not to comply, the company is fined. First-time fines for minor violations on companies with one to 25 workers in 1994 were increased fivefold by the old Congress to $25,000.[12] They rise dramatically for serious violations by large companies. No U.S. business can be sure it has fully complied with an OSHA inspector's interpretation of the mammoth code. OSHA can enter a business at any time. OSHA is interpreter, judge, and jury of all alleged violations. OSHA keeps all fines to support itself.

HAVE WORKERS BENEFITED OVER 30 YEARS?

Over the last 30 years, workers have received benefits 263% above their earned productivity, because of COLA. The raises have not increased workers' purchasing power; however, the growth in benefits is the highest in the world. Except for the loss of several million good jobs, workers have not paid for any of the following benefits since 1965:
1. The right to sue almost anyone for discrimination, harassment, wrongful dismissal, equal opportunity of employment, and other newly defined rights
2. The benefits of cleaner air and water; the protection of birds, fish, animals, snails, clams, worms, and beetles
3. The benefits of a welfare system, for those who do not work
4. The benefits of a retirement system presently paying out two to five times more than was earned
5. The right to send the bill for these benefits to our children, with the hope they will pay for it

Japan's workers received none of these benefits. Their wages only rose when their productivity did, while our dollar depreciated 400% against the yen. Unions must soon realize that their fate and the fate of the companies they work for are inexorably bound together. The enemy has been runaway COLA, hatched by the old Congress, which has driven the cost of our manufactured goods twice as high as our international competitors. The costs driving economic friction and COLA include the national debt, runaway litigation, EEOC, OSHA, EPA, welfare, lobbies, and runaway government spending. Until COLA drops, U.S. manufacturing jobs will decline and outsourcing will expand here and overseas. Union attempts to stop or reverse this trend will only accelerate the decline of U.S. manufacturing. Ironically, strong powerful manufacturing corporations, free of burdensome and wasteful government, is the only real hope U.S. workers have of a brighter future. Real wage increases will come when all workers strive for quality and efficiency at work, and reforming government.

CREATING JOBS IN AMERICA

An April 1994 article in *Scientific American* by Paul R. Krugman and Robert Z. Lawrence, states that real wages doubled from 1945 to 1973. They have risen only 6% since then. The authors state that if many nations compete worldwide and each of their productivity rates and wage rates increase 3%, they will continue to compete unchanged if their currency exchange rates remain constant. If one country's productivity increases only 1% and wage rate increases the same, they will still compete equally. If, however, this country's wage rate increases to 3% the country will become less competitive, and lose jobs or reduce its currency value. **We have lost both**.

They discuss the concept in international trade that when a rich country with a skilled labor force trades with a poor country with many unskilled workers, the pay of the skilled workers in the rich country increases and in the poor country it decreases. At the same time, the wages of unskilled workers of the rich country decrease and in the poor country they increase. **U.S. unskilled labor rates will fall.**

Their research shows the share of U.S. domestic spending for manufactured goods has dropped 12% from 1970 to 1990. The output per hour of manufacturing has increased 30% since 1984 or 3% per year. The efficiency of nonmanufacturing output—including clerical, legal, government, and other services and construction—has grown only 5% since 1984, or 0.5% per year. It is this larger portion of our GNP which is keeping our total productivity increase to 0.7% per year. **The increased wage inequality, decline in manufacturing, and slowdown in income growth is overwhelmingly the consequence of domestic causes**.

Since 1973 real (constant dollar) wage increases (6%) are just slightly higher than non-manufacturing output (5%) since 1984. There is too much economic friction in our economy. The share of manufacturing in GDP is declining because people are buying relatively fewer goods; manufacturing employment is falling because companies are replacing workers with machines and making better use of those they retain. Wages have stagnated because the rate of productivity growth in the economy as a whole has slowed, and less-skilled workers are suffering because a high-technology economy has less and less demand for their services.

Because the cost of living has rapidly increased above worker productivity over 30 years, some suggest we repeal NAFTA and erect trade barriers as a means of keeping and creating jobs. It sounds reasonable because millions of well-trained and well-educated workers have been replaced in Asian rim countries. Our present surplus of these workers will continue to drive wages down until we again become competitive. We can't build a tariff wall around the United States, because our trading partners will surely retaliate.

Can we or anyone in the world compete with Japan? The answer is yes, but it is absolutely necessary to change the power structures of our country. Congress, government, education, the legal system, unions, management, and the public must quickly change from their present form into a new, more enlightened, efficient, competitive social-economic system.

Government overregulates business and industry and causes them to be less competitive in comparison to China, Taiwan, Korea, and Japan who give business protection. OSHA, EEOC, and EPA need to change from adversary and bounty hunter to a resource for business in finding the most reasonable and effective ways to protect workers and the environment without threats or penalties. Industries should only be responsible for cleanups of sites they knowingly polluted.

More and better jobs depend on achieving a booming export economy that demands a large amount of investment capital and internationally competitive prices. Our federal government needs most of our available investment capital and can't allow interest rates to rise because of what it will do to interest payments on the debt, which has been increasingly funded with short-term notes.

Instinct tells us to act. Reason tells us to think. Our labor costs have been driven far beyond worker productivity by laws and regulations passed by the old Congress. We have been made internationally uncompetitive. When we accept the fact that COLA has hidden the excesses of government, we can adopt worker productivity as the pay index. Taxpayers can then enjoy reduced costs of living as all Americans push government to rescind the least needed laws, regulations, and government overhead and waste that burden the economy. Temporary worker companies charge a 30% premium on the workers' pay to cover compliance with these laws and regulations. Major corporations like John Deere must offer early retirement, and then hire back workers using temporary services at a 30% premium. Seasonal employers must add these costs to their cost of goods and services. Big activist government has done no favors for workers, business, or the economy. Regulations now steadily increase unemployment. If business is to create jobs, profit, and salaries quickly, the laws and regulations that most hinder small business and international corporations must be rescinded.

Labor and business have dissipated too much time, energy, and capital over the years in confrontation. We can learn from Japan that labor and management, working together, can make world-class products at very competitive prices. Unlike Japan, we have a land full of natural resources. Labor and management must shake hands, forget old animosities, and work together for their company's and our nation's good. In reality, the fate of labor is tied to its employer. If South Africa can end a century of bloody conflict using mediation, we surely can use mediation to solve our problems. We need to create "unified companies," whose owners share the profits of productivity equally with their employees, both salaried and hourly. They may be privately owned, partnerships, and corporations. The goal of these companies must be quality and efficiency. They should expect both labor and management to make regular suggestions on forwarding these twin goals. Unified companies should receive a 1% reduction in FICA taxes. Workers would have no reason to strike. These companies would do well to strive for long-term rather than short-term market share and profit goals. There are many examples of these successful competitive companies such as Lincoln Welding, Gore Corporation, Jeldwen, and Wal-Mart. The economy will rapidly improve when labor and management work together and government unburdens business.

Our legal system takes too much out of our economy. All tort litigation should be changed to require mediation, using basic common law. The federal government must balance the budget and pay back half of the debt within 10 years as we stimulate the economy. Corporate welfare must end along with regulatory penalties on business and industry.

The majority of the National Association of Business Economists who met in early November 1995 agreed that if the budget were in balance in 2002, they would expect faster growth in the real GDP over that period. Roger Brinner, chief economist with the forecasting firm of DRI/McGraw Hill, estimated that balancing the budget would raise America's yearly output an extra 2.5% over the next 10 years. That would mean an average of an extra $1,000 a year for each American family. He adds that the economy would create 2.4 million more jobs by 2005 than if the deficit remained unbalanced.[13]

Who heeds not the future will find sorrow close. —Confucius

Chapter 8.   Japan

THE NEW CREATION

In his book, *The Reckoning,* David Halberstam provides great insight into the early history of Japan's amazing productivity. When World War II ended, the United States dictated a new constitution, signed by Japan, which provided among other things that the people be free to organize unions. By 1949 communist-dominated unions were established throughout Japan. Nissan's 8,500 union workers received a year's pay for nine month's work, and built fewer than 12,000 vehicles a year. The union called many strikes over wages, management control, promotions, and additional union rights. It ruled the shop floor, and continually subjected managers to endless hours of verbal abuse. Production was down, payroll was high, and Nissan was losing a great deal of money. The company needed modern equipment to compete. Most workers feared but respected the union's power. Some of the workers believed the union's actions would destroy the company. The stage was set for a change.

Nissan needed a loan from the Industrial Bank of Japan (IBJ). Nissan's president believed the unions were destroying Japan's economy, and so did the industrialists and the IBJ. The president decided to cut the workforce by 1,760 employees. The directors were afraid to challenge the union. The IBJ was impatient. Japan's industrialists believed modern equipment placed a ceiling on wages. The union believed workers came first. This was a fundamental division of a capitalist society. How would money be used and to whose benefit? Nissan borrowed over $1,000 per employee for severance pay and promised the bank that there would be a new and harder line from management. The company fired the union leader and the radicals. A strike was called on May 25, 1953, and the union leader proclaimed he was for union rights or death. Resolution of five years of struggle was at hand. Three Nissan workers dissented with the union and backed the company's right and need to tighten its belt. They became a critic and the target of the radicals. They were threatened. It took considerable courage to challenge the union, but soon they had 40 people who began to meet and form a loyal union, which was constitutionally permitted. Nissan management borrowed money to fund this union as a partner.

The strike drew crowds of 5,000 to 6,000 people. Nissan's president let the union exhaust itself. He had special loans from the IBJ. The union assaulted any worker, or his family, who opposed them. The company hired thugs to protect the second union. Japan's banks persuaded Nissan's competitors not to take advantage of Nissan's strike and they agreed. For nine weeks nothing was resolved. The new union of 40 workers, with a slogan, "Those who love the company love the union," was working. Meanwhile over 7,000 union workers were on strike. The 40 workers agreed to recruit 10 workers each to attend an open meeting and 400 came . By September the new union had over 3,000 members and by the end of 1953 the new union had control of the factory floor. Nissan put loyal workers in key jobs. All of Japan's industries quickly followed the new pattern that unions and management have a common need to work together in harmony to achieve success. Modernization of equipment would come first. Japan, 20 years later, had a highly efficient industrial machine, and Japanese workers have enjoyed full employment. In 1973 Leonard Woodcock, head of the UAW, went to Japan as a guest of the Japan Auto Workers Union. He did not understand the union speeches about the terrible times of 1953, and the vows that it must never happen again.[1]

QUALITY SUCCEEDS

Quality did not arrive in Japan on a divine wind. It came in the person of Dr. W. Edwards Deming with a single-minded goal to create a system of making ever better products ever more efficiently. He was primarily responsible for developing quality control in U.S. defense industries during the war. He found American industry was irresponsibly focused on quantity instead of quality, after World War II, and was scorned by every major corporation in his country. He believed quality required total commitment at the top which would, in turn, filter down to the bottom. It had to be the sole purpose of a company. Japan was well aware of our superior products and production during the war. After World War II, Japan continued to produce shoddy products. In 1950 Japanese industrialists desperately wanted to succeed. Their backs were to the wall. They had half our population packed on a mountainous island the size of California and few to no natural resources. That year a Dr. Deming lecture was arranged in Japan; it was attended by all 45 of Japan's major industrialists. Deming outlined his quality control program to them and told them they could meet and beat America in some of their products within five years. The industrialists had no alternatives. They fully accepted his concepts. Within months, Deming received thanks from many of these Japanese corporations because of large increases in productivity and quality. Japanese industries consider a complaint a gift from God, and proceed to eliminate the problem forever. We have begun to believe in quality, and our products are rapidly matching theirs. It is ironic that the man behind Japan's quality and efficiency, and known to everyone in Japan, went unrecognized in America for decades. It took 30 years before American industry realized its loss.[2]

PROTECT INDUSTRY FIRST

I went to Japan in 1970 and was amazed to find you could buy their products cheaper in the United States. Japan has a goal to be first in the world economically. In just 25 years, they became a superpower while we became a superdebtor. They blocked out foreign competition by means of regulations. Japan has dealt with six presidents and has made each administration believe that barriers and restrictions to trade will be removed; however, most remain. Their regulations guarantee success to large corporations with few national competitors. They regulate agriculture, air travel, discount stores, housing, banks, and many other things. Their people want many of these regulations ended such as rules rigging stockbroker commissions, rules slowing the construction of retail centers, and rules raising national air travel prices which subsidize international flights. Japanese cannot buy aspirin over the counter. The *Wall Street Journal* quoted a MITI (Ministry of Trade and Industry) official as saying, "we must deregulate or die."

Capitalism has different forms. Japan protects and encourages the producer versus the consumer and they lead world savings. We protect the consumer versus the producer and we have led consumption and debt at the expense of saving. Japan has no land and no natural resources. It succeeds because it protects its only resource, its industries. They provide business incentives, close their home markets, and charge higher prices at home to fuel the foreign market. They then install a bureaucracy to protect the producer. Winners are guaranteed. Can any country compete with this system?[3]

Japan has no reason to change, except to get more competitive because they do not want to lose an economic war with Korea. Financially Japan has moved from one of the weakest countries in the world after World War II, to the strongest. We have done the opposite. In 1995 our largest bank, Citibank, had $205 billion in assets. Japan had four banks with assets ranging from $826 billion to $588 billion.[4]

The Japanese government selects strategic product markets they wish to develop and eventually dominate. They then fund and develop a research and development consortium, and patent any new technologies. They then allow Japanese corporations to use this research and compete freely. Capitalism in Japan is not perfect. Because the door was opened to fund basic common strategic research, there have been huge and continuing illegal payoffs by corporations to politicians, who direct the spending of government funds toward research benefiting specific corporations. As a result of this, Japanese people believe their political system is corrupt. Power to favor specific special interests in any country will always produce bribes and corruption.

A DOMINANT ECONOMIC POWER

Japan, a tortoise in 1950, is relentlessly achieving its goals, while America, the confident hare, carelessly dissipates its assets. Consider the following:

1. The Japanese education system provides almost double the education contact hours per year as ours does. All first grade students know their grades and tests will determine their future. Their average students test better than our best 10%. They have 16% more teachers and one-third of the nonteaching staff per thousand population. Their students clean the schools daily and learn patience, responsibility, and cooperation.[5] We have 14 times more incarcerated prisoners per million people than Japan does.

2. Japan (and Germany) spend 50% more than we do for nonmilitary R&D. Japan now obtains five times more U.S. patents per year than it obtained 25 years ago. They have nine times more robots per 100,000 workers than we have.[6] Japanese corporations strive for ever higher quality, productivity, and market share.

3. Japanese workers and management have identical goals. They have no labor management strife. They work for one employer for a lifetime, and offer over 30 suggestions a year for product improvement. Most are accepted and incorporated in a better product.

4. Japan has kept most high-tech, retail, and insurance companies out of their markets. Business and industry are considered a national asset and are protected by laws and regulations preventing competition.

5. Japan believes that lawyers generally produce only economic waste. We have 26 times more lawyers, per million people, than they have.[7] They believe in mediation, which is quick and simple. Our system of laws and regulations, costs our support households over $6,000 in liability and other insurance, defensive medicine, court costs, and higher costs of taxes, goods, and services each year. Japan has dramatically less crime and fewer repeat criminals, and they can walk their streets safely.[8]

6. Japanese households save and invest 17% of their income, which remains tax-free.[9] We save only 2.8%, and savings are taxable.

7. The yen has appreciated 400% against the dollar in 25 years. Japanese households average $200,000 net worth while ours average $36,000.[10] They have become the bankers of the world. They hold $480 billion of our debt.

8. Japan has evolved a highly competitive industrial democracy. It has been running an annual $130 billion trade surplus with the rest of the world for decades. Accepting Japan's legal philosophy based on mediation and protection of business alone could eliminate much of the difference in our economies.

9. Japan's prime rate at the end of a four-year recession is 0.5% while ours is over 8%. Japan doesn't need to stimulate the economy because unemployment is only 3%.

10. They spend little on defense compared to the United States, which spent $600 billion in 1995.

11. From 1980 to 1990, Japan's manufacturing capacity grew from 52% of ours to 78% (an increase of 50%) and the United States lost millions of jobs.

JAPAN'S FUTURE

Time reported that Tokyo's most influential politician, Ichiro Ozawa, wrote a book *Blueprint for a New Japan* in which he stated, "We need to change in at least three ways:

1. We must establish political leadership. We must show who bears political responsibility in Japan, what they think, and what their larger visions are.

2. We must decentralize. Except where absolutely necessary, power should be transferred from the national to the local governments.

3. We must abolish excess regulations. We should preserve only the minimum number of rules necessary to govern economic and social activity, and adopt fundamentally laissez-faire policies."[11]

Ozawa recently has developed elaborate proposals to deregulate the economy and cut taxes 50%. Japan's politicians, corporations, and workers apparently understand their problems better than ours do. If Ichiro Ozawa can convince Japan to follow his course, especially points 2 and 3, they will leapfrog us again by correcting their government faults before we correct ours.

OTHER CONSIDERATIONS

Do our high CEO salaries make us uncompetitive? High salaries are outrageous for companies with poor performance. Salaries need to relate to performance. Japan's CEOs have huge expense accounts, and corporations have given their CEOs $40 million houses, tax-free. Our CEO salaries, compared to Japan's, have little to do with productivity and success.

Is NAFTA important? Past history tells us that Japan will protect industry some way. We must compete with many foreign labor costs until rescinded legislation and a stimulated economy bring down our cost of living. We must move in this direction, because Korea is overtaking Japan with quality goods at lower prices.

Will the dollar continue to lose value against the yen? We have moved from over 360 yen per dollar in 1970 to a low of 80 yen per dollar in 1995. Economic theory tells us that for every 1% reduction in the value of the dollar, $1 billion in trade is lost. The dollar has dropped 400% against the yen in 24 years. In the long run, the dollar will continue to drop, unless we change.

The United States, and other countries, sustain an annual trade deficit of $130 billion with Japan. We, and others, export meat, fish, and timber to Japan in exchange for high-tech manufactured products. This transfers highly paid manufacturing jobs to Japan.

LET'S CHANGE DIRECTIONS

Japan's success has been in great part due to our failures. Japan invested early in technologies that improved efficiency. This drove the cost of living up for five years, but paid great dividends ever since. We know a house divided cannot stand; however, labor and management have dissipated their resources while better products at better prices from Japan took our jobs away. Our unemployed become an additional burden. Our legal system devastates and penalizes our economy, primarily in indirect costs. Our regulations are overly expensive, make us uncompetitive, drive up the cost of living far above productivity, hurt business, and cost jobs. Too many of our corporations favor short-term profit instead of long-term market share. Too little R&D is spent developing new products. We consume too much and save and invest too little. Their lobby funds ($60 million last cycle) to the old Congress have been repaid with favors. Our educational system is clearly inferior. We have not been able to open up Japan's markets. Our trade deficits are not sustainable to Japan or the rest of the world.

From our perspective, Japan is on the rise. In reality, we are falling. If we want to compete with Japan, we must quickly reverse everything listed in the preceding paragraph. Japan can wait until our economy collapses and then buy us out for ten cents on a dollar. Time is not on our side. We have treated our industries as greedy and dangerous, and they have responded by going elsewhere, where they are wanted. We must change philosophy and treat our industries as our most important national asset, and then totally change our labor, legal, and regulatory environment. We must relentlessly pressure Japan to open its markets, but not count on them doing so. We are in an economic war with Japan, which we cannot afford to lose. We must compete, not complain. However, this time Japan has a quality, productivity, and education edge. They will compete fiercely for their only national asset, their industries.

"The future belongs to those who plan for it." —Unknown

Chapter 9   Education in the United States

U.S. EDUCATION IS FAILING

Education is hopelessly behind and has not produced enough focused, enthusiastic, inventive, creative, persistent, problem-solving minds needed to create new industries and eventually jobs. Students have not trained and exercised their minds but wait to have ideas poured into them. They go to school 1,170 hours per year and a recent AP study showed they watch TV over 1,000 hours per year. A public television program "Does TV Kill?" reported 3,000 studies linking TV violence and viewers who became kickers and hitters. One study estimated 10,000 fewer homicides would occur if there was no TV. By teen years, the average student spends many more waking hours thinking about or doing things with the opposite sex, music, sports, cars, and TV than they invest in education. The hormone-enriched students have few thoughts of their own responsibility for getting an education and preparation for the world of work.

The best 10% of our students test out lower than the middle 10% of Japan's students in math and science. Our education system delivers 6.5 hours of class a day for 180 days (1,170 hours) per year. Japan delivers 1,893 hours per year to each student (62% more). Their students go to school 8.5 hours per day, 5 1/2 days per week, 243 days per year. After school, their students have an hour of homework and then go to Juku School two hours for three to four nights per week. They help serve lunch. Japanese students understand that a job is not a right, it must be earned. A 1995 AP dispatch described the anger of Japanese parents about eliminating school classes one Saturday a month. German students go to school 230 days a year, 50 more than our students. They have school on Saturday. More and more of our students are physically out of shape and endangered by sex, drugs, violence, and TV. A 1983 study by the National Commission on Excellence in Education stated in conclusion, "If a hostile power had attempted to give America the bad education system it has today, we would have viewed it as an act of war."[1]

In l960 we spent $2,035 per student (in 1994-adjusted dollars). In 1994 we spent $4,247 per student ($1,120 were Department of Education funds), which was higher than any developed nation, and our SAT scores declined by 80 points (10%). Ron Grossman (*Chicago Tribune* April 9, 1995) reported the College Board decided to dumb down the test a total of 95 points in math and verbal in early spring of 1995. The new "recentering" allowed a student who did very well last year, but missed a few questions and received a score of 730, to get 800 on this year's test—the same score as a student who answered every question right in 1994. In 1994 after "recentering" the board announced that students' SAT scores were up. It was reported by the Scholastic Aptitude Test administrators that since l987 the number of SAT candidates with A- or better averages in school had risen 13 points. These same students then tested 12 points lower in verbal and 61 points lower in math. The United States presently does not rank in the top 20 nations in the world in math and science achievement.

In 1993 the AP reported the Paris-based 24-nation Organization for Economic Cooperation and Development showed 3.1% of OECD nations' workers are teachers while only 2.6% of our workforce are teachers. The United States had the highest percent of the workforce in nonteaching education jobs at 2.9% while countries like Japan and Netherlands had less than 1%. The nonteaching jobs include administrators, guidance counselors, food service staff, nurses, bus drivers, coaches, and custodians. New York State has more school administrators than all of Western Europe, which has a population 20 times larger. U.S. education costs per student are the highest in the world. In 1991 our 13-year-olds scored significantly lower than any other large industrialized country in math and science. A 1993 report shows our 17-year-olds ranked last in algebra and biology, and were 11th in chemistry out of 13 nations tested. Students from Singapore, Britain, and Canada were comparatively off the scale. Only 1% of American high school seniors ranked as high as Canada's top 25%. Education director Dick Riley released results showing 90 million Americans (47% of our adult population) possess only rudimentary literacy skills. We spend too little of our education funds for teachers, and too much for nonteaching. An earlier 1985 report said in conclusion, "If a foreign power wanted to undermine the United States, it would give us the education system we now have."

ACT results released in February 1995 show the majority of America's high school students can't do better than C-level work in their first year at college. It is an open secret that most schools and colleges now give better grades for poorer performance. Stanford University recently discovered that 50% of their letter grades were As and 42% were Bs, totaling 93% of all grades. Harvard discovered that 91% of their students had B- or better grades.[2] There were no Fs. Our colleges consume 250% to 300% more of our GDP than they do in any G-7 country except Canada. Our yearly costs also average 195% higher.

During World War II, everyone knew our national interest was to defeat Japan and Germany. The government and the media motivated all to produce war equipment and train men to win the war with the least possible loss of life. We are in an economic war with Japan, Korea, and other big seven nations and have lost millions of jobs. We will lose more unless we understand the magnitude of our education problem and create an education strategy to compete with, and beat, any education system in the world.

JAPAN'S EDUCATION PROGRAM

In order to move their economy forward after World War II, the Japanese created a unique education system, much different from ours. They stressed achievement, conformity, and responsibility. In 1970, when traveling, we saw squadrons of schoolchildren in identical uniforms. Virtually every school employee was a teacher. There were no layers of administration, and there were no custodians to be seen. The children cleaned their schools every day before they went home. Twelve years of this taught them to care for and respect public property. Parents were highly involved in their children's education. Children from age six understand that their future life and work after they graduate will depend on how well they study and succeed with their schoolwork. Good grades open the doors to good universities, where good grades at the best universities are rewarded by good jobs with the best corporations. They have quality education and their economy is rapidly expanding. Japan has a national education objective to produce highly educated scientists and engineers for its high-tech industries. Their students almost never watch TV. Japan, with half our population, now graduates 10,000 more engineers per year than we do. In 1990 the top four U.S. patentees were Hitachi, Toshiba, Canon, and Mitsubishi.[3] They have an education system that is achieving their national goals.

MOTIVATED TEACHERS ACTIVATE LEARNING

It is well known that the most important factor in a good education is a good teacher. The opposite is also true, and many teachers' performances pale compared to TV entertainment. I met and watched many great teachers practice their profession. The best were truly inspirational. I have recently talked to many of these teachers, educators, and principals and I have become aware that there presently are substantial numbers of ineffective teachers, who are hard to remove or improve. Many of these best educators now view public education as defective, in part, because of defective teachers and administrators. Teachers must radiate enthusiasm for learning, and become motivators and colearners instead of dispensers of information (to be tested later). Students' measured learning performance should become a measuring stick for teacher performance and pay. Kentucky has recently raised its test scores 20%. Teachers are paid more, and rewards are based on student performance. Better community support has been the result.

A recent address by James L. Melsa, Dean of the College of Engineering at Iowa State University, revealed the new paradigm of the Engineering College. He quoted Peter Drucker: "Every organization has to prepare for the abandonment of everything it does." The college is forming a new philosophy of education:

1. The programs must be learning-based;
2. The experience must be practice-oriented; and
3. The program must demand active involvement of the student.

Melsa said, "The shift from a teaching-based program is much more than a simple semantic change. In the teaching-based program, we focus on the teacher—the sage on the stage. In a learning-based program, we focus on the learner—the student—and the teacher becomes the guide on the side. In the teacher-based model, the teacher works hard and the students rest—some might suggest listen. In the learning-based model, the students work hard and the teacher listens and guides. Learning can take place in a wide range of ways: co-op experiences, laboratories, design projects, case studies, hallway conversations, and of course even in classrooms. We should focus on evaluating learning not teaching. Otherwise, the outcome of our attempt to transfer knowledge may be, I taught, but the students didn't learn. Think about the meaning of *taught* in that sentence. Most schools throughout the ages have spent endless hours trying to teach things that are better learned than taught. The teacher must motivate, direct, encourage, coach, and serve as a knowledge resource."

He continued, "The successful school of the future will empower students with motivation and discipline of continual learning. In the knowledge society, students must learn how to think and how to learn. We must reinforce the students' native thirst for knowledge and create a lifelong curiosity and desire to learn." In summary he said, "If we keep on going the way we are, we will miss the road to the future."

PARENTS MUST HELP THE PROCESS

Parents must take a more active role in their children's education. Many children start school and college unprepared. Retaking college courses is expensive. The Education Resources Institute in September 1995 estimated borrowing for college has jumped 50% since 1992, from $16 billion to an estimated $24 billion in 1995.

Two children in my extended family began school one year late, with exceptional results. Children not ready for school should generally wait a year. Their chances of success are much better. A 1995 study by Dan Goodman, described in his book *Emotional Intelligence*, asserts a 5-minute test of four-year-old children is a better predictor of a child's success as an adult than IQ scores. The tester brings the child into a room and says, "I must do an errand for a few minutes. You may eat this marshmallow, but if you wait until I come back, I will give you another marshmallow." Those who wait, succeed in life. Parents must take responsibility to teach their children to use their minds for their own benefit at the expense of quick gratification. Parents frequently don't take enough interest in their children's school, the teachers, the subjects taught, and the performance of their school standard evaluations. Many families and single parents send their children to school without breakfast, and think of school as a baby-sitting service. Too many students are in school only because they and their friends are required to be there. It is useless to point the finger of blame at anyone, because almost everyone but the children are at fault. We must be concerned that since forming the Department of Education, education has regressed. As Pogo once said in a comic strip, "We have seen the enemy and he is us." Education needs rethinking.

MORALITY, ETHICS, AND RESPONSIBILITY

A 1995 AP article, "Truth About Lies", reported that University of Virginia students lied to their parents every other phone call home. The Air Force Academy recently decided they needed an "ethics" course because the arriving students don't understand the necessity of ethics. Another AP article reported that the U.S. Naval Academy in 1992 investigated possible cheating by 133 cadets. Most repeatedly lied, before being presented with irrefutable evidence. Eighty-one finally confessed to breaking the 42-year-old honor code. A recent survey showed only 4% of parents have their children do regular chores. The same parents overwhelmingly did chores themselves.

These chores taught duty, obligation, and responsibility, all concepts many parents have not instilled in their children. Is it any wonder that the child feels no responsibility for his education, or that teen pregnancies are exploding? Our lower expectations of children, in order that they gain self-esteem, have only led to lower performance. It is past time to challenge students, expect more, and teach respect and responsibility for one's own future. Challenging students increases their performance in proportion to the challenge.

The *Miami Herald* studied student cheating. It concluded, "National surveys consistently find 60% or more of students engage in at least one form of cheating. This year, a national study of business students at 35 universities found 95% reported cheating in high school or college."

The National Education Goals Panel in November 1995 reported, "More teachers report being threatened or injured by students now than in 1990, and more teachers say classroom disruptions are interfering with teaching and learning."

On April 29, 1994, Margaret Thatcher gave a speech at Storm Lake, Iowa. She stated, "The greatest threat to freedom is crime and violence." She blamed TV violence and the failure of schools to teach "fundamental principles and religious values" and added, "schools shouldn't be entirely blamed because courts have erected a wall keeping religion out. Every government has a duty to pass legislation on public decency, particularly to protect the young."

There are few highly motivated, responsible, self-directed, educated young people who can think and communicate in the workforce today. Indeed, this type of person is a rarity, an endangered species. We need to provide a stimulating, challenging environment with highly motivated teachers so that more undermotivated students will succeed. We must produce a better product than the product of the last half century. We need to change the status quo.

We are graduating too many unmotivated, irresponsible, and uneducated people with defective thinking, reasoning, and communication skills. We have no goal to win. Our students go to work unprepared. They have come to believe their parents and the government will take care of them. Nothing could be further from the truth. A good steady job is very scarce today. Companies who have them can be very selective about who they hire. These jobs will go to the highly qualified. How then do we change our education system to produce this highly qualified person?

THE DEPARTMENT OF EDUCATION

The Federal Department of Education has presided over the decline of our education system. The department's administrative expenses eat up 13% ($30.4 billion) of our total education costs plus 12% ($26.8 billion) used for discretionary programs.[4] One program, the National Education Standards and Improvements Council, prepared national standards of U.S. history as part of the president's Goals 2000 program. A *Wall Street Journal* article by Lynne V. Cheney had this to say: "National Standards divides American history into 31 general standards and does not encourage anyone to linger over American achievements. The Great Depression is addressed in three standards, yet not a single one directly mentions the U.S. Constitution except to ponder the paradox that the Constitution sidetracked the movement to abolish slavery. John D. Rockefeller is accused of unethical and amoral business practices in direct violation of the common welfare. Counting subjects mentioned, McCarthyism had 19 references, and the Ku Klux Klan had 17. Lincoln's Gettysburg Address had one mention. Harriet Tubman, an African-American is mentioned six times. Civil War General and U.S. President Ulysses S. Grant had one mention; Robert E. Lee is not mentioned. The famous midnight ride of Paul Revere is ignored, as are Alexander Graham Bell, Thomas Edison, Albert Einstein, Jonas Salk, and the Wright brothers. One of the few congressional leaders actually quoted is Tip O'Neill, calling Ronald Reagan a cheerleader for selfishness. These standards were rejected by the Senate 99 to 1."

The Goals 2000 program was supposed to be a bipartisan standard to test the performance of our nation's schools. Widely published (November 1995) results of nationwide history tests of 22,000 high school students, released in November 1994, revealed 57% had no basic knowledge of history.[5] The Department of Education has set history back.

An old business adage says, "If it ain't broke, don't fix it." This has evolved into today's new concept: "If you are still doing things today the same as last year, it is time to reevaluate why you do what you do, and how you could do it better or more efficiently." Education, politics, government agencies, and the legal system steadfastly resist the changes necessary to prevent economic disaster. Only external pressure and incentives will produce change.

A NEW NATIONAL EDUCATION STRATEGY

U.S. students need 445 additional hours of better learning each year in order to compete with European and Asian rim countries. The Department of Education should be terminated, and $20 billion of their $58 billion funds should be sent directly to states who would raise the total yearly education contact hours to 1,615 hours. It could increase 2,950,000 teachers' salaries, averaging $34,000 to over $40,000.[6] As an alternative, schools could hire more teachers, assistants, or aids. Each state should develop its own education expansion programs; however, teacher performance, as measured by student testing each year, must become half of the increased teacher compensation and their reason to increase measured learning.

The school year should be two weeks longer. Schools would operate from 8:00 A.M. to 5:00 P.M. This would give every student four more years of education (by today's standards) plus a year of service, cleaning, and learning personal responsibility at school. Children would be at school while parents work. The change would give students 38% more access to computer, science, and vocational equipment and 38% less TV time. Full Employment recipients might work in a study hall or library, grade papers, take attendance, perform administrative duties, supervise the playground, and clean the building. The completed program would graduate students who could provide industry with quality, responsible, and well educated workers. Students would be able to move into vocational training at ninth grade. They could test out of several years of expensive college courses, college costs would be reduced $10 billion, and student loans could be halved. Graduates could begin work years earlier and pay wage taxes longer, and the country could save the remaining $38 billion budget of the former Department of Education.

FOUR YEARS OF ADDITIONAL EDUCATION PROGRAMS

In 1990 a corporation I founded considered developing a two-week youth summer camp designed to solve problems, adapt to change, and increase self motivation, responsibility, perseverance, and creativity. We believed the program would supplement missing portions of youth education and would improve their success in life. Later the local school administration asked for new education ideas. We submitted most of this program and were informed it was filed (and forgotten).

1. In early grade school the following concepts should be learned and understood: truth, honesty, responsibility, respect, courage, persistence, self-discipline, and compassion. These concepts should be reinforced in reading, stories, history, videos, and discussions throughout a student's education. Students who fight, kick, or trash should become rest room custodians.

2. Educators must uncover the talents, activities, or interests of each student, then encourage and praise any substantial success. It is important that every student have an interest, succeed at something, and feel pride in success.

3. Students must learn that they alone are responsible for their future. The best jobs will go to exceptional people who have made the most of education opportunities. A positive attitude and an education history of accomplishing difficult projects will assure them success.

4. Students should learn how to set lifetime goals. They can achieve most goals, once set. They must understand the importance of setting priorities regarding family, siblings, friends, education, morality, TV, reading, athletic activities, alcohol, and drugs.

5. Everyone can make positive contributions to our society. Early, all should know that society does not tolerate abusers, bullies, and cheats. Teachers and student committees should deal with offenders quickly and decisively. Daily school cleaning should be done by students.

6. Minds must be stretched with obstacles and adversity so that the students feel frustration and challenge. A successful conclusion gives students perseverance and self-reliance. The greater the struggle, the greater the reward. Adversity develops imagination.

7. Schools must raise their expectations of student performance about one letter grade by simply setting the mark higher and encouraging students to exceed their own expectations.

8. Understand that failures of nature and business accrue because of an inability to adapt to change. Develop creative and innovative thinking in small groups with problems such as how to build a better bike, kite, paper airplane, or mousetrap-powered model car. Use these small group projects to develop communication skills and consensus building. Analyze how creative thinking works.

9. What type of problem does the scientific method work best for? Why does this method work? What does IQ measure? What does SAT measure? Why are these measurements useful to you? How do they relate to you and a job? Teach how to Discuss, Observe, Analyze, Plan, then Act.

10. Have students contract to write several papers a year about topics in 1 on the preceeding page, subjects of special interest to the student, or mutually selected special projects. This will develop their abilities in research, organization, thinking, and communication.

11. Develop responsibility with absolutes, and don't vary from them: on time, as contracted for, absolutely clean, complete silence, orderly, and wait until everyone is served.

12. Discuss "sayings" such as: "You become what you think." "What do you wish you had done when everything goes wrong?" "Survival of the fittest." "The more things change, the more they stay the same." "Don't knock the competition." "Nothing succeeds like success." "I can make a difference." This teaches students to think before talking or acting.

13. Have students develop their positive personal assets:
- Personality—honest, positive, outgoing, communicative, enthusiastic, fun, determined
- Mental—focused, alert, logical, creative, organized, tenacious
- Work habits—careful, efficient, precise, alert, anticipate and avoid problems, suggest improvements, reliable, prompt, cooperative, good attitude, initiative, team player
- Appearance—clothes, self, eyes, hair, strength, athletic abilities, health

14. High school students should search for a career track and develop life-after-school skills; create good academic records; prepare a job application; determine which jobs will be most in demand; know what employers want to see; prepare for job interviews; know what questions to expect; make out an income tax form, car purchase agreement, car insurance and life insurance policies; balance a checkbook; and know how to shop smart for clothes, groceries, and nutrition. They should learn about staying healthy, drugs, sex, marriage, children, divorce, responsibility, respect, restraint, hard work, and determination.

15. Expand all the standard school subjects such as history, English, math, and science into college level courses like Recent World History and Current Federal Government and Economics. If students had understood federal economics years ago, we might have acted more responsibly decades ago and avoided the present debt crisis. By ninth grade, students should elect a college or vocational track. Classes requiring special equipment or training such as molecular biology and nuclear physics would have to wait for college or vocational school.

16. Consider requiring that students wear school uniforms to improve behavior. It works in Japan, and their constitution is copied from ours. It works in many U.S. parochial schools, and it works at Long Beach, California, according to the *Los Angeles Times*. In the first year after enacting a dress code, school fights are down by half, suspensions are down a third, and criminal activity is down at all schools, in all neighborhoods.

SHOULD EDUCATION OR JOBS COME FIRST?

American history and world economics have shown that added education increases lifelong earnings. There is a widening gap between those with high incomes and those near poverty levels. It has been suggested that we fund more low-income students to help them through college. This argument runs into the fact that required economic downsizing has accumulated an estimated six million graduates (the equivalent of all graduates of all the colleges and universities in the United States for three years) who are presently unemployed or underemployed. Business and industry have not been able to generate enough college graduate jobs to absorb the supply in great measure because of the effects of unprecedented legislation passed by Congress over 30 years. Artificially funding additional college graduates would simply make a bad situation worse. Many of these estimated six million existing graduates are now in the untenable position of paying off college loans with low-wage jobs. A much better solution is for Congress to fund, directly to the states, an additional 445 hours of education each year in the public and private primary and secondary school systems. This will gradually add one more year of education for all students every three years. All artificial funding of higher education will increase graduate unemployment until Congress rescinds old legislation pulling our economy down. Job expansion must precede education expansion.

Were we directed by Washington when to sow and when to reap, we should soon want bread.
—Thomas Jefferson

Chapter 10. Federal Agencies and Employees

MY EXPERIENCE WITH FEDERAL AGENCIES

Over the last 40 years I have dealt with six federal agencies: HUD, FHA, EPA, U.S. Forest Service, Postal Service, and the U.S. Air Force. Almost all of the people I dealt with were congenial; however, every part of the federal system, its policies, and procedures convince me that all of these agencies are very ineffective in accomplishing their tasks.

As a second lieutenant almost 40 years ago, I had my first look at government in action. I was working in the installation engineer's office of a TAC air force base. We prepared annual requests for new construction and repair of the base. I was given orders by the chief civilian administrative assistant to always ask for more funds than were asked for the previous year and to always spend everything that was approved. We received approval of resurfacing all base roads with blacktop and after that was accomplished, we received approval to replace all base water lines (which were mostly under the streets), requiring tearing up the newly paved streets. The pipes were almost plugged by calcium deposits. New pipes were installed and the old pipes were then stored adjacent to the stockade where they were lifted over a fence with a crane and prisoners pounded the deposits out with large hammers. The pipe was next welded by a prisoner sentenced to 30 days in the stockade. A seeding request and a few sprinkler heads was the foundation of a new irrigated base golf course. Because it was easier to get rehabilitation funds than new construction funds, one building was totally rebuilt from the foundation up including a new floor slab, all with government approval. There are countless ways federal agencies can expand projects and themselves and their costs without being detected by government watchdogs.

Working with HUD on a project, we designed and built a nine-story elderly housing tower with a central service core and a minimal donut-shaped corridor around it. It was very inexpensive and substantially reduced the space needed for corridors. On a second project with a different office, another similar innovative solution was proposed and rejected by HUD because it was not like other standard solutions. Although the innovative solution would cost less, we were obliged to redesign a standard solution.

My experience with the Forest Service has been pleasant but exasperating. It started in 1960 when our family acquired a cabin with an outhouse on leased land with a 99-year lease in a national forest. We receive a review yearly on the condition of our property and notice of any violations of Forest Service rules. In 1961 we were advised that outhouses were no longer permitted and we must add a bathroom to the cabin with "indoor plumbing," and fill in the pit and remove the outhouse. We submitted plans for the addition and they were approved including the location of the well, septic tank, and drain field. We did, however, request to use a concrete septic tank. This was refused and we were told to use a 575-gallon steel tank, which we agreed to do.

The Forest Service did give us permission to fill in the pit and floor the outhouse and use it for tool storage. We completed the work that summer. The next summer we got a letter saying that we had to paint the green outhouse to match the cabin which was brown with green window trim. We had a visit next summer with the forest ranger and permission was granted to allow us to let it stay green as it had been for the previous 10 years. It was also rather out of sight behind some green brush. Within a few years of owning the cabin we were advised that the 99-year lease would be changed to 20 years and renewable at the Forest Service's discretion. There were no options; if you didn't sign the lease you had no lease. I distinctly felt like I was being treated the same way our government treated Native Americans years ago. Before long we were notified that the yearly lease would increase and it quickly rose 10 times the amount of the previous lease and is now 16 times higher. In 1979 an arsonist burned our cabin to the ground. We intended to rebuild from the foundation up. We were told we had to furnish complete site and contour plans or they would not be reviewed or approved. They also noted we had a 575-gallon steel septic tank which they said was not allowable, and would have to be replaced or we would have to use an outhouse. I mentioned that outhouses were banned years ago and the ranger replied, "not anymore." It was all irrelevant because the water and sewer systems were each 100 feet away and undamaged by the fire. When I reminded them that their office required me to install that specific steel tank, it was grandfathered into approval. Our new cabin is weathered cedar with brown trim. Last year we were asked to paint the former outhouse brown—we did.

Lessees in the forest are required to obtain a permit from the Forest Service to cut firewood. Trees to be cut must now be dead and down to preserve the ecology. They formerly could be cut if they were dead. Roads comprise less than 1% of forest land. There was an average of one dead birch tree hanging over the road every 200 feet on the five mile access road to the highway in 1995. Birch makes excellent firewood the first year it dies, and is of no known use to animals because it rots within 3 years. These dead trees fall without notice, and are a clear and present danger to people and vehicles on the road. Lessees have asked for three years to cut dead trees along the road. No permission has been given. This would make the trees easy to harvest, make the roads safer, and save the Forest Service the time and expense of removing dead wood from the roads. A change is rational, but it is not permitted by the regulations.

In early 1980 I helped plan the construction of a ski area in Illinois. We knew that approval of a sewage system was our first priority. It would need approval of the County Department of Health, DNR, and EPA. Each agency wanted a different system: septic tank, sewage lagoon, and treatment plant. They would not compromise. Two weeks before opening in December, we had no approvals. We forced a decision which then required us to build a lagoon 400% larger than necessary with a structure for a possible future treatment facility. The lagoon has never held a foot of water. All government agencies want the power to say yes or no, and they frequently conflict with each other.

THE NECESSITY OF EFFICIENCY

Business must search for creative solutions to remain competitive. Government rejects creative solutions because they don't conform to existing regulations. Business cannot break contracts, but government can. Government agencies have no interest in making their operation more efficient. Indeed, the GSA system encourages government employees to make things complicated, keep extra records, analyze unimportant information, and hire as many people as possible. The reason for this is that GSA promotions are frequently related to how many people work for you in layered management.

Joseph Spear, syndicated columnist, has this to say: "In 1935, one-fourth of all Americans lived on a farm (63 million); today, only one-fiftieth of us do (5.2 million, 12 times less). In those six decades, the Department of Agriculture workforce has nearly tripled, from 44,000 to 123,000. One of the department's functions is the operation of 11,000 field offices throughout the country. One of these offices in Georgia serves 17 farmers. In Clay, West Virginia, a Department of Agriculture field office serves a single commercial farmer. The office director earns $35,000 a year. He has an assistant who makes $8,000. A *Washington Post* reporter who visited the office for a day heard the phone ring five times."

Business in the 1990s is much different than it was in the 1980s. The new main forces of change include striving for quality, customer satisfaction, and reinventing or reengineering the corporation to operate differently, more efficiently, and more effectively. Many layers of management and many workers are now absent from these new streamlined corporations and their final products are better and less costly. Ironically, the waste of our political system and government agencies is the primary reason many corporations faced the necessity to change or go out of business.

THE UNMANAGEABLE FEDERAL BUREAUCRACY

Government agencies have no pressure to change. Reengineering corporations to produce breakthrough efficiency must be pushed by the people in charge of the business. In the government's case this must be the voters, the Congress, and the president. The other necessity is to bring "outsiders" in to consult with an equal number of "insiders" or in this case people who run the agencies. It is only when you have outside people asking: why do you do this? why don't you do a task another way? why is it needed or how else could it be done more efficiently? that you make any progress doing necessary work more effectively. There will never be any progress in making government agencies change until they are given a mandate by the voters or the Congress that all federal agencies must reduce their total spending by 5% for five years, assuming zero inflation. The present system will never make any substantial improvement in effectiveness without external pressure. There have been 11 attempts to trim government (mostly by presidents) and reduce the number of departments, but the bureaucracy continues to grow.

The federal government runs 400 programs to give subsidies to individuals. Fifteen programs account for 97% of the transactions.[1] The other 385 programs make only 3% of the transactions. Agencies want to protect their departmental turf regardless of savings. It's time to consolidate or decentralize them to states. Agencies will resist. First it would be an admission that the existing managers and workers are functioning inefficiently. Second, streamlining government would imply fewer workers and reduction of GSA ratings or managers. Both of these are more than enough incentive for agencies to continue to oppose any changes. The following example by Knight Ridder newspapers is an example of unacceptable business practice and everyday government practice violating laws passed in the Carter administration.

When a veteran Labor Department legal secretary rebuked a young part-timer for not filing promptly, she was struck and her jaw was broken. She fired the part-timer. Firing a government employee is almost impossible. After the knockdown, a representative of the American Federation of Government Employees intervened in the assailant's behalf. Ultimately the assailant was given a permanent job and a $3,890-a-year raise. Firing someone is so time-consuming, and repercussions so fearsome, that getting tough doesn't pay. Statistics show that in a federal office of 100 workers, one worker would be fired for serious misconduct every 10 years; one would resign under pressure every 15 years; and one would be fired for incompetence every 70 years. Pentagon statistics show that 23 times more soldiers are dismissed for incompetence. The statisticians said, "Once a new worker passes the probation period, they have a job as long as they want it." Dense civil service protection, strong union representation, and a flood of bias claims (12 times more than the private sector) make efficient management of government impossible. A specialist said that few workers get fired and none stay fired. About half of the government workers who make EEOC claims allege bias because they are black, Hispanic, women, or over 40. Others claim to be whistle-blowers, physically handicapped, or victims of ethnic, religious, or reverse discrimination. This list demonstrates that everybody can be a victim.

Richard Reeves, a syndicated columnist, in 1994 said, "Who loses? The taxpayers, of course, but also the public employee unions. It is, in fact, impossible to defend what is happening coast to coast. The unions are destroying themselves by not sharing the public interest in fairness, enforced by common sense rather than contract clauses, in all aspects of relations between governments, public servants, and ordinary taxpaying citizens. Instead, many public unions treat such things as the spoils of old wars—making public service a battle against taxpayers."

A federal government dishwasher complained that the water was too hot. The supervisor asked her to wear rubber gloves and she got a rash. Was the temperature of the water turned down or the employee given other instructions or another job? No! She was classified as permanently disabled and entitled to collect full on-the-job disability pay for the rest of her life.

Government employees generally have salaries similar to private industry; however, the benefits are much higher. The fringe benefits, including retirement, vacation, and health care, are 76% higher than the private sector. Federal workers take 1.6 times the number of sick days and 1.4 times the number of vacation days. They retire earlier and get pensions three to six times better than private industry. With a federal job you can retire after 35 years at age 55 at 67% of full pay, get four weeks vacation after three years, six weeks after six years, be entitled to 13 days of sick leave annually, and expect to be promoted twice as fast as workers in the private sector. Taxpayers, not workers or government, pay for 80% of these pensions. Federal civil service benefits are 259%[2] higher than the private sector employees who have a pension. Half have none. Government employees have five times more retirement benefits than average Americans. The annual cost of civil service pensions has increased from $2.8 billion in 1970 to $261 billion by 1998. This $258 billion increase is now over $5,000 per support household. Federal pensions are growing much faster than the cost of living. The Senate Bipartisan Commission on Entitlement and Tax Reform reported in 1994 that our national debt was understated by $14.4 trillion.[3] A substantial portion is due to unfunded promises regarding federal retirees. Why hasn't Congress curbed these excesses? Federal unions and employees are powerful in Washington, and over 400 congressmen in 1984 were receiving these same benefits. Future congressmen will also receive them.

GRACE COMMISSION FINDINGS 1984[4]

An unmanageable and unchangeable system of federal workers is only one of the government's problems. President Reagan's Grace Commission's report showed in 1984:

1. The Health and Human Services Department has routinely paid out Social Security benefits to some 8,000 dead people.

2. The Urban Mass Transportation Administration spent $10 million to buy new computers to keep track of the $25 billion it controls in active ongoing grants. Despite the new computers, the agency has been unable to close its accounting books since 1979. No account reconciliations have been done since 1977. The UMTA has no central ledger showing who owes what to whom. So even with the computers, the agency has to compute its financial data by hand.

3. The Veterans Administration has a hospital construction staff of 800 employees. The Hospital Corporation of America, a private company, does the same amount of work with a staff of 50. Because of the bureaucratic layering at the VA, it takes seven years to finish a project, versus two years at HCA. Overhead costs at the VA are four times greater than at HCA and other private sector companies.

4. Most of the subsidized mortgage loans made by the government in 1982 went to people who could have bought homes without government help. The typical mortgage revenue bond buyer had an income between $20,000 and $40,000 a year. Some 53% were among the more affluent half of the families in their states with earnings over $50,000 a year.

5. The government operates over 300 accounting systems and over 200 payroll systems. Each agency has developed its own software and many run on totally different and frequently obsolete computer systems. This leaves government managers with the time-consuming problem of reconciling incompatible information.

6. The Postal Service processes over 20 million checks per year at over a dollar a check. If it used a commercial bank to process the checks, it could save $20 million a year.

7. The government operates 238 grocery stores (commissaries) including six in Washington DC. They cost an average of $3 million each to operate per year. They could be leased to private industry and make money while providing better service.

8. The power marketing administration of our government is the world's largest producer of hydroelectric power. It has supplied power mostly to western and southern states since 1930. Its costs have exceeded its revenues almost every year since it started, and it supplies power at 40% of the wholesale costs that private utilities charge. If these plants were purchased by private utility companies or co-ops they would not need to be subsidized by the taxpayers, saving $7 billion per year, and their sale to electric companies could reduce the debt.

9. The Army Corps of Engineers spends over $ billion per year dredging harbors and rivers for the shipping industry and receives less than one-fourth that amount back in revenues. Why not have the shipping industry pay for all of it?

Three recent AP reports show little improvement. In November 1994 the AP reported $14 billion of government equipment was held by or being given to NASA contractors because of inadequate record keeping. Books cannot be audited, planning is unrealistic, and budgets are hopelessly unrealistic. In February 1995 they reported the Park Service doesn't collect enough information to tell where its limited resources can be best spent to protect the federal property it oversees, according to the Government Accounting Office (GAO). Overall the information contained in the financial statements was not accurate, reliable, or supported by the accounting system. Park property values were overstated by more than $90 million because of accounting errors. In September 1995 they reported the national computer system set up in 1985 at a cost to date of $23 million to track hazardous materials has a huge error rate that makes it almost useless. A spot check in the Dallas regional office turned up 15,000 mistakes by 45,000 hazardous waste contractors.

As a year-end 1992 reward, the government paid out employee bonuses of $487 million. The Social Security Administration, with 65,000 employees, handed out 50,000 bonuses averaging $640 each.

THE VALUE OF WORKING SMARTER

Russia learned that a large centralized bureaucratic government is doomed to fail. Politicians have not learned this lesson. The Grace Commission focused on the concept of privatizing everything possible in government. This is an excellent concept. In addition, everything that is not privatized (and most government will not be) must be put on the same mandate that most manufacturers have been under for 10 years. This mandate is to trim fat, simplify, cut the layers of management, computerize, cut payroll, and improve quality. Better quality at less cost must be the only means for federal workers to receive higher pay. Increased efficiency must be the only means of pay increases for five years. Lee Iacocca, past president of Chrysler Corporation, firmly believed that any corporation could trim 10% from its yearly costs. The federal government is easily capable of exceeding that amount.

A 10% national (NST) plus 3% average state sales tax combined with a revised FICA tax, could replace all federal, state, and local income taxes plus gift and estate taxes. They would reduce costs to government, individuals, and corporations, $165 billion a year. It would save over 4 billion hours of despised paperwork. Both taxes can be adjusted to be fair to all segments of the economy. Employees earning less than $8 per hour would pay no FICA tax and would receive an increased minimum wage or 4% wage increase (11.65% gain). Employees with wages above $8 would pay 7.65% FICA tax. Employers would pay an added 4% FICA tax to replace all business income tax and save $24 billion. All households could average over $1,400 less tax or expense after making their yearly purchases. The states could collect their own and federal sales tax while the federal government collects the FICA taxes. The extra state administered collections could go to Washington or stay in the state to fund full employment, education, or other state-administered federal programs. The FICA tax would be called a government service tax (GST) aimed at restoring the trust funds the government borrowed for decades (see Appendix A).

Citizens Against Government Waste is a bipartisan group advocating reduction of government waste. This group has its roots in the Grace Commission. They have proposed, line item by line item, a reduction of $1.3 trillion over five years. This alone is enough to repay the Social Security funds that the old Congress borrowed in the last 30 years. Appendix B lists all line items saving over $9 billion in five years. This proposal should be passed by Congress on an up or down vote without amendments.

Abandoning the Department of Education and spending $20 billion on block grants to schools, raising the number of school hours 38%, would go a long way toward enabling our students to catch up with the rest of the developed countries in the world.

Use funds from the Departments of Energy and Housing to rebuild structurally sound housing units in cities where the streets can be made safe. Workfare residents with professional supervision can learn skills and build or remodel their own housing. Energy funds can help subsidize heat costs for these projects as well as low-income heat subsidies. All remaining funds can be used to reduce the debt.

We have not learned from the past. The Department of Labor could do much more to encourage management, professional, salaried staff, and labor to work together for common corporation goals of quality and efficiency in such a way that workers and salaried staff would share equally, with stockholders, in profit gained. Success at this effort would do more good than a century of labor management strife. We must focus on this goal to again become the greatest economic power in the world, and to continue to do good. Had we, in 1975, recognized that government hindered sound economic growth, we would have made the changes recommended in this book, and we would have no federal deficit today.

Ask not what your country can do for you, but what you can do for your country.
—John F. Kennedy

Chapter 11.   Welfare or Full Employment

THE WELFARE CATASTROPHE

In the mid-1960s President Johnson and the majority in Congress believed that providing money to the poor would cure poverty, and through legislation declared a "War on Poverty." In 1965 welfare cost $3.31 billion per year ($66 per support household).[1] It now costs $375 billion per year ($7,500 per support household).[2] Now the vast majority agree the "War on Poverty" has failed. Despite spending $5 trillion[3] on poverty since 1966, the poverty rate has only dropped from 14.7% to 14.5%, and more people (39 million) are now living in poverty.

The welfare system is abused many ways, because the government can't possibly check on everyone daily, weekly, or monthly. Some welfare recipients who live in Chicago collect their Illinois welfare check, catch a bus for Milwaukee, and collect an identical welfare check from Wisconsin. Between 1987 and 1993 one New York recipient obtained 17 identification cards and collected welfare benefits under 15 names while claiming 78 fictitious children and received $450,000.[4] She was discovered when she applied for multiple passports. Massachusetts discovered that it was paying Medicaid for fertility drugs to welfare mothers. Another 1995 report showed AFDC and SSI cost over $130 billion this year ($2,600 per support household).[5] SSI pays an average of $5,200 to parents of 770,000 children who misbehave in school.[6] The agency insists there is little abuse; however, a network investigation estimated only 30% of the children qualified, and 81% of the children were coached by their parents to misbehave.[7] The Agriculture Department investigated 4,644 stores and found violations in half. The department kicked 1,400 stores out of the program. In 841 cases, store workers bought food stamps from agents posing as recipients. Abusers siphon off at least $1 billion a year. The Postal Service also arrested 79 people last year for theft of food stamps. A much better way must be found to aid those in need.

In reality the War on Poverty was a catastrophe. It has destroyed millions of individuals and families and has wreaked havoc on our communities and our civil discourse. Giving money to the poor has caused dependency, destroyed the work ethic, eroded educational pursuits, and has been a major factor in single parenthood, illegitimacy, crime, and substance abuse. How did this happen? There are many reasons. Let me give you an example:

Alice is 16 years of age and has dropped out of school. She lacks work and social skills. There are few opportunities, and no public assistance for her. However, if she becomes pregnant, she will receive between $15,000 and $25,000 in money, goods, and services. She keeps this public assistance if she meets two criteria. She must not work and she cannot marry an employed male. Alice quickly learns that she or her husband would need to make close to $10 an hour to break even. Therefore, Alice decides not to work or get married. Initially, from an economic standpoint, Alice has made a rational decision. She gets to stay home with her child and she receives more money than working full-time can provide. Alice does not realize that she is depriving herself of developing work and social skills, which will eventually trap her and her child in economic and behavioral poverty.

Robert Rector of the Heritage Foundation describes behavioral poverty as "a breakdown in the values and conduct that lead to the formation of healthy families, stable personalities, and self-sufficiency. Behavioral poverty is a cluster of social pathologies including a dependency and eroded work ethic, lack of educational aspiration and achievement, inability or unwillingness to control one's children, increased single parenthood and illegitimacy, criminal activity, and drug and alcohol abuse."

Many studies correlate giving welfare benefits to illegitimate births, disintegration of families, and reduced work. The tragedy is the adverse effect of single parenting on their children. In general, children raised by a single parent on welfare are more likely not to achieve the adequate emotional stability and sufficient educational skills as those raised in two-parent families. Children raised in welfare are far more likely to commit suicide or to be involved in drugs and crime. Finally, children raised in welfare are far more likely to have illegitimate children and unstable marriages. Conservatives say the problem is one of the most serious threats to American society and that while welfare may not cause illegitimacy, it is its "economic lifeline."[8]

Particularly hurt is the black community where illegitimate births are now 64% and 80% in the inner cities (up from 28% in 1965). Inner city black family life has been torn apart. Neither the grandmother, mother, nor new teenage mother has had to work or had a father image in the family. Many of these women are too unstable to hold down a job. More than 40% of the males age 35 and under are in jail. Throughout America gangs control the inner city, making money on drugs and prostitution. What has happened to the black population in the inner city is tragic and frightening. More frightening (because of the numbers) is the fact that illegitimate births in the white population are now escalating faster than the blacks, and the resulting behavioral poverty and dysfunction will soon reach levels that the nation simply cannot afford.

The result of behavioral poverty is the crime, violence, and fear that disrupt our communities and prohibit interaction with strangers. America is very guarded and afraid. This is very different from the America of the 1950s.

How can we break the despair and dependence that we forged more than 30 years ago that led to the high levels of sex, drugs, abuse, and violence? What incentive and disincentives can move the inner cities back to peaceful living spaces? Valid solutions are needed to decrease single-parent families and increase two-parent families.

It is time to require that single pregnant teenagers finish high school and live at home except in unusual circumstances. They must apply for Medicaid and support six months prior to the expected birth. The mother must agree to remain drug and alcohol free and be tested until the baby's birth. Crack and fetal alcohol syndrome babies may require that the mother make child care payments for life. The father must be named and verified by blood type in order for the mother to receive support. Both must support the child until age 18, unless it is put up for adoption. This can automatically be picked up by a new national computer system and each citizen's ID card.

THE FULL EMPLOYMENT SOLUTION

The "Full Employment Program" was conceived in 1976 to educate both policy makers (national and state) and the public of the benefits of work. Recently these same individuals formed the "American Institute for Full Employment," with offices in Klamath Falls, Oregon, and Washington, D.C.

The concept is simple. Instead of giving money and benefits to people on AFDC, food stamps, and unemployment, provide them a job with private and public employers. A Full Employment job pays, at least, the minimum wage (in Oregon recipients average $5.57 per hour) and has the medical and child care benefits that welfare provided. The money that previously went to keep the parent idle and keep the family in poverty, is now used to reimburse the employer for providing the job.

Employers have enthusiastically provided more employment opportunities than needed and it has been quickly determined that there will be enough jobs to make "Full Employment" a practical reality. In addition, dramatic reductions in welfare caseloads and costs have been achieved. Persons normally on public assistance for extended periods of time, have quickly found jobs on their own, or through the program's transitional jobs. The Oregon version of the Full

Employment Program has been tested in six counties since mid-1995, and is now being implemented statewide. Oregon has reduced the Aid to Families with Dependent Children (AFDC) cases by 12% during a period of time when requests for assistance have continued to rise and surrounding states have continually increased their caseloads. With the mandatory work requirement, Oregon has found that of all people directed to the Full Employment Program, 80% find work on their own, or otherwise exit the program. This means that the program is very cost-effective and over time will substantially reduce the cost to society. The state of Oregon is saving millions of dollars.

The program should encourage the individual to ultimately find work that is rewarding and self-fulfilling. The habits and skills developed by working will provide the participant the opportunity to enter the regular workforce and continue lifelong learning, achievement, and success. Work will assist people out of economic and behavioral poverty. Only work works. A quick phaseout of all existing "something for nothing" programs is essential. Time will soon undo the destructive forces put in place by past ill-conceived welfare programs.

THE REASON FULL EMPLOYMENT WORKS

Essential to all meaningful relationships, social or legal, is that there must be an exchange of something of value. Recipients of public assistance must work and earn an income, and therefore make the same value decisions the rest of society makes such as allocating time between leisure and productive activities, investing time and money in developing income-generating skills, and the number of children we can support. These socioeconomic alternatives permeate our lives, and must be part of the lives of those receiving public assistance.

A public assistance program must create positive incentives for the participants to develop skills, become employed, and earn an income which gives them the freedom to make their own decisions about marriage, homes, children, and careers. This is the opposite of the present system, which prolongs and traps people in the welfare system, dictates what grants they receive and where they live, and discourages marriage and family formation.

The best place to develop the skills and knowledge to exit poverty is in the workplace. Empirical studies have found that on-the-job training for unemployed workers, displaced workers, and welfare recipients is the most effective means of assisting unemployed or underemployed persons. Research clearly establishes that early attachment to work improves the earnings and employability of any citizen including welfare recipients.

Programs allocating substantial funds to education, training, and support services, do much worse than those that focus primarily on immediate job placement. Reports show that despite much higher outlays for education, training, and services in Alameda County, California, than in the San Diego and Riverside programs, earnings gains for recipients were lower. A 1988 GAO study shows an overhaul of the training programs for welfare recipients cost $13 billion over seven years and resulted in only 1% of all on welfare going to work. The study shows that these teenage mothers are the least likely to earn their way off welfare.

OTHER DETAILS OF THE PROGRAM

Any person seeking work goes to an employment center, where a job placement specialist will quickly analyze the person's skills and interests. Persons capable of finding regular employment are directed to the job that best suits their desires and talents. For persons unable to procure regular employment, a subsidized job is provided. A job placement specialist matches the participant with an employer. Key is knowing the skills and attitude of the participant, and the job and expectations of the employer. The job placement specialist must have credibility with both the participant and the employer. When problems arise the job placement specialist must intervene, either removing the participant or rectifying the problem.

The employer provides a job, the training necessary to perform the job, and a mentor. The mentor is a fellow employee, who is readily available to the new employee, explaining the rules and expectations of the business as a fellow worker.

All employers, public or private, who pay unemployment taxes are entitled to participants. The participant is a temporary employee of the employer, and the state reimburses the employer for the wage and all employment expenses. Paychecks from an employer prevent fraudulent double payments from two welfare offices.

Employers will not be allowed to lay off or replace current workers with program participants. Nor can they use workers from the program to work during a labor dispute or require that program workers join or not join a bona fide union. The pay, hours, and working conditions cannot be substantially less favorable to the worker than those for comparable work in the community. In short, employers can employ Full Employment Program workers to expand their workforce and increase production, but not as a money-saving device at the expense of regular employees.

Participants are placed in limited-duration positions, where they earn at least the minimum wage without loss of benefits. In Oregon the average hourly wage paid to participants is $5.57 which is higher than their minimum wage of $4.75. Of the participants that complete the program, 80% are hired by their Full Employment employers. All but a very few find permanent employment and are enthusiastic about the chance to prove themselves in a "real world" work situation. They are pleased to be earning more money, and appreciate receiving a paycheck rather than an AFDC allotment, food stamps, or an unemployment check, all of which carry a stigma.

Changes in "behavioral poverty" can be measured by a typical anecdote. "I cannot begin to express just how much the ...program has helped. I could have very easily been one of those mothers who stayed home and watched soap operas all day...Thanks to the wonderful program AFS had to offer me, I am now a working mother and setting a better example for my daughter than the couch potato example she was seeing." The participant was hired by her Full Employment employer as a receptionist, and the firm will be paying for her to attend real estate classes.

EVERY STATE SHOULD HAVE THE FULL EMPLOYMENT PROGRAM

Congress should immediately enact a minimum list of state requirements for supporting those now on welfare and terminate federal welfare and unemployment agencies. The state requirements should be concise enough to fit on a single sheet of paper. Each state should then formulate its own consolidated implementation program. Any disputes regarding compliance could be quickly and inexpensively resolved with mediation.

If every state had the Full Employment Program the consequences could be enormous. Removing 9.3 million households from welfare plus all unemployed workers would reduce federal, state, and local costs a total of $375 billion ($7,500 per support household).[2] It would directly add $100 billion to $180 billion to the national personal income, and would increase the national GDP twice that amount ($200 billion to $360 billion) as this new money enters the economy and generates more jobs. FICA contributions would increase federal revenues by $20 billion to $36 billion, and most would be paid by the employer. A national sales tax on the purchases of these workers will add $12 billion to $20 billion to federal revenues. Full Employment will reduce health, drug, and alcohol penalties on the economy. The program will also substantially reduce crime costs when there are no unemployed in the United States. Oregon's Full Employment program works.

AP reported in January 1996 about the first 8,000 Illinois welfare recipients notified in November 1995 that they must report to state offices and begin looking for work. Half didn't show up for the initial meeting.

Wisconsin has had welfare reform since 1987. Recipients are required to work, look for work, or attend education classes. Their funding is reduced if they don't. AP reported that when they apply for work, they meet with a financial and employment planner to determine if they have the experience or training to get a job. AFDC caseloads have dropped 32% since the program began, and are expected to drop to 52% by 1997. Costs are falling in inflation-adjusted dollars except for medical assistance. Participants in a proposed new "Wisconsin Works" program are guaranteed medical coverage, child care, and transportation on a sliding scale for up to two years, or five years in a lifetime.

It is hard to predict how many of the people who enter these programs will never be able to hold a job. It is equally hard to determine how many will become fully employed, or are now receiving welfare who don't really need it. What *is* predictable is that these programs work. They remove families from welfare and into jobs, and the benefits to themselves and the economy are enormous. Removing just half of these families from the costs of welfare could save $187 billion in taxes ($3,750 per support household) and create 4.7 million additional jobs. This is reasonably attainable.

89

We enact many laws that manufacture criminals, and then a few that punish them. —B. R. Tucker

Chapter 12.   Sex, Drugs, and Violence

WHAT HAS HAPPENED IN FORTY YEARS?

Decades ago sex wasn't on the radio, in the newspaper, or much talked about. Drugs were introduced in the 1960s, along with birth control pills and the sexual revolution. The 1960s had an oversupply of pampered children, who required instant gratification. Sex, drugs, and instant gratification have walked hand in hand ever since. The media and entertainment industries, along with too many adults, looked at all of this as harmless fun.

The media industries slowly opened the door to debauchery. Ratings ruled profit, and the industries increasingly destroyed our moral environment of abstinence, restraint, and responsibility. We have required other industries to restore our physical environment at their own expense. It may be time to require cleanup again.

A 1995 survey by *USA Weekend* of 65,000 respondents showed 97% believed that prime time network TV is too racy, vulgar, and violent. There are few third grade children who haven't watched many naked romantic embraces on TV. They are portrayed as accepted and exciting. The sponsors of the survey enlisted the help of journalism majors from American University School of Communication to monitor prime-time TV of the four major networks for five days. They counted 370 incidents of violence, vulgarity, and sex during those 15 hours on four networks, or one incident every 9.7 minutes on each. Students watch over 1,000 hours of TV a year. At that rate they are reminded 6,186 times a year[1] that vulgarity, sex, violence, rape, incest, infidelity, homosexuality, and abuse are accepted as part of life.

All societies have some crime and illegitimate births; however, many movies, song lyrics, and TV programs rob children of their innocence. They glorify violence, vulgarity, casual sex, and the swampy morality of Hollywood. Impressionable youth desperately need moral if not religious roots relating to responsibility, patience, compassion, honesty, restraint, diligence, self-worth, and abstinence. Youth ages and becomes society. If it were all "harmless fun," we could look aside; however, drugs now cost our society $126 billion, and welfare costs are $375 billion.[2] Crime costs $250 billion.[3] All of these costs overlap; however, all three now cost each support household a minimum of $8,000 a year.

A more serious form of vice for money has evolved in most inner cities. Drugs are used to prey on runaway teenage girls and hook them into prostitution. Inner city welfare recipients are regularly coerced into sex, which frequently leads to disease, pregnancy, and even death.

SEX

Recent trends were reported in the *Journal of the American Medical Association*. One in 10 youngsters ages 10 to 16 queried nationwide in 1993 reported being sexually assaulted or abused within the previous year.[4] The assault rate was three times higher than the rate reported in the

National Crime Survey in 1991. Being a victim of sexual abuse or assault is linked to higher rates of alcohol use, sexual promiscuity, and other risky behavior. And 34% of sexually abused eighth and tenth graders said they had planned suicide within the previous year.

California state statistics indicate that in 1990 more than half the fathers of children born to 11- to 15-year-old mothers were adults (18 or older). Among mothers ages 11 and 12, the fathers were, on average, 10 years older, which means much of the sex involved comes under the legal heading of rape. In addition 60% of girls who had intercourse before age 15, and 74% of those who had sex before age 14, say they have been forced into sex. The National Committee to Prevent Child Abuse in 1993 reported one million cases of child abuse including 150,000 sexual abuse cases.

DRUGS

The loss of a human brain is a terrible thing. Drugs kill as does violence associated with drugs. Marijuana use among eighth graders has more than doubled since 1991.[5] There is an overall increase in drug use among teenagers, federal statistics published in 1994 indicate.[6] A friend's substance abuse is directly related to adolescents' own use of alcohol and other drugs. A Department of Health and Human Services study showed women on welfare are three times as likely as other mothers to abuse, or be addicted to, alcohol or drugs. Children are more apt to use drugs or alcohol if a parent does and adolescents who do drugs and alcohol become sexually active sooner. The combination ends all interest in education and they become six times more likely to live in poverty. Too many children of welfare recipients become pregnant and keep their babies because illegitimacy no longer carries a social stigma. Adolescent mothers then exist in an ever more dangerous environment just like their mother.

Sex and drug abuse produce other terrible results. Children with fetal alcohol syndrome and crack babies frequently have major behavior problems which exasperate the mother, who already has drinking or drug problems. Many of these children have no concept of right or wrong, no ability to have eye contact, moderate to severe learning disability, attention deficit disorder, facial and other deformities, and no ability to give back any love or affection. As a result, many of these children end up in institutions because they are difficult to love or care for. Caregivers are paid to tolerate them. What a waste. The experiments with sex and drugs in the 1960s have turned rabid now with AIDS, crack, and FAS babies.

CRIME

The Justice Department in March 1994 projected that 75% of Americans will be victimized by violent crime at some time in their lives. A 20-year-old male today stands a better chance of being murdered than a serviceman in World War II. Society and inner cities are threatened by escalating crime and violence. Many inner cities are losing control of their streets and their residents daily face street gangs, intimidation, guns, drugs, and death. Some have suggested we not sell any more guns, legalize drugs, make friends with gangs, and legalize prostitution. Then we won't have problems. This is a prescription for social chaos and spreading destruction. Inner city problems are so large they must be treated as a war zone, or an area under martial law, until complete block by block law and order can be restored. Black teenagers are being devastated by violence. Black teenage males have one chance in nine of being the victim of a violent crime each year. The murder rate of black youths is seven to 10 times higher than white youths.

Many categories of crime paused for two years; however, from 1960 to 1990, violent crime increased 450%[7] and every category of crime is much higher than 30 years ago. You can expect that one of every six homes will be broken into. Young boys age 13 to 17 are more violent than ever and violent crime is predicted to rise soon. A crime-related injury now costs $41,000. The total cost of injuries alone totals $20.4 billion a year according to Health Affairs.

INNER CITY PROBLEMS

Inner cities have four festering problems. The major industries are welfare, prostitution, drugs, and crime. The last three of these produce big money, role models, and hope. Crime really pays well now. According to Heritage Foundation, a criminal has only a 1.2%[8] chance of doing time for committing a crime. Welfare is just a way of life where the government pays a mother $16,000 per year as long as she doesn't work. There is no plan. There are no jobs; there is no hope. Is it really any wonder that 80% of inner city children are born to unwed mothers, and that crime, drugs, prostitution, and gangs are the growth industries of the inner cities? Gangs have the potential to make the Mafia look like a church association. They have all the trappings of secrecy, brotherhood, violence, and an absolutely cold-blooded need to take, kill, and achieve power. There are multiple gangs now in cities 10 times smaller than the Mafia ever considered. It is absolutely necessary to make crime and gang membership unprofitable and undesirable as rapidly and with as much innovation as possible. It should be approached like Desert Storm with much planning, devastating swiftness, and overwhelming force.

In summary there is too much sex and violence in the media, movies, and lyrics. There are too many drugs, lethal weapons, and gangs on the streets. There is little or no moral instruction at home or in school. Education levels are low and dropout rates are high. Two-parent families are declining and too many single mothers are without jobs and living on welfare. Too much welfare housing is now in dangerous areas. The criminal justice system leaves too many criminals on the streets. There are not enough jobs in the inner cities. All of the above problems must be stopped and reversed using carrots and sticks.

A PROGRAM OF RESTORATION
To be successful a plan needs the following elements:

1. It has been shown that alcohol and tobacco can harm society, and their advertising has been restricted in the media. There is linkage that explicit media exploitation of sex, drugs, and violence is very harmful to some members of our society. Our children watch TV over 1,000 hours per year, slightly fewer hours than academic studies. Movies, music, and prime-time programs are filled with immoral content. Children and adult minds are "wired" or programmed by what they see, read, hear, and perceive as significant. With this massive exposure to the above "entertainment," it should be no surprise that the incidence of these crimes and problems is increasing and harming society in the process. It should also be no surprise that most TV, newspapers, magazines, and radio believe confrontation, violence, and sex sell best, and they will continue these programs. It is time that the media voluntarily accept substantial restrictions which should give all media an equal playing field. If the media cannot or will not accept such restrictions, they should be legislated—similar to not shouting FIRE in a crowded theater and not showing drinking of alcohol or allowing cigarette commercials on TV. These are not restrictions on freedom of speech. They are restrictions in the best interest of society. The media endangers our most important national resource, our minds. Media pollution needs a giant cleanup. An alternative would be to require the media and entertainment industries to clean up the moral swamp they created by imposing taxes based on content.

2. Control of inner city streets and confiscation of all handguns without permits must be the first order of business. With careful planning and overwhelming force, drugs, crime, and prostitution should be moved off the street overnight, and offenders should be quickly prosecuted. This first effort must get control of all weapons possible and make the streets safe. It will fail if the pressure is applied gradually. It must be approached city by city with all-out force to convince gangs that they cannot win. The force should stay in place substantially beyond the time when violence subsides. The program should start with no more than one city at a time, at its request, and fully authorized as a federal test site. Special federal military units with additional training should be authorized to reinforce local police. The first city to be cleaned up should have less than 500,000 population. Things will go wrong, but we must plan it, do it, try it, and fix it until the streets are safe. The goal is to stop all drugs, crimes, and violence COLD. This pressure and a modification of laws to increase society's rights to a peaceful environment will produce substantial results quickly. Without peace on the streets, inner city crime and violence will continue to grow. The force should be kept in place to assure that criminal activity is both risky and unprofitable. Once the streets are safe, the foundation is laid and a rehabilitation program can begin. A foundation must be prepared before you build a building.

3. Get tougher on drugs and crime. Make conviction of wholesaling drugs a capital offense, along with loss of all assets. Conviction of retailing drugs should require a five-year mandatory sentence and confiscation of all assets. The fence, who distributes stolen goods, should lose all assets and be given a mandatory sentence. Increase penalties each year for selling and distributing drugs. Islamic countries protect society and have no drug problems because of severe penalties. Criminals' rights and society's rights to life, liberty, and the pursuit of happiness frequently clash. Society's right to life, liberty, and the pursuit of happiness must prevail. Allow cars to be

searched, make juvenile records available, and double sentences for violent crimes, carrying weapons, and lying. Cars are regularly searched by game wardens and immigration agents. Make it illegal for anyone with a criminal record to own or carry a gun or other dangerous weapon. Double sentences for offenses using dangerous weapons or lying under oath. Everyone must carry a national ID card with picture and fingerprints to trace criminal records.

4. Provide adequate counseling, comfort, and refuge for children and adults who are abused or who want to report criminal activities.

5. The day care, Head Start, and education programs will be changed to care for the children of Full Employment parents. A day care, Head Start, education program from 8:00 A.M. to 5:00 P.M. for children from age one can prepare children for school. Safe schools with expanded hours can provide an advanced education for high-technology jobs. They can reinforce morals, cooperation, responsibility, achievement, hope, and success. From age six, a school program adds four years of education. It can provide the student with many more skills to cope with a much more complex world. The Full Employment mother will be able to count on this system to care for her child while she is at work. Work will provide self-esteem. The mother may be an education or day care assistant. The program will establish a work ethic for the children. There is no substitute for a solid two-parent family; however, this program will give welfare children education, skills, and hope. Two-parent families will be given priority for existing and new housing.

6. Full Employment mothers will have a job eight hours a day. They should work at their highest possible level for private industry or government. They may work at any private business or publicly operated day care facilities, schools, building rehabilitation, city projects, or recycling operation. Welfare recipients can demolish or rehabilitate inner city buildings a block at a time and provide minigovernment or authority to police themselves. Vacant buildings can be renovated using little over material costs as a practical workfare training program for construction jobs. Eliminate all vacant buildings unless they can be closed up tight. All areas between welfare housing and schools must be made crime free.

7. New businesses and industries that locate within inner city designated areas and provide substantial employment should be exempt from city and state taxes except for service, water, sewer, and garbage. Each job they create near low-income housing can take one person off the welfare rolls.

Inner cities had high unemployment during the Great Depression over 60 years ago. Just prior to the Depression most people bought cars for cash. In 1929 the stock market crashed and many banks failed. Many people lost their homes and lifetime savings overnight. A fourth of the country's workers had no jobs. The situation was desperate. The government and our society at that time was conservative. Our national debt then was 20,000 times less than now. President Roosevelt, elected in 1932, faced unemployment at an unprecedented scale and desperate families calling for something to be done. He proposed, and Congress passed, numerous WPA, CCC, and other federal programs to develop national parks and build dams, bridges, roads, and public buildings as long as they required major amounts of labor. Work was all done at minimum wages and frequently the men were working far from their families. The men worked hard, lived in barracks buildings, and sent most of their money back to their families. The wives and children made do as best as they could and accepted help, food, and clothes from friends and churches. With hope and a program, it was a terrible experience but it didn't produce riots, violence, or major crime. We are too far in debt to repeat this type of massive bailout without destroying our currency and everyone's savings with runaway inflation. The country, and especially inner cities, need crime-free streets, jobs, and hope. Revised laws and regulations can provide all three.

For youth, the future is long, the past short...It is easily deceived, because it is quick to hope.
—Aristotle

Chapter 13. Generational Discrimination

A BROKEN ECONOMY

The old Congress enacted a massive body of legislation which increasingly discriminates against young Americans. All legislation that benefited Congress, lobbies, lawyers, and welfare recipients, directly penalized farmers, business, and manufacturers. It raised the cost of living 263% above worker productivity, made our products uncompetitive, and was the primary cause of losing international market share and terminating thousands of businesses and millions of manufacturing jobs. In addition to this damage, Congress ran up an unprecedented $5 trillion national debt and $14 trillion of retirement promises to be funded by future generations.

Baby boomers born from 1946 to 1964 grew up with expansion and had jobs; the bust generation, from 1964 on, has only had discrimination. Major companies and unions must lay off by seniority rather than efficiency. Young (newer employees) are laid off first without considering their contribution to the company. This practice is pure discrimination. Demographer William Dunn writes in his book that between 1980 and 1990, the baby busters' income declined 10.8%. From 1960 to 1970 hardworking employees were promoted every 18 to 24 months. Today, promotions come every five years on average. At least 54% of 18- to 24-year-olds live with their parents. From 1973 to 1990 the poverty rate doubled for households headed by people under age 30. Over a third of college graduates cannot find jobs requiring a college degree in their field upon graduation. The equivalent of three years of all U.S. college graduates are available for hire but are unemployed or underemployed, because of lost U.S. jobs, a deficient education system, and federal laws and regulations. Young people under 35 are 10 times more likely to be unemployed than those over 35. Young people now will average 13 employers over their lifetime. People born in 1930 averaged five employers. This means at least eight more relocations or disruptions which frequently involve selling a house, realty costs, and moving. Many young people, unemployed or marginally employed, have less or no health insurance coverage. They face starting over many times at a lower or equal level.

Our children's education is not comparable with most major countries. A University of Michigan study found that in the fifth grade the highest scoring mathematics classes ranked lower than the lowest scoring Asian classes. In June 1994, the *Minneapolis Star Tribune* reported that at Iowa State University, Michael Pederson, a mechanical engineering student, graduated with a 3.77 grade point average and a rank of ninth in a class of 309. Michael had no job or serious prospects for one. Neither did 40% of his classmates. A recent Iowa Department of Labor survey revealed that 70% of college graduates who cannot get a job in their major take a job that does not require a college degree. Salaries of those hired are down 2% from last year and down 7.4% since 1969.

Pederson's class and many others before him are both angry and disappointed. They have done everything they were supposed to do to earn a degree at great expense and for nothing. Many of these graduates will become underemployed and drift into temporary jobs where they will be the last hired and the first fired. They are postponing marriage and paying off college debt as best they can. Our education and economic system has failed these graduates, and Congress has given them a $5 trillion debt (over $100,000 for each employed graduate).

In addition to discrimination regarding employment and insurance, a young working couple earning $30,000 pay over five times more federal tax than a retired couple earning $30,000 with average Social Security and a modest taxable pension. Recent studies including one OMB study show that children born after 1990 or 1992 will pay 71%, 82%, or 90% of their lifetime income in net taxes. No other generation has ever been asked to contribute anything close to this amount. This provides a sound argument that our national policy consists of foisting financial obligations on to future generations.

UNFUNDED OBLIGATIONS AND GENERATIONAL DEBT TRANSFER

The Bipartisan Commission on Entitlements and Tax Relief shows the federal government's unfunded liabilities for just four programs—Social Security, Medicare, civil service retirement, and military retirement—were $14.4 trillion to 17.2 trillion by 1993. This is several times larger than the national debt. These promised entitlements can't possibly be funded at their present levels. The negligent old Congress failed to address the generational burden they foisted on future generations—a burden they can't possibly carry. Most currently retired Americans receive Social Security benefits that are two to five times greater than the actuarial contributions they and their employers made. Even more disturbing, estimates show that the payback for Medicare hospital insurance programs is five to 20 times greater.[1]

Retirement costs are driven by several forces:

1. People now live 15 years longer than they did when Social Security started. To be fair to the next generation, my generation should have paid more FICA tax or raised our retirement age.

2. Medicare is rising faster than Social Security. The rise is due to better drugs, medical equipment and procedures, and better doctors. Senior citizens live longer. The rapid rise of Medicare is equally driven by aggressive malpractice lawyers, product and medical liability insurance, and the need for doctors, hospitals, and manufacturers to all practice defensive medicine which adds 20% to our immense health care costs.

3. Federal employee benefits are much greater than the best corporation retirement plans. Both are much greater than Social Security, and the government agencies have not put their 50% contribution in the fund as all other employers have.

4. The 263% rise in the cost of living induced by the old Congress and its debt is driving the above forces out of sight.

5. The investment return on money paid into retirement insurance and the forecasted future ability of the government to pay these obligations are totally unrealistic.

An additional five years of work will increase Medicare and Social Security payments 10% to 12%. Life expectancy is now 76.3 years instead of 61.7 in 1935. Additional work years will reduce Social Security payments 40%. Delaying retirement five years can reduce unfunded obligations 50% of $17.2 trillion, or $8.6 trillion. Lengthening the minimum years of work is an easy method of assuring those younger than 60 that their retirement coverage will last for life.

The old Congress failed to tax or restrain spending and dipped into trust fund surpluses which could have earned $4.3 trillion, including dividends, since 1965 if invested at Standard and Poor's average rate. This investment could easily double again before the baby boomers retire. The old Congress could have reduced the $17.2 trillion shortfall to $12.9 trillion with a balanced budget. Instead the baby bust generation is being asked to make interest and principal payments on unfunded obligations of $20 trillion, or $400,000 per support household. They can't.

The generational debt transfer can be mitigated by balancing the budget, reducing federal government costs, collecting and investing government's share of retirement payments, having a single Social Security retirement program for all, extending the retirement age, requiring that mediation replace litigation, rescinding those federal laws that most drive COLA, and investing FICA surpluses in the private economy. Control of the above will allow retirement for all.

If those of us over 40 don't now feel a need to eliminate discrimination of children and young adults, the result may change your mind. In the last 20 years the old Congress has spent more than $4 for every $3 of income. In times of relative peace it borrowed $1.4 trillion from Social Security, Medicare, Medicaid, and other trust funds, and left only an IOU for future generations to pay. The number of workers supporting one retirement beneficiary has decreased from 42 in 1945 to three now, and it is projected to decline to two by 2030. With two workers per retiree, support households can't possibly pay for the present levels of Social Security, Medicare, and Medicaid, **and they won't**. They will hold the elderly in contempt for allowing the legal, lobby, and political system to neglect and financially abuse them.

A DISINTEGRATING SOCIETY

In the last 30 years the divorce rate has increased over four times. These breakups removed many families from support households and put them in poverty and welfare. Children pay a high emotional price for these breakups which are helped by the media and movie stars who frequently portray marriage and sex as casual. The economic necessity of two working parents has also increased marital problems.

A million young people age 12 to 19 die yearly due to violence. It is the leading cause of death for this age bracket. Guns must be banned for all in this age bracket for their protection. TV, movies, dramas, music, and other media trash depict excessive sex, drugs, violence, and other perversions, which give them huge profits and cause our society to grow more coarse, confrontational, amoral, and dangerous every year. Crime costs our economy $250 billion yearly. These powerful industries could, and should, promote positive social behavior and reduce crime. The industries should eliminate 80% of the present level of sex, drugs, and violence voluntarily. If not, ban it because it is hazardous to society. The more sex, violence, and trash we see, the more profit they make. Make it unprofitable. If it reduced crime only 25%, our economy could save $62.5 billion yearly. That amount would be a good starting point for a tax.

EMBRACE CHANGE AND RESTORE OPPORTUNITY

It is time to eliminate debt transfer, discrimination, and violence thrust on the next generation, and change antiquated laws relating to retirement, lobbies, the legal system, the education system, regulatory systems, welfare system, and others. We need to strengthen marriage. More than anything, we need to leave our children with a government and economic system that can compete in the world. They need to be unburdened from the debt Congress carelessly piled up during the relative peace of the last 30 years. Finally, we need to develop a plan to create productive jobs and hope. Anything less will be inadequate.

Jerry Holbert Reprinted with permission of Newspaper Enterprises Association, Inc.

BABY BOOMERang

Balance

Government, even in its best state, is but a necessary evil; in its worst state
it is an intolerable one. —Thomas Paine

Chapter 14. Reforming Government to Suit Our Needs

REASON TO CHANGE

Our national debt can easily enslave our children. The debt was produced by an old Congress, far more concerned with reelection than national prosperity. Lobbies and special interests have been generously rewarded by Congress for their political contributions. Government and our economy are on opposite sides of a teeter-totter, and the economy, for 30 years, has been left in the air. COLA makes the process possible and invisible. Our industries have become uncompetitive because the cost of living has grown 263% higher than worker productivity over 30 years. It passed unprecedented laws and regulations that reduced our national export industry labor force by over 50% since 1970. Our misguided education system is no longer in the top 20 nations in the world. Inner cities have become hopeless centers for crime, drugs, prostitution, and welfare recipients. Drugs are out of control and destroying thousands of lives daily. Crime feeds drug habits. Between 60% and 80% of most inner city births are by unwed mothers. Children are trying to raise children. Federal government waste and abuse is extensive. The old Congress, the media, and the legal profession have profited from excessive confrontation and all make our economy less productive. Extensive laws and regulations cost jobs and weaken the economy. Government has become overly intrusive in our lives. The war on poverty has not reduced those living in poverty, and welfare has failed. The old Congress, from World War II until 1994, radically altered entitlements so that they now cost 52 times more, in inflation-adjusted dollars. Those on welfare and those in jail don't work. Our country has become amoral and self-centered. For several years our total personal national savings has not equaled the added interest on the national debt, and the debt is rapidly rising while our savings rate is going down. The old Congress spent too much and did not tax enough to fund these newly given entitlements. The national debt grew from $300 billion in 1965 to $4,960 billion now. We owe it to our children to change the old course of government.

Some years ago Milton Friedman, in a talk at the Washington Press Club, said America should understand that 40% of our population now depends on the federal government for a living. He said that when over 50% rely on government, they can vote themselves any benefits they want until the government and economy are bankrupt. He commented on the budget crisis of January 1996, by saying "The freshman Congress is too timid." France and Sweden tried and failed to reverse their socialist course. Without change, economic collapse is inevitable.

It is time to get involved; educate people about the government, economy, and trust funds; and support national candidates who favor continued change in the following areas:

1. Reduce government waste. Support bipartisan unamended Citizens Against Government Waste proposals.
2. Fund congressional elections and prohibit all lobby funding of elections and all funding from outside of a legislative district.
3. Change COLA to WPI (worker productivity index).
4. Support reducing the economic cost of federal regulations on our economy by 25% in five years.
5. Use discretionary spending only for "absolutely necessary" projects.
6. Revise and simplify criminal justice and change tort litigation to required mediation.
7. Eliminate corporate welfare.
8. Require the federal bureaucracy to streamline and reduce its size and costs 5% a year for five years by privatization, decentralization, and elimination.
9. Revise our out-of-control retirement system by reducing the cost of living and raising the retirement age.

A TIME TO CHANGE

The Chinese character for crisis is made from two characters, danger and opportunity. Most people avoid both crisis and danger, and given a choice they will pursue opportunity to avoid both. We must now use this opportunity to change what has been wrong with our government and economy since 1960, in a new and substantial way. We were invited to do this by the Constitution, which says:

We hold these truths to be self-evident, that all men are created equal, that they are endowed, by their Creator, with certain unalienable rights, that among these are life, liberty, and the pursuit of happiness. That to secure these rights, governments are instituted among men, deriving their just powers from the consent of the governed, **that whenever any form of government becomes destructive of these ends, it is the right of the people to alter or to abolish it, and to institute new government, laying its foundation on such principles, and organizing its powers in such form as to them shall seem most likely to effect their safety and happiness.......when a long train of abuses and usurpations, pursuing invariably the same object, evinces a design to reduce them under absolute despotism, it is their right, it is their duty, to throw off such government, and to provide new guards for their future security.**

When Americans fully understand why and how our political system and economy has failed, they will support creative changes and insist the changes be made quickly. The debt crisis has given us an opportunity to reexamine everything. The budget must be balanced and half the debt should be paid off in 10 years. Using federal costs, in terms the public understands, we know that those households who pay over 95% of all federal personal income tax total 50 million, or half of our households. **A billion dollars amounts to $20 for each of these support households.** The $4.96 trillion national debt means $99,200 to them and will grow $6,000 a year for years, primarily because of interest on the debt. A $10,000 reduction can balance the budget and cut the federal debt in half in 10 years. The other half of all U.S. households, who pay the last 5% of all personal income tax, can carry no more burdens. This half of our households, earning less than $22,000, desperately needs an environment that reduces taxes, government excess, and COLA. **Taxes will kill the economy, while rescissions of laws and regulations, when they eliminate economic waste, will stimulate it.**

SPECIFIC RECOMMENDATIONS

The old Congress was not rational when it spent funds it didn't have for unnecessary projects to boost the economy. These debts are now destroying jobs and our economy. **Citizens Against Government Waste proposed a very large bipartisan reduction of federal expenditures. This report should be put to a single yes or no vote without amendment by Congress. All savings from canceling these programs should be earmarked to repay the $1.4 trillion borrowed from the Social Security and Medicare trust funds within five years. Congress should then resolve to allocate new federal spending only to those projects which are "absolutely necessary."** Many federal agencies overlap and have no reason to change. Congress should give them a reason. GSA ratings and regulations should be changed so that increased wages depend on

98

increased quality and productivity. **The new Congress should further ask itself four questions of every department and agency in the federal government.**

1. Is it absolutely necessary?
2. Can it be consolidated or given to the states to administer without mandates?
3. Can it be privatized?
4. Can the problems it solves be accomplished in an entirely different manner at less cost?

Our cost of living increase over the last 20 years and the total national debt are a result of the excesses of the above items. COLA was the mechanism that allowed these buildups to happen. Business, especially small business, can be more productive, invest more in R&D, and generate jobs faster by rescinding many excessive federal government programs and regulations. Substantial cuts will make goods less expensive and reduced federal borrowing will change inflation to deflation. Then the definition of **COLA should become worker productivity increase at each workplace.** All workers will then strive to maintain or improve quality and become more efficient in order to receive higher wages. Everyone will want to focus on and eliminate waste in business and government. **A special reduced FICA tax status should be set up for a new class of company known as a unified company.** In these companies all labor and management share, with stockholders, profits from better products at lower prices.

Many regulations have studies showing the cost to save a life. Limited funds dictate we mediate regulations or lose our economy. We squander vast resources on some programs, and have none for others. Safety and waste must be balanced or many will die unnecessarily. Regulations were created for lobbies, haphazardly, and with little relation to cost or benefit. Spending billions to save one life and not spending thousands to save another makes no sense at all. **It is time to set a dollar figure to save a life, which we are absolutely sure we can support** and eliminate all laws and regulations above that figure, and start to adopt those below.

Lobbies and pork have caused much of the damage to our economy. Lobbies cost the support household at least $6,000 in goods, services, and taxes. Would you feel comfortable in a trial against a lawyer who gave the trial judge 40% of his reelection funds? Lobbies gave congressmen 40% of their reelection funds, and the bills, laws, and regulations reflect special interest favors. The economic costs of these laws and regulations have fluctuated between 1% and 13% above productivity for 30 years. They are a major reason our economy is 263% less productive.

Election campaign funds should be financed at $6 per support household after Senate candidates raise $600,000 and House candidates $100,000 in contributions not to exceed $200 per person. Government would then fund $3 million and $300,000 respectively with total campaign expenditures limited to $4 million and $500,000 respectively. All lobby and special interest funding would be prohibited. This should similarly be adopted for presidential and state elections. Congress should then establish term limits of three in the House and two in the Senate. Congress can then look impartially at any special interest legislation that should be rescinded.

Our expensive, and failing, education system is a product of the old Congress and the Department of Education. Our SAT test scores are falling, and our students do not rank in the top 20 nations of the world. Japan schools its students 723 hours a year more than we do. The Department of Education has a budget of $30.4 billion plus $26.8 billion discretionary spending ($1,144 per support household). Approximately **$20 billion of those funds could be better used to expand our student education 445 contact hours from 1,170 to 1,615 hours (from 8:00 A.M. to 5:00 P.M.) with a 190-day school year**. This will give students 5,785 more hours of education equivalent to 4.94 more current years of school. One year of these hours would be used to learn responsibility and duty by cleaning and picking up at school. Every teacher's salary can rise $6,000, or funds can be used to add more teachers or teacher aides. **The funding should be given to states in grants and continue based on improved student test results.** Low tests may reduce grants or require changes in staff or methods. By ninth grade, students would move into a technical or college track. This proposal adds 38% student access time to computers and audio visual, science, and vocational equipment. This saves $37 billion annually in federal expenditures and all students have four more years of better education at no added cost or years. College years and loans will be smaller. All will have more productive after school years. School should also become a place where moral values are learned, and where prayers are heard more frequently than foul language. The media needs to curb its exploitation of sex and violence, which affect the minds of youth and adults alike. The Constitution offered domestic tranquility and the pursuit of happiness. Media excess, like smoking, is hazardous to our health; freedom of expression must be returned to freedom of speech.

The time has come to eliminate the IRS and all state and local income taxes, gift taxes and inheritance taxes, and replace them with a 10% national sales tax, an average 3% state sales tax, and a revised employee wage tax of7.65% on all wages below $8 per hour. Employers will pay a 4% additional FICA tax to replace all their income taxes. The $165 billion savings should all go to taxpayers except $24 billion which corporations and employers will save. The added disposable income should greatly stimulate the economy.

We must quickly revise all federal retirement programs into a single medical / retirement program. Early and regular retirement ages must be extended over a 10-year period to accommodate longer life expectancy. Retirees must work a minimum number of years to receive full benefits. We must replace litigation with mediation and reduce the national debt, cost of government, and ultimately the cost of living. Finally, if necessary, raise premiums.

The American Trial Lawyers Association is the most powerful lobby in Washington. One of every 10 people there is a lawyer. Congress has handsomely repaid gifts from this lobby with laws regulating the environment, discrimination, OSHA, justice, and many others. Laws have grown complex and contradictory. Lawyers have received over 40% of the $75 billion cost of Superfund sites cleanup to date. Lawyers have increased eight times faster than the population since 1965. They and Congress have no incentives to mediate or make trials short. Indeed they both thrive on confrontation. Simple laws, justice, and mediation not requiring lawyers should replace the present expensive and time-consuming system.

National, tort, and many criminal disputes should be mediated instead of going to trial. Mediation should be required on civil disputes unless both parties choose to litigate. The support household can save at least $6,500 per year in taxes, goods, and services by using understandable common laws and mediation instead of the present legal system. Upon presenting the facts, the sides will give the mediators their single mediation compromise. The mediators will then select one. On intractable national issues, the country should vote on two final alternatives. Mediation can be quick, inexpensive, and final. Fees should not exceed 10% of any settlement. A judgment should not be overturned unless it violates one of the 12 or fewer laws that take precedence over all laws. These are detailed in Chapter 6.

Over $1.4 trillion of surplus **Social Security trust funds** generated for baby boomers' retirement has been looted by the old Congress for their past projects. As they retire, their children will have to carry a normal load of retirees plus the added size of this generation. They will also have to pay back the funds spent by the old Congress and they will have to do this triple increase with only two workers per retiree. We allowed this to happen, and we presently support retirees with three workers. **It is up to the current generation to replace the missing $1.4 trillion funds within 10 years.**

Welfare and the War on Poverty have failed. Both have produced terrible results, especially in inner cities. **Welfare dependency should be replaced with required Full Employment.** All receiving support and all prisoners should perform 40 hours of work a week to partially support their needs or expense. All unemployed, over 18, and not living at home should be given a Full Employment job. There should be a job and a paycheck for everyone who wants to work when the economy is freed from excessive regulation, litigation, and special interests. These employers, both public and private, will be reimbursed minimum wages. The employer must add over a dollar plus on-the-job training, and must hire or release workfare employees within nine months. After six months the employer must give these workers one paid day a week to look for other work. Reasonable time off for interviews will be provided. With full employment, many agencies can be combined into a one stop place to go for anyone unemployed. Prisoners can build detention facilities, and Full Employment workers can rehabilitate inner city housing, staff day care centers and schools, recycle, clean off graffiti, clean and do laundry, as well as work for private businesses.

To prevent future budget abuse **an independent CPA / computer firm should be set up to receive and disburse all funds.** It should be designed to operate with a picture ID card with fingerprints for all citizens, and should be renewed every five years. The card will reference transactions with employers, Social Security, federal tax records, marriage, divorce, death, criminal records, medical records, blood type, and allergies, all keyed in with a social security number. Children will need these cards to go to school. Spouses can track delinquent child support payments; all entitlements will be tracked. Illegal aliens will have no cards. The firm will forecast future needs, and financially secure all trust funds using citizen cards as the control. Failure to make this change will further cause Congress to play games with our treasury and trust funds. This system should be easy to modify and should be developed for sale to other countries. All Social Security and federal employee trust funds must be actuarially repaid before the baby boomers retire.

A CALL TO ACTION

Patrick Henry was right. A strong central government has become an oppressive, cumbersome, unmanageable bureaucracy which has used the ruse of general welfare to displace states' rights and generate enormous debt and ruinous taxes.

We live in an imperfect world with a changing environment. We have been poorly served by the old Congress that would commit our children and grandchildren into bondage in order to retain money and power. The laws, regulations, national debts, and obligations they have passed to us and our children are unprecedented. They are destroying our economy, jobs, and society in order to achieve elusive ivory-tower perfection by means of massive and burdensome laws and regulations. Many powerful members of Congress want to continue this dangerous course until we become bankrupt and destitute.

Knowledge is power. You now understand the information supporting the changes Congress must make. The Constitution invited citizen-led changes to secure life, liberty, and the pursuit of happiness. Creative and unconventional thinking is a rarity in Washington and it is desperately needed to restore America's future. Every effort will be made to get a copy of this book in the hands of every member of Congress. Your letters and votes count. Tell your congressman which changes on pages eight and nine you most favor.

Time is short. The debt imperils us. We need to act, embrace change, become more informed, and talk to friends about the changes necessary in society, government, and the economy. Lend this book to them. Support candidates committed to change with your time and your money. The economy must be restored to its original condition in order to assure a bright future for our children and grandchildren. Don't rest until this work is done.

A rising tide lifts all boats -John F. Kennedy

Every organization has to prepare for the abandonment of everything it does. -Peter Drucker

Chapter 15. The Positive Values of Change

In order to understand the proposed changes and develop the inertia to overcome the status quo, why not think of two competing countries, both identical to the United States. Which country would you want to live in?

Country A

1. The GDP is $7 trillion.

2. The debt is $5 trillion, rising $300 billion per year including borrowed trust funds. $14.trillion of unfunded retirement and Medicare promises along with welfare entitlements will continue until we become insolvent.

3. Federal CSRS workers, after 35 years of work, can claim retirement benefits and receive up to two-thirds of their last five years average annual pay annually at age 55. These funds are only partially funded by federal employees and not at all by the government. All other workers can retire at 62 with benefits less than half that of these federal workers. Retirees will rely on their children and grandchildren to pay 82% of their lifetime wages in federal, state, and local taxes. Unfunded retirement obligations are $15 trillion and rising.

4. The legal system will remain as is and add many new laws per year making it more complex and expensive than present. The system, and its consequences, costs support households over $10,000 per year for tort law, defensive medicine, crime, and associated insurance costs. Expanded laws will identify more victims. Added regulations will penalize industry and result in more unemployment.

5. State and local business and government will continue to comply with all existing laws and regulations that cost the support household $13,000 per year. Government will add 5,000 additional regulations per year. Unemployment will grow in proportion to the number of new regulations enacted.

6. Retain antimonopoly laws.

7. Retain the Department of Education, and our existing education system, which has much higher nonteaching educational jobs than any other country and provides ever lower educational performance. Continue all our present policies relating to our youth, college, and young workers. Give them inferior education, keep them in poverty, make it difficult to enter the labor market, and discriminate against them with seniority. Do not correct the bombardment of their minds with sexual gratification, abuse, drugs, violence, and confrontation. Leave our children with a debt of $99,231 and increasing over $6,000 each year.

Country B

1. The GDP is $7 trillion.

2. The debt is $5 trillion and falling $200 billion a year. All future promises and entitlements will be funded completely and actuarially. Everyone on welfare will be on Full Employment.

3. All workers, including federal, can claim full Social Security benefits at age 70 after contributing to FICA or Full Employment for at least 35 years. Early reduced benefits start at age 65. This time extension is primarily due to a 16-year increase in life expectancy since 1935. Unfunded retirement obligations are $9 trillion and falling.

4. Mediation will replace the present tort system. It will cost less than England, Canada, or Germany. No legal fees over 10% of judgment or settlement are permitted. All damages of any kind must show intent or irresponsible behavior. The cost of appeals will be paid by the loser as a percent of the change from the mediated judgment. Perfect decisions are not required. Society's rights will come first. Criminals will be assured of double sentences for lying or carrying a lethal weapon. Everyone will understand all of the 12 or fewer simple laws. The tax drop and cost of living savings to the support household and business they work for will be over $6,000 per year.

5. Federal regulations will be simplified, reduced, or eliminated to stimulate the economy. Many regulations such as banking and highway would have minimum or no changes. Other regulations such as trucking and economic regulation should be further deregulated saving the support household over $2,000, of $13,000 per year, in reduced living costs.

6. Allow similar businesses or industries to do joint basic research and patenting.

7. The Department of Education will close and $20 billion will be sent to states to increase the school year 450 hours. There will be more teachers, and students will do most custodial work. Students will be in school while parents work. They will have the equivalent of four added years of education with more emphasis on responsibility, creativity, mediation, life skills, math, science, and engineering. They will learn that the rest of their life will depend on what they learn in school. This saves $740 education costs per support household.

8. Keep all departments of government operating unchanged and expenditures rising faster than COLA.

9. Allow campaign funding by PACs, corporations, unions, lawyers, and special interest groups that results in legislation favoring their interests.

10. Continue to use antiquated unrelated federal computer systems which are decentralized and don't talk to one another. Continue to use over five million different computer programs (one for every 50 people in the United States). Have no way to read or understand true government income, expenditures, overexpenditures, and errors by department for years if ever.

11. COLA will remain as is, primarily fueled by entitlements, regulations, the legal system, crime costs, and government inefficiency. The increase will be in the range of 3% in the near future and increasing rapidly in the long term. Because of our inefficient economic system, we will become less competitive compared to other nations.

12. Congressional committees and committee chairpersons will operate as usual with federal expenditures exceeding income 20% to 35% per year. Committee chairs and the entire Appropriation Committee will receive a disproportionate share of discretionary spending funds. Continue to use off-budget spending to conceal the transfer of FICA and other trust funds to current spending. The Appropriation Committee and its chairperson will be able to dictate programs and policies as well as demand conformity. Expenditures and laws will grow until the economy collapses.

13. Continue freedom of speech, art, expression, protest, and their portrayal in the media with continued graphic exploitation of unabated sex, drugs, violence, and confrontation.

14. Continue our present nonpolicy toward sex, drugs, and welfare, especially in the inner cities.

15. Federal income taxes will increase, or remain, until the government is bankrupt early in the next century.

8. Adopt the Citizens Against Government Waste report to make government more efficient and less costly. Privatize all possible federal operations. This will reduce the government costs $5,200 per support household.

9. Make all lobby contributions to candidates a crime. Consider them a bribe causing expulsion from office and replacement with the runner-up candidate. Federal elections will be funded from taxes. The savings to business and taxpayers are over $5,994 per support household.

10. Form an independent CPA /computer firm to receive and post all income and write all federal checks. It must connect all usable computers and programs and replace obsolete computers and programs. They will integrate all government financial and department data into a single system to track all government information monthly. The computers will rely heavily on and refer to each citizen's personal ID card.

11. COLA will be redefined as "increase in productivity" of your employer, either government or private. The real cost of living will go down several percent for several years as the least beneficial and most costly laws and regulations are replaced. Reduced economic friction will lower the cost of products, services, government, and insurance while paychecks go up (or down) with each employer's increase in productivity. An increase in productivity will then be every worker's goal.

12. Congressional committees will be combined and reduced one third. Committee chairpersons will rotate annually. No special appropriations could go to the chair's district that year. All funds sent out of committee must be passed by line item as being "absolutely" necessary. Balance the budget, reduce the debt $200 billion a year, and limit congressional terms.

13. Freedom of speech will be limited, as is shouting FIRE in a theater. Graphic exploitation by the media of sex, drugs, violence, and confrontation will voluntarily stop or be stopped by legislation. Their influence on us and our children is too important.

14. Use overwhelming force to remove sex, drugs, and violence from the inner cities. Then rebuild the inner cities using Full Employment and increased education.

15. A sales tax plus a progressive wage tax will replace all income taxes, saving all households an average of over $1,400, with remaining benefits going to employers and reducing the cost of government.

Footnotes:

Introduction

[1] *Nations Business*, April 1994, p 79.   1995 *Budget of the United States Government* Analytical Perspectives, p 24-25
Minneapolis Star Tribune, August 22, 1993. Source: Lawrence Kotlikoff, Boston University.
Time, Feb. 21, 1994. Source: 1994 Federal Budget, Administration Future Tax Projections, p 44.

[2] Henry W. Rouff: *Century Book of Facts*. The King Richardson Company, 1902, p 459.

[3] See chart 3 in Chapter 3 "Charting History."

[4] *Issues 94*, Abridged Edition, Heritage Foundation, 1994, p 34. Source: U.S. Department of Justice. "The Case For More Incarcerations," October 28, 1992.

[5] See Chapter 9 "Education."

[6] Albert Tuijnman, educational statistician for the 24 nation Organization for Economic Cooperation and Development.

Chapter 1.

[1] *Budget of the United States Government* Historical Tables 1996 p 90.

[2] IBID p 90.

[3] Peter G. Peterson: *Peterson Facing Up* Simon & Schuster, 1993. p.108 ($14 trillion) Senate *Bi-Partisan Commission on Entitlements and Tax Reform* 1994. $14.4 trillion unfunded entitlements. "Truth in Spending Needed for Budget to be Balanced" *Washington Times*, 22 January 1996. Accrued federal obligations for civil and military pensions, Social Security, and Medicare are $17.2 trillion.

[4] J. Peter Grace: *Burning Money* Macmillan Publishing Company, 1984, p.13.

[5] See Chapter 3. Charting History. *Social Security Trustees Report* , 1995, p 122 & 123.

[6] U. S. Commerce Department report 5 July 1994 Foreign debt up 9.4% from 1992 now is $555.7 billion.
Harry E. Figgie, Jr.: *Bankruptcy 1995*. Little Brown, 1992. p 93 (1991 debt $441 billion).

[7] *Statistical Abstract of the United States* Department of Commerce 1994 brief, population and households. Projected from 1990 and 1993.

[8] IBID p 343 1991 data $19,600 inflated to 1995.

[10] One billion dollars divided by 50 million households = $20.

[11] *Issues '94* special abridged edition, Heritage Foundation 1994, p 57 $375 billion ($7,500 per support household).

[12] $2.4 trillion amortized over 10 years at 6%.

[13] Henry W. Ruoff: *Century Book of Facts* King Richardson Co, 1902, p. 472.

[14] IBID p 459.

[15] IBID p 592.

[16] *Budget of the United States Government* Analytical Perspectives 1996, p 90, $4.962 billion / 50 million households = $99,231 per support household. "Truth in Spending Needed for Budget to be Balanced" Joseph DioGuardi and Michael Granof *Washington Times* 22 January 1996, The obligations are understated by $17.16 trillion.

[17] *Budget of the United States Government* Historical Tables 1995, p 87, gross debt. *Budget of the United States Government* Historic Tables, 1992 p 82, 1989 table 5.1, and 1977, Budget brief p 62. *Historical Statistics of the United States Colonial Times to 1970* p 1124 $8.94 billion.

[18] *Budget of the United States Government* Analytical Perspectives, 1996, p 212 $333.6 billion.

[19] Laurence Kotikoff Economist at Boston University quote *Minneapolis Star Tribune* 22 August 1993 p 11A.

[20] *Statistical Abstract of the United States* Department of Commerce 1993 p 451.

[21] Thomas D. Hopkins, Former Deputy Administrator of OMB Office of Information and Regulatory Policy conference report: *Regulatory Policy in Canada and the United States*, P 5 lobby costs ($300 billion per year)
Jonathan Rausch: "The Parasite Economy," *National Journal*, 25 April 1992, p. 984 lobby costs ($300-700 billion per year).

[22] *Nations Business*, July, 1994, p 26-29 source OMB.

[23] Melinda Warren: Center for Study of American Business, Washington University, St. Louis, Mo. $16.6 billion.

[24] See page 1 of Appendix B.

[25] *Budget of the United States Government*,1995, p 94 $760.1 billion total entitlements less welfare $375 billion ($7,500 per support household) (*Issues '94* Heritage Foundation p. 57) = $385.1 for Social Security, Medicare, farm subsidies, interest, and misc.($7,700 per support household).

[26] *Budget of the United States Government*,1995, p 94 $435.1 billion = $8,702 per support household.

[27] IBID p. 25 Federal pension income $4.6 billion - outgo $37.8 billion = -$33.2 billion ($664 per support household).

[28] *Budget of the United States Government* Analytical Perspectives, 1996, p 212, Interest on the Public Debt is $333.6 billion = $6,672 per support household.

[29] *Budget of the United States Government*, 1996, p 61, Budgets of Agriculture, Commerce, Energy, Housing, Labor, Treasury, and EPA total $534.24 billion ($10,685 per support household) and proposed savings of $70 billion ($1,400 per support household).

[30] See chart 3 in Chapter 3. For 10 years COLA has averaged 1.5% higher than worker productivity. Federal expenditures are $1.574 trillion (p. 61 1995 budget) times 1.5% = $23.6 billion or $472 per support household.

[31] Thomas D. Hopkins, Former Deputy Administrator of OMB Office of Information and Regulatory Policy *Profiles of Regulatory Costs* Report to the U.S. SBA, November 1995, total 1995 regulatory costs: Table A-4, $669 billion and Table B-4 $416 billion ($13,380 and $8,320 per support household).

[32] Thomas D. Hopkins: Report of a conference *Regulatory Policy in Canada and the United States*, May 1992, p 5.

[33] Election campaigns average half a million dollars for representatives every 2 years, and $4 million for senators every 6 years. Assuming they each have an opponent with equal funds, this would cost $335 million for representatives plus $133 million for senators = $468 million every year. This should be reduced 20% to $374 million. The candidates must raise $67 million of this amount. The remainder ($307 million) cost the support households $6 per year.

[34] Paul J. Grant: "Tort reform in the 1990's," *Quality*, January 1991. Costs are $120 billion or $2,400 per support household. Rowland Evans & Robert Novak: "America's Most Powerful Lobby," *Wall Street Journal*. tort economic costs $130 billion/yr. Stephen Magee: "The optimum number of Lawyers," *Law and Social Inquiry* Journal of the American Bar Assn. Fall 1992, p 674, yearly economic cost $660 billion ($13,200 per support household). Peter G. Peterson: *Facing Up*, Simon & Schuster, 1993, p.182 2.6% of GDP (7.1 trillion) $182 billion ($3,640 per support household).

[36] *Issues '94* , special abridged edition, Heritage Foundation, 1994, p 43 Cost to victims alone $150 billion. NBC January 25, 1995 "America the Violent" crime costs $250 billion a year, including buildings, law enforcement, and detention.

[37] *Historical Statistics of the United States Colonial Times to 1970*, p. 210 and USA Statistics Brief US Department of Commerce 1970 to 1994 tables of CPI and total economy output per man hour.

[38] Rowland Evans & Robert Novak: "America's Most Powerful Lobby," *Wall Street Journal*.

[39] Peter G. Peterson: *Facing Up*, Simon & Schuster, 1993, p.182 (2.6% of GDP $7 trillion = 182 billion) see also footnote 34.

[40] IBID p 175, and Dan Quayle speech.

[41] IBID p 182, also see footnote 34.

[42] IBID Chart 1.2.

[43] *Budget of the United States Government* 1995 Dept. of Education, 57 billion total for authorized and discretionary.

[44] See Chapter 10 2.9 million teachers paid $5,900 each or equivalent plus benefits and FICA tax.

[45] *Statistical Abstract of the United States* Department of Commerce, 1994, p.450.

[46] *Statistical Abstract of the United States* Department of Commerce, 1994, summary p 451.

[47] *Budget of the United States Government*, 1995, p. 14, 1995 est. $7.9 billion.

Chapter 2.

[1] *Webster's guide to American History*, G & C Merriam Company Publishers, 1971, Virtually all references to dates, places, events and quotes from 1774 to 1800 are arranged chronologically.

[2] IBID, p 68.

[3] Norine Dickson Campbell: *Patrick Henry*, Patriot and Statesman, 1969.

[4] Larry Burkett *The Coming Economic Earthquake*, Moody, 1991, Chapter 2., The Great Depression p 25 & 264

[5] IBID p 73-79.

Chapter 3.
All footnotes in this chapter are included on the charts.

Chapter 4.

[1] See chart 3 Chapter 3.

[2] *Historical Statistics of the United States* Colonial times to 1970, p 144 - 162. *Statistical Abstract of the United States* , 1994, p 451 plus summary.

[3] Center for Study of American Business, *Occasional Paper 155* p 24.

[4] "Judgement Calls,"*Newsweek* January 31, 1994, p 51.

[5] IBID

[6] Peter G. Peterson: *Facing Up*. Simon & Schuster 1993, p 182.

[7] Representative Don Manzullo, Illinois.

[8] Glenn Bailey: "Litigation Abuse is Destroying My Company" *Wall Street Journal* , July 15, 1992, p A 13.

[9] Jack Anderson and Michael Binstein: *Washington Post*.

[10] Center for the Study of American Business *Policy Study Number 127*.

[11] Todd G Buchholz with Carol M. Cropper *Forbes* 1994.

[12] Office of Management and Budget.

[13] *Washington Week in Review*, May 13, 1994.

Chapter 5.

[1]Dr. Ravi Batra: *Surviving the Great Depression of 1990*. Dell Publishing, 1988, p 111.

[2] J. Peter Grace: *Burning Money* . Macmillan Publishing Company. 1984, p 13 2.1 workers *Status of the Social Security and Medicare Programs* Social Security Boards of Trustees report April 1995. p122-123 2.2 workers by 2025.

[3] Peter G. Peterson: *Facing Up*. Simon & Schuster, 1993, p 78.

[4] J. Peter Grace: *Burning Money*. Macmillan Publishing Company, 1984, p 70.

[5] IBID p 72.

[6] *Los Angeles Times* June 1994.

[7]*Issues 94*. Abridged Edition, Heritage Foundation, 1994 p 94.

[8] See Chapter 4.

[9] *U.S. News and World Report* , January 30, 1995.

Chapter 6.

[1]Peter G. Peterson: *Facing Up*. Simon & Schuster, 1993. p 175.

[2]Gina Kolata: *New York Times* June 22, 1995. p 1A.

[3]*New York Times*, April, 1994.

[4]Knight-Ridder Newspapers source U.S. Census Bureau.

[5]Peter G. Peterson: Facing Up. Simon & Schuster, 1993. p 116.

[6]George Will: *Washington Post* Writers Group.

[7]Mary Ann Glendon: Harvard Law School, author, *A Nation Under Lawyers*.

[8]Mike Royko: Syndicated Columnist.

[9]Larry Rather: *New York Times* .

[10]Peter G. Peterson: *Facing Up*. Simon & Schuster, 1993. chart 1, 9.

[11]IBID p 182.

[12]Rowland Evans and Robert Novak: *Wall Street Journal*. "America's Most Powerful Lobby."

[13]See WPI chart Chapter 3.

[14]Mike Scanlon: *AP* January 1, 1994.

[15]Jan Crawford: *Chicago Tribune* .

[16]Heritage Foundation *Issues '94* Abridged Edition, 1994. p 43 Victims only, $150 billion for economic damage, pain and suffering.

[17]IBID p 34 table 1.

[18]IBID.

[19]*AP* November 13, 1995.

[20]*New York Times*, July 31, 1994.

[21]*AP* reports.

[22]IBID.

[23]IBID.

[24]Dianne Williamson: *Worchester Telegram*.

[25]News hour with Jim Lehrer, Dec. 11, 1995.

[26]Peter G. Peterson: *Facing Up*. Simon & Schuster, 1993. p 182.

Chapter 7.

[1]*Statistical Abstract of the United States* Department of Commerce, 1994, p 413. Source Bureau of Labor Statistics monthly labor review November 1993.

[2]The total of yearly differences in the CPI and WPI from 1971 to 1981.

[3]*AP* January 17, 1995.

[4]Peter G. Peterson: *Facing Up* , Simon & Schuster, 1993, chart 1.2.

[5]*Statistical Abstract of the United States* Department of Commerce, 1971, p 219, and 1994 p 413 (1992) the total of seven major manufacturing jobs: primary metals, fabricated metals, industrial machines, electronics, transportation, instruments, and misc. The totals were compared with total employed.

[6]Wayne B, Gray "The Cost of Regulation OSHA, EPA and the Production Showdown "*American Economic Review* , December 1987.

[7]*Time* May 16, 1994 p 71, 72.

[8]*Time* Oct 24, 1994 p 54.

[9]*Wall Street Journal*, Milo Geyelin October 5, 1994 plus Barry Bearak *Los Angeles Times*.

[10]*Time*, October 24, 1995 p 55.

[11]David Halberstam: *The Reckoning,* William Morrow and Company, 1986. Chapter 51.

[12]*Nations Business*, September 1994 p 8.

[13]Suneel Ratan *Time* May 22, 1995 p 35.

Chapter 8.
[1]David Halberstam: *The Reckoning*. William Morrow and Company 1986. The above three paragraphs are a summary of chapters 7 to 10.
[2]Rafiel Aguyao: *Dr. Deming*. Fireside, 1990. The paragraph summarizes the book.
[3]Joseph Gorman CEO of TRW corporation speech at Cleveland City Club Forum.
[4]*U.S. News and World Report* April 10, 1995 p 60.
[5]See chapter 10.
[6]Peter G. Peterson: *Facing Up*. Simon & Schuster, 1993, chart 3.7. *Nations Business*. June 1994, p 41 Japan has 400,000 robots, U.S. has 45,000.
[7]IBID p 175.
[8]See Chapter 7.
[9]Peter G. Peterson: *Facing Up*. Simon & Schuster, 1993, chart 3.5 (1995 U.S. personal savings at 2% of GDP $7.1 trillion=$142 billion=2.8%).
[10]Seigfried H. Sutterlin Fullbright Scholar Author Munich in the cobwebs of Berlin, Washington and Moscow U.S. household net worth $40,000. Japan and Germany above $200,000. U.S. Census bureau 1991 $36,623 (U.S.), down $4,849 from 1988.
[11]*Time* June 19, 1994 p 38.

Chapter 9.
[1]Peter G. Peterson: *Facing Up*. Simon & Schuster, 1993, p 56.
[2]John Leo Universal Press Syndicate.
[3]Peter G. Peterson: *Facing Up*. Simon & Schuster, 1993, Chart 3.7.
[4]*Budget of the United States Government* 1996 HistoricalTables p 61.
[5]Knight Ridder News Service Dec. 8, 1995 National Assessment of Educational Progress.
[6]Economics and statistics division, Bureau of Census p 162, table 240 & p 165, table 245.

Chapter 10
[1]J. Peter Grace: *Burning Money*. Macmillan Publishing Company, 1984. p 108.
[2]Peter G. Peterson: *Waking Up*. Simon & Schuster, 1993. Chart 4.15.
[3]Bipartisan Commission on Entitlements and Tax Reform, Final Report, p 79.
[4]J. Peter Grace: *Burning Money*. Macmillan Publishing Company, 1984. p 4, 5, 136, 155

Chapter 11.
[1]*Budget of the United States Government* 1995 Historical tables p 154-174.
[2]*Issues '94* Abridged edition, Heritage Foundation, 1994 p 57.
[3]IBID p 57.
[4]Seth Faison: *New York Times*.
[5]Norman E. Zuckerman: Editor in Chief of *U.S. News and World Report*, January 16, 1995, p 68.
[6]AP February 1994.
[7]Prime Time Live: October 13, 1994.
[8]AP June 1994.

Chapter 12.
[1]*USA Weekend*. June 2, 1995 p 4.
[2]*Issues '94* Abridged Edition, Heritage Foundation, 1994 p 57.
[3]NBC January 25, 1995 "America the Violent" Crime costs $250 billion. *Issues '94* Abridged Edition, Heritage Foundation, 1994 p 43 $150 billion for just economic damage and pain.
[4]AP report of *Journal of the American Medical Association*.
[5]AP report of Douglas J. Besharov with American Enterprise Institute.
[6] IBID.
[7]*Issues '94* Abridged Edition, Heritage Foundation, 1994 p 34 450%. Minnesota Public Radio 500%.
[8]*Issues '94* Abridged Edition, Heritage Foundation, 1994 p 41.

Chapter 13.
[1]Peter G. Peterson: *Waking Up*. Simon & Schuster, 1993, p 106.

Appendix A

Change all income taxes to a sales and wage tax

Our seven million word IRS tax code has been distorted by lobbies and special interests. Only 8% of all calls to IRS get answers and 20% (8 million) of the answers are wrong. OMB estimates income tax preparation wastes 4.2 billion hours. The Tax Foundation Special Report estimate is 4.96 billion hours.

Federal personal, corporate, and FICA taxes raised 93% of all federal revenues in 1995. In billions per year they were: personal $590, corporate $125, and FICA $492 (half from individuals and half from corporations). Unfortunately, the annual cost to comply in billions is:

	Collected	Compliance cost[1]	Congressional Compl. Est [2]
Business income tax	$125	$86 (69%)	$130 (104%)
Personal income tax	$590	$42 (7%)	$65 (11%)
IRS operating cost [3]		$28	$14
State income tax rev. & costs[4]	$173	$10	$10

Wasted compliance costs are $166 (18.5%)—to $221 (24%). I have used the smaller estinmate. A sales tax will collect $125 to $300 billion in revenues the IRS presently fails to collect from criminal and hidden income.

Americans spend 96% of their income and invest only 4%. Wages generally parallel income until retirement. All FICA, medicare, and federal retiree trust funds have been borrowed by Congress. **All personal and corporate income, estate, and gift taxes** (federal, state, and local) **could be easily replaced and made progressive using the existing FICA tax collection system in combination with a 10% national sales tax and an average 3% state sales tax** (each state would set its own rate to match its services and collect both sales taxes and transfer a federal payment monthly). Federal and state governments will receive more tax revenues from business because business is relieved of immense compliance waste shown above.

Workers earning less than $8 per hour will receive all pay with no deductions plus an additional 4% paid by the employer or higher minimum wage (11.65% more). Employee FICA taxes from this level to $62,700 will remain the same. Employees above that level will pay 7.65% because it now replaces a major part of the income tax. Employers will pay 4% additional FICA tax to replace all income taxes. The revised FICA tax will be called a Government Services Tax (GST). A 10% National Sales Tax (NST) plus average state sales tax of 3% will collect all remaining revenues lost by all federal and state income, gift, and estate taxes. The NST will be collected on all goods and services except for resale and non profit. No savings will be taxed. Commissions on investments will be taxed. All but 5 states now collect income and sales taxes. The state can easily collect the added sales taxes and forward the federal portion monthly.

There are many benefits:

1. The average taxpayer will save over $1,400 and employers will save $24 billion at no loss of federal or state revenue. There are alternatives on p 109 of a higher NST.
2. The underground economy will now contribute from $32 to $100 billion NST revenue.
3. Over $165 billion will be saved in income tax compliance costs.
4. Both of the above will reduce the cost of goods including the NST and state sales tax.
5. The 10% NST and 3% state sales tax will be apparent and remind citizens of government costs.
6. No tax on investment income will directly increase investments.
7. Gift and estate taxes will be eliminated.
8. The changes will stimulate our economy which will be over $180 billion more efficient.
9. We will be rid of 4 to 5 billion grudging hours of wasted time collecting documents and preparing income tax forms. The IRS income tax division will be obsolete.
10. Taxes are easily collected with each paycheck or purchase using systems in place in 46 states.

In 1995 1% FICA tax on wages of $3,455 billion =$34.6 billion. 1% NST = $58 billion.

---

[1] See note 3 p 109
[2] Treasury Dept. estimates (coming from Congressman Archer's office)
[3] See note 4 p 109
[4] See note 5 p 109

PROPOSED CHANGE OF ALL INCOME TAX TO A SALES AND WAGE TAX

For simplicity all proposed state sales taxes are averaged. Each state will assign its own % of taxes to match its services.

Description	Support HH	Other HH	Corp	Federal	State	Local
1. Eliminate federal personal income tax	$561	$30		($590)		
2. Eliminate the IRS				$28		
3. Eliminate private and corp. inc. tax accounting	$41	$1	$86			
4. Eliminate federal corporate income tax			$125	($125)		
5. Eliminate state personal income tax	$125	$4			($130)	
6. Eliminate state and local corp. income tax			$30		($27)	($3)
7. Eliminate local personal income tax	$12	$1				($13)
8. Eliminate state income tax divisions					$9	$1
9. Eliminate state and federal estate and gift taxes	$17			($12)	($5)	
10. Taxes collected and costs of collecting 1 to 9	$756	$36	$241	($699)	($153)	($15)
Total tax plus cost of compliance	**$1033**		collected	**($867)**		
11. Needed federal, state, and local taxes (line 10)	**($867)** billion					
12. Total possible compliance savings	**$166**					
13. Existing 1995 FICA tax amounts	($202)	($44)	($246)	$492		
14. Tax all wages above $62,700 7.65%(+6.3%)	($20)		($20)	$40		
15. Raise Bus. FICA tax 4% to replace all inc. tax			(138)			
Workers under $8/hr. pay no FICA & get 4% raise	$67			72		
16. Total FICA changes for HH, corp, and fed govt.	($20)	$23	($158)	$111		
17. New total sales tax revenues needed	($756)					
18. Personal disp. inc. is 74% * GDP (7.1 tril.)	$5240					
19. Bus. consumption of fixed capital	$455					
20. + corp & indiv. sav. (line 3) to disp. inc.	$128					
21. Total tax base of all goods and services	$5823					
22. Add 10% fed. + avg. 3% state sales tax =**13%**	($757)		-line 17=$30			

Description	Support HH	Other HH	Corp	Federal	State	Local
23. Base for sales tax as portion of line 21	$4774	$594	$455			
24. Distribute FICA and sales tax to govt entities	($621)	($77)	($59)	$558	$154	$15
25. Billions of gain per entity	**$116**	**$25**	**$24**	**$0**	**$1**	**$0**
% Savings per entity	21%	69%	10%	0$	1%	0%
26. Savings per household in dollars	**$2318**	**$507**	Avg. savings all households =**$1412**			
Alternate gains using a sales tax of 13.5%	$92	$22	$22	$29	$1	$0
14%	$68	$19	$20	%58	$1	$0

Notes by line

1. & 4. est. pers. and corp. inc. taxes shown in federal budget. Pers. inc. 61.4% of GDP. Other HH inc. 5% of $590 billion = $30 billion.

2. 1996 Budget of the United States Analytical Perspectives p 430

3. Profiles of Regulatory Costs Thomas D. Hopkins p 21, use $26 hourly cost * $123 billion and $60 billion

5. Lines 5-8 Statistical Abstract p 298 inflated 25% to 1995 data compared to 1996 U.S. Budget Analytical Persp.

9. Same as above except increases 9% since 1992

13. 1996 Budget of the United States Analytical Perspectives table 2.4. Other HH pay 7.65% x $562 billion

15. Other households gain $67 billion more from employers (7.65%+4%) to pay 13% sales taxes.

18. 1994 Statistical Abstract of the U.S. p 451 1993 disposable pers. inc./GDP = 73.8%x$7.1 trillion GDP =$5,240

19. 1995 Survey of Current Business U.S. Dept of Commerce p 8 Business consumption of fixed capital = $455 billion

23. Corp. line 19. Other 5% x lines 18+ 20. Support 95% x lines 18+20.

OTHER CONSIDERATIONS '90&91 DATA (billions)	other HH	%AGI	Support HH	%AGI	source line 18
Adjusted gross income	$440	100%	$2965	100%	
Mortgage interest deductions	$11	3%	$189	6%	
Contribution deductions	$3	1%	$58	2%	
State and local income tax deductions	$11	3%	$77	3%	

Appendix B
Citizens Against Government Waste Report *Prime Cuts 1994*

The following are major cuts in government spending which save over $9 billion over 5 years. The complete full list is available from the bipartisan Citizens Against Government Waste in Washington, DC.

America is more than $5 trillion in debt. The federal budget deficit was $305 billion last year. Each day, while Washington dawdles over deficit reduction, the nation slips nearly a billion dollars closer to bankruptcy.

Taxes consume nearly 40% of our pay, but Washington wants more. Each time taxes have risen, spending has grown even more. Waste, inefficiency, and mismanagement remain pervasive in the federal government, claiming 44 cents of every individual income tax dollar. Symbolism and shell-game accounting won't cut it anymore. The people are demanding dramatic, tangible action to restore America's fiscal well-being.

Citizens Against Government Waste (CAGW) has compiled a comprehensive catalogue of private and public-sector reform recommendations called "Prime Cuts." CAGW estimated in 1994 the federal government squandered $186.8 billion on pork, bureaucratic bloat, and programs that are poorly managed, have failed or outlived their usefulness, duplicate other programs encroach on state and local responsibilities, enrich special interests at the expense of families, or are simply extravagant. Government waste and interest on the national debt consume all personal income taxes collected.

To determine the Waste Tax, The bipartisan CAGW examined waste cutting recommendations from government sources such as the Congressional Budget Office and the Office of Management and Budget, as well as private sector sources such as the Grace Commission, and totaled the nonduplicative savings.

Until the 556 recommendations outlined in this document are implemented, taxpayers should not be asked to fork over another cent. These waste cuts can reduce the deficit and save taxpayers more than $1.3 trillion over five years.

Prime Cuts Menu to Cure the Waste Tax, 1994

	PUBLIC SOURCES	5 year savings in $ millions
1.	Congressional Budget Office	560,395
2.	National Performance Review	4,540
3.	President Clinton, Vision of Change for America	10,878
4.	Current Congressional Proposals	313,455
	PRIVATE SOURCES	
5.	Grace Commission	110,649
6.	Citizens Against Government Waste	301,941
	TOTAL	**1,301,858**

Savings per support household per year　　　$5,208 in 1994 dollars

No.	Partial List of Recommendations over $9 billion for 5 years	5 Yr Sav. in $millions
	Congressional Budget Office—1994 Options	
DEF 04	Focus theater missile defense efforts on core systems which include Theater Defense Missiles, Patriot Advanced Capability, and Theater High-Altitude Area Defense system.	18,470
DEF 14	Reduce the number of Army light divisions, which were not even needed in Operation Desert Storm	12,600
DEF 35	Reduce funding for U.S. forces stationed abroad by increasing host nation support in countries such as Italy, Germany, the United Kingdom, and Spain	12,540
DEF 37	Reduce and reshape DOD's civilian work force ratio, which was 1.9:1 in 1992, to match that of the early 1980s, in which the ratio of military personnel to civilian personnel was 2:1.	24,820
DOM 01	Cancel the international space station program	10,400
DOM 30	Eliminate the CDBG program, which generates primarily local benefits that should be funded by state and local governments	15,650
ENT 06	Lower target prices for subsidized crops by 3% annually; in addition to reducing the deficit, this would encourage farmers to respond to market prices, rather than to government benefits, in making their production decisions	11,050
ENT 22	Reduce subsidies for Stafford Loans by requiring students to pay in-school interest and raising the loan origination fee to 5%.	11,090
ENT 25	Reduce from 50% to 45% the floor on the federal share of Medicaid, AFDC, and Foster Care and Adoption Assistance payments for high-income states	36,000
ENT 28	Gradually eliminate the disproportionate share adjustment for hospitals in Medicare's prospective payment system; data on hospitals' costs provide only limited support for any such adjustment	12,550
ENT 29	Reduce Medicare's payments for the indirect costs of patient care that are related to hospitals' teaching programs by reducing the teaching adjustment payment to 3%	13,550

110

No.	Partial List of Recommendations over $9 billion for 5 years	5 Yr Sav. in $ millions
ENT 35	Increase the SMI co-insurance rate from 20% to 25%	16,250
ENT 37	Collect 20% co-insurance on all home health and skilled nursing facility services under Medicare.	20,450
ENT 39	Increase the premium for physicians' services under Medicare SMI from 25% to 30% of program costs.	17,370
ENT 41	Bring federal employee retirement benefits in line with private practices; defer COLAs until age 62, limit some COLAs below inflation, modify salary base used to set pensions, restrict agency match on Thrift Plan Contribution to 50%, and raise employee contributions.	10,690

Congressional Budget Office 1993 Options

DEF 30	Eliminate payments for independent research and development, an indirect and inefficient way to generate defense-related research; substitute $7.5 billion in direct R&D grants for basic DOD research.	14,740
ENT 37	End Federal Employees' Health Benefits program's pay-as-you-go policy and prefund federal retirees' health insurance to improve management and provide a better view of government operating costs.	11,600

Current Congressional Proposals A. A Common Cents Plan

GM 23	Cut federal workforce by 252,000 over the next five years	26,700

The Fiscal Responsibility Act of 1994

AGR 16	Eliminate the Conservation Reserve Program, which pays farmers to leave lands idle, to reduce environmental damage encouraged by other subsidy programs	9,300
GM 03	Sell most of the government's 340,000 non-tactical, non-postal vehicles.	9,250

The Republican Budget Initiative, Fiscal Year 1995

PC 4	Create a privately-owned air traffic control corporation	32,523
GM 34	Freeze overhead expenses for five years	27,641

Republican Members, House Budget Committee

H 1-5	Reduce the use of emergency rooms as primary care facilities by allowing states to establish managed care for Medicaid similar to Arizona's program	10,000
H 3-8	Institute malpractice limits and hold supplementary medical insurance rates at 93%, except primary care.	14,900

Legislative Sources Members, 103rd Congress

S 457	Prohibit direct federal financial benefits and unemployment benefits for illegal aliens and end federal mandates for states to provide for illegal aliens	14,000

President's Private Sector Survey on Cost Control (Grace Commission)

FSP 01	Improve targeting of means-tested benefits by requiring federal, state, and local agencies to issue a form similar to a W-2 form, showing the subsidy payment for each beneficiary, with a copy going to the IRS	24,500
OSD 09	Realign or close redundant or unneeded military bases.	15,500

Citizens Against Government Waste (Cato Institute, Mr. Marvin Gross, Heritage Foundation, Department of Health and Human Services Inspector General)

DOE 01	Transfer DOE nuclear weapons testing and development to the Pentagon; consolidate remaining DOE functions with Department of Interior to create a Department of Natural Resources.	10,000
GM 02	Prohibit the use of outside consultants, who have become an unaccountable "shadow" government	24,500
GM 04	Sell increasing portions of the government's direct loan portfolio to the private sector.	30,000
HHS 03	Extend beyond 18 months Medicare Secondary Payer (MSP) provisions for end-stage-renal-disease beneficiaries; apply MSP to retirees of currently exempt state and local government agencies	10,765
PBGC 01	Increase company-sponsored contributions to the PBGC; freeze the guarantee for unfunded plans; amend bankruptcy laws to improve PBGC	13,100
PROC 01	Reduce Pentagon waste; eliminate unnecessary procurement regulations; require defense contractors to share cost overruns with the government; link DOD salaries and promotions to a manager's ability to complete programs on schedule, within budget	49,000
TREAS 01	Prevent future taxpayer bailouts; limit deposit insurance to $100,000 per depositor per bank; limit coverage to the original principal investment; establish risk-based premiums; measures losses as they accrue; allow interstate banking and branching	15,500

Total CAGW savings with 5 year savings over $9 billion=$606,959 billion

Appendix C.   Abbreviations

ABC	American Broadcasting Corporation
ACT	American College Test
AFDC	Aid for Dependent Children
AP	Associated Press report
ATF	Department of Alcohol, Tobacco, and Firearms
CAFE	corporate average fuel economy
CAGW	Citizens Against Government Waste
CBO	Congressional Budget Office
CCC	Civilian Conservation Corps
CETA	now Job Training Partnership Act , JTPA
CFC	chlorofluorocarbon (freon)
COLA	cost of living adjustment
CPA	Certified Public Accountant
CPI	consumer price index
CSRS	Civilian Service Retirement System
DDT	An insecticide prohibited by the federal government
DNR	Department of Natural Resources
EEOC	Equal Employment Opportunity Commission
EPA	Environmental Protection Agency
ERISA	Employment Retirement Security Act
FHA	Farm Home Administration
FICA	Federal Insurance Corporation of America
GAO	Government Accounting Office
GDP	gross domestic product (total of all goods and services)
GED	general education degree
GNP	gross national product (GDP with factored income re. other countries)
GSA	Government Services Administration
HUD	Department of Housing and Urban Development
NAFTA	North American Free Trade Association
OECD	Organization for Economic Cooperation and Development
OMB	Office of Management and Budget
OSHA	Office of Safety and Health Administration
PAC	political action committee
R&D	research and development
REA	Rural Electrification Administration
SAT	Scholastic Aptitude Test
SSI	Supplemental Security Income
TAC	Tactical Air Command
VAT	value-added tax
WIC	Women, Infants and Children program
WPA	Works Projects Administration
WPI	worker productivity index
WWI &II	World War One and Two

Appendix D
The RepublicanContract With America. September 27, 1994

As Republican members of the House of Representatives and as citizens seeking to join that body we propose not just to change its policies, but even more important, to restore the bonds of trust between the people and their elected representatives.

That is why, in this era of official evasion and posturing, we offer instead a detailed agenda for national renewal, a written commitment with no fine print.

This year's election offers the chance, after four decades of one-party control, to bring to the House a new majority that will transform the way Congress works. That historic change would be the end of government that is too big, too intrusive and too easy with the public's money. It can be the beginning of a Congress that respects the values and shares the faith of the American family. Like Lincoln, our first Republican president, we intend to act "with firmness in the right, as God gives us to see the right." To restore accountability to Congress. To end its cycle of scandal and disgrace. To make us all proud again of the way free people govern themselves.

On the first day of the 104th Congress, the new Republican majority will immediately pass the following major reforms, aimed at restoring the faith and trust of the American people in their government:

FIRST, require all laws that apply to the rest of the country also apply equally to the Congress;

SECOND, select a major, independent auditing firm to conduct a comprehensive audit of Congress for waste, fraud or abuse;

THIRD, cut the number of House committees, and cut committee staff by one-third;

FOURTH, limit the terms of all committee chairs;

FIFTH, ban the casting of proxy votes in committee;

SIXTH, require committee meetings to be open to the public;

SEVENTH, require a three-fifths majority vote to pass a tax increase;

EIGHTH, guarantee an honest accounting of our federal budget by implementing zero base-line budgeting.

Thereafter, within the first 100 days of the 104th Congress, we shall bring to the House floor the following bills, each to be given full and open debate, each to be given a clear and fair vote and each to be immediately available this day for public inspection and scrutiny.

1. THE FISCAL RESPONSIBILITY ACT—A balanced-budget/tax-limitation amendment and a legislative line-item veto to restore fiscal responsibility to an out-of-control Congress, requiring them to live under the same budget constraints as families and businesses.

2. THE TAKING BACK OUR STREETS ACT—An anti-crime package including stronger truth-in-sentencing, "good faith" exclusionary rule exemptions, effective death-penalty provisions, and cuts in social spending from this summer's "crime" bill to fund prison construction and additional law enforcement to keep people secure in their neighborhoods and kids safe in their schools.

3. THE PERSONAL RESPONSIBILITY ACT—Discourage illegitimacy and teen pregnancy by prohibiting welfare to minor mothers and denying increased AFDC for additional children while on welfare, cut spending for welfare programs, and enact a tough two-years-and-out provision with work requirements to promote individual responsibility.

4. THE FAMILY REINFORCEMENT ACT—Child-support enforcement, tax incentives for adoption, strengthening rights of parents in their children's education, stronger child-pornography laws, and an elderly dependent care tax credit to reinforce the central role of families in American society.

5. THE AMERICAN DREAM RESTORATION ACT—A $500 per child tax credit, begin repeal of the marriage tax penalty, and creation of American Dream Savings Accounts to provide middle-class tax relief.

6. THE NATIONAL SECURITY RESTORATION ACT—No U.S. troops under U.N. command and restoration of the essential parts of our national-security funding to strengthen our national defense and maintain our credibility around the world.

7. THE SENIOR CITIZENS FAIRNESS ACT—Raise the Social Security earnings limit which currently forces seniors out of the work force, repeal the 1993 tax hikes on Social Security benefits and provide tax incentives for private long-term care insurance to let older Americans keep more of what they have earned over the years.

8. THE JOB CREATION AND WAGE ENHANCEMENT ACT—Small business incentives, capital-gains cut and indexation, neutral cost-recovery, risk assessment/cost-benefit analysis, strengthening the Regulatory Flexibility Act and unfunded mandate reform to create jobs and raise worker wages.

9. THE COMMON SENSE LEGAL REFORM ACT—"Loser pays" laws, reasonable limits on punitive damages and reform of product-liability laws to stem the endless tide of litigation.

10. THE CITIZEN LEGISLATURE ACT—A first-ever vote on term limits to replace career politicians with citizen legislators.

Further, we will instruct the House Budget Committee to report to the floor and we will work to enact additional budget savings beyond the budget cuts specifically included in the legislation described above, to ensure that the federal budget deficit will be less than it would have been without the enactment of these bills.

Respecting the judgment of our fellow citizens we seek their mandate for reform, we hereby pledge our names to this Contract with America. **(end of contract)**

Index